Ezili's Mirrors

EZILI'S MIRRORS

IMAGINING BLACK
QUEER GENDERS

Omise'eke Natasha Tinsley

Duke University Press   Durham and London   2018

Library of Congress Cataloging-in-Publication Data
Names: Tinsley, Omise'eke Natasha, [date] author.
Title: Ezili's mirrors : black queer genders / Omise'eke Natasha
Tinsley.
Description: Durham : Duke University Press, 2018. | Includes
bibliographical references and index.
Identifiers: LCCN 2017036325 (print) | LCCN 2017056618 (ebook)
ISBN 9780822372080 (ebook)
ISBN 9780822370307 (hardcover : alk. paper)
ISBN 9780822370383 (pbk. : alk. paper)
Subjects: LCSH: Gender identity—Haiti. | Blacks—Sexual
behavior—Haiti. | Legends—Haiti. | Feminism. | Homosexuality. |
Queer theory. | African diaspora in art.
Classification: LCC HQ1075.5.H2 (ebook) |
LCC HQ1075.5. H2 T567 2018 (print) |
DDC 305.3097294—dc23
LC record available at https://lccn.loc.gov/2017036325

Cover art: Didier William, *Ezili toujours konnen*, collage, acrylic, and
wood stain on panel, 36 in. × 48 in., 2015.

For my daughter, Baía Tinsley,
who is all the black girl magic,
all the Ezili that fill my life.
I love you more today than I
did yesterday—and tomorrow,
I'll love you even *more*
than I do today

CONTENTS

ACKNOWLEDGMENTS

Because this book is a praise song for the world-making, mirror-breaking power of black queer artists, my first thanks go to those who so generously shared their work with me. Sharon Bridgforth, the mermaid we black queer folk have been waiting for, not only sent multiple versions of her work-in-progress and a beautiful set of black mermaid oracle cards. She hosted me with utmost grace and care when I followed her to New York to see her work, came to my house to sit with my mermaid art for photos, and offered support and watery conversation from near and far. Nalo Hopkinson made my dreams come true when she answered our request to give the keynote presentation at the University of Texas's symposium "Mapping the Afro Imaginative: Black Queer Diaspora Studies and the Work of the Imagination." Once there, she was kind enough to indulge me in conversation about Jeanne Duval, light-skinned black cisfemmes, Beyoncé, and her own black mermaid art, all punctuated with a rich laugh I won't soon forget. When I met Ana Lara at a writers' workshop with Sharon Bridgforth and Omi Oshun Jones in 2005, I asked for a copy of the unpublished novel she came to talk about—*Erzulie's Skirt*—and her vision of La Mar has colored my imagination ever since. She also kept me safe when spirits came knocking at my head at the Transnational Black Feminist Retreat she brilliantly organized in Santo Domingo. Cindy Elizabeth's vision of Whitney and our black queer foremothers grounded and lifted me as I wrote this, and I'm honored her vision has become part of this volume. Working with Cindy has been an incredible, unexpected gift I hope to carry into the future.

Because this book is a love song for black feminists, my deepest thanks also go to scholar-sister-friends who worked in black feminist solidarity with me as I moved through the dazzle of Ezili. Since my arrival at the University of Texas, I've had the privilege of working with the African and African Diaspora Studies' Black Queer Diaspora faculty focus group not only to plan our symposium, "Mapping the Afro Imaginative," but also to share and offer feedback on each other's work. Lyndon Gill, Matt Richardson, Xavier Livermon, Omi Jones, and Charles Anderson have been incredible interlocutors and coimaginers. Special thanks to Jafari Sinclaire Allen, who visited our group, read our work, and was the first and last person to help me believe this black queer song to Ezili could become a book. Jafari, without you *Ezili's Mirrors* would not be. Grounding me in imagining black women could have a divine future are my colleagues in the Center for Women's and Gender Studies' Black Feminist Research Collective: Kali N. Gross, Daina Berry, and Matt Richardson and Xavier Livermon once more. Juana Rodriguez, my old graduate school colleague and fabulous femme role model, was kind enough to answer questions about black feminist/black queer work at Berkeley as I formulated this project in homage to our shared mentors VèVè Clark and Barbara Christian. Sallie Ann Glassman responded generously to the questions I asked her virtually and in person about Marie Laveau, and my ancestors thank her along with me. Carlos Decena shared his own work on—and admiration of—Ana Lara's fiction to help make the conclusion of this book what it is, and his support has touched me throughout the process.

As I looked in Ezili's mirrors, many colleagues were kind enough to issue invitations so their communities could engage my work. E. Patrick Johnson cared for and fiercely supported an early version of my work on MilDred Gerestant that now appears in his anthology *No Tea, No Shade*. Lisa Armstrong, Nathalie Batraville, Dasha Chapman, Nadège Clitandre, Sarah Harsh, Rachel Lee, Yolanda Martinez-San Miguel, and Marcia Ochoa provided me with wonderful, much-appreciated opportunities to share work and receive feedback that changed how I imagined and worded this book. Vanessa Agard-Jones, Jennifer DeClue, Erin Durban-Albrect, Alexis Pauline Gumbs, Mario Lamothe, Liza McAlister, Claudine Michel, Juliana Hu Pegues, and Beth Povinelli served as brilliant interlocutors for the versions of this work that I was able to present and taught me so much about Ezili's beauty and precision.

And as I struggled to write what I saw in Ezili's mirrors, my beloved family on Wayward Sun Drive reflected back why black queer lives and loves matter in the most daily, intimate of ways. My husband, Matt, the only one for me, greeted me every morning I wrote this as my lover and coparent, yes, but also shaped this book long before I struck a key to write it. We met as the two out queers in VèVè's seminar in August 1997—remember?—and he's been my friend, colleague, and indefatigable supporter ever since, continually pushing me out of my comfort zone and keeping me safe in my truth and high heels. And my daughter Baía: what can I say? Being her mother is the most empowering thing I've done as a queer black femme, and make no mistake: she's my first and last image of black women's divinity. Nothing has cemented my commitment to radical black feminism—to the world-changing importance of black women loving each other—than parenting a fiery, irreverent, imaginative, bear-hugging, laughing black girl who keeps me accountable to this world and its future, and this book is only possible because she taught me to see the world in this way. Last but not least, my gratitude to our many animal companions and especially Dulce, who purred by my side while I wrote not one but two books and insisted on being in the photo with Baía. Dulce, sweetness, you were right as always.

READ THIS BOOK
LIKE A SONG

Read this book like a song. No never, ever like a book of theory. Creating theory, Barbara Christian told me years ago, means "fixing a new constellation of ideas for a time at least."[1] She refused to fix constellations & so do I. This is a book in motion—in singing, falling, faltering, weeping, hip-circling, moaning, yellow-boning, following, insisting. The motion makes me dizzy sometimes, trying to sing & move at the same time. It may make you dizzy, too. I want it that way. So we can lose our bearings & find new ways to make sense, together & coming-apart-at-the-seams.

Read this book like a song. One day I sat down in front of my keyboard & decided to play language. With the rise & fall of her beautiful voice Barbara's essays told me to do this, too. To string words in the tradition of black women whose "language, and the grace and pleasure with which they played with it" sounded all the ways that "sensuality is intelligence, sensual language is language that makes sense."[2] No language is neutral & English is not a language made for me. Geechee & Creole would be my languages if there were any women alive in my family to teach them to me. Since there aren't, I try to do something unexpected with the words & letters & sounds I have at my disposal.

Read this book like a song. This song for Ezili is written in many voices. Read it like you listen to a song by my favorite group, Destiny's Child. Every chapter has three voices. The most serious font—this one—is the one I was trained to write in, the voice of academic knowledge & close textual readings. Imagine it's the book's Beyoncé, the voice easiest to recognize. My favorite font—this one—is the voice of spirit knowledge, the mark of vignettes telling stories of Ezili's manifestations. Think of this as the Kelly of my song, the quiet power that holds black women together but we don't ever publicly acknowledge enough. The last font you'll see—this—is the voice that speaks with black feminist ancestors, those who dropped knowledge & walked the path of Ezili before us. This is the Michelle, the voice you didn't expect to show up & who sings more quietly than the others, maybe. Sometimes the voices will confuse you. Like Destiny's Child, too: Weren't there voices that used to be there then just went away? Why is Beyoncé singing again when I wanted to keep hearing Kelly? Follow the voices you like, trace them back from one break to another. Listen to them in & out of order, always, & know their stories are partial, incomplete, & fractured. In writing them, I practiced living with—making melodies from—the disjunctured & syncopated, the sounds of black queer world making.

Read this book like a song. This is the bridge.

FOR THE LOVE OF LAVEAU

Water is eternal summer, and the depths of winter, too. When I arrived on the west bank of the Mississippi River in August 2005, everything, *everything* in my life was midsummer, bright, and new. I had just moved to Minneapolis to start a new job at a new university, was living in a newly painted apartment by a glinting lake I ran around every new morning, was newly single, and every day wore new white clothes and answered to a new, seven-day-old name, Iyawo, the name of a priest newly initiated in the Ifa tradition. So who would be surprised that even though I hadn't finished my first book—literary criticism caressing the writing of Caribbean women who love women—I was suddenly inspired to research a new, second project. An analysis of twenty-first-century Caribbean fiction by queer writers, the project seemed bright and shiny as beaches and I rushed into it headlong, in one weekend penning an article that I thought would become the introduction to my next book.

But the longer I sat with this book the more choked, the more stagnant it became. The directions I followed and answers I found seemed too easy, too pat—and while this apparently pleased funders and tenure committees, it left me cold and uneasy. So I went back to texts I'd gathered for my project and other texts I'd loved in the past ten years, looking for what unexpected things they might have to say about Caribbean lesbian, gay, transgender, and queer experience that I was still missing. I quickly found my answer: *nothing.* This was because the vocabulary I had been using to describe these authors, the descriptors that they used for their own identities—queer, lesbian, transgender—appeared nowhere in their work. *Nowhere.* No characters, no narrators, no one in the novels used these words. Instead they talked about many kinds of desires, caresses, loves, bodies, and more. And over and over again, they talked about something that was such a big part of my life, but that I never expected to find in most queer fiction: spirituality, Afro-Caribbean religions. Not one of these authors wrote about "queers," but almost everyone wrote about lwa—that is, about the spirit forces of the Haitian religion Vodou. And, finally, finally tuning into this other vocabulary, I was fascinated by the recurrence of one figure, who multiplied herself in these texts as if in a hall of mirrors: the beautiful femme queen, bull dyke, weeping willow, dagger mistress Ezili. Ezili is the name given to a pantheon of lwa who represent divine forces of love, sexuality, prosperity, pleasure, maternity, creativity, and fertility. She's also the force who protects madivin and masisi, that is, transmasculine and transfeminine Haitians.[1] And Ezili, I was coming to see—Ezili, not queer politics, not gender theory—was the prism through which so many contemporary Caribbean authors were projecting their vision of creative genders and sexualities. Finally, five summers later and into the middle of a winter, I was coming to see.

That winter, discarding plans so carefully laid out in grant applications, I decided I wanted to write a book that would be a reflection on same-sex desire, Caribbeanness, femininity, money, housing, friendship, and more; I wanted to write a book about Ezili. My loving, unfinished meditation on Ezili would open space to consider how, as Karen McCarthy Brown writes of the pantheon, "these female spirits are both mirrors and maps" for transfeminine, transmasculine, and same-sex-loving African diaspora subjects.[2] And it would reflect on Ezili as spirit, yes, but also on Ezili as archive. That is, I wanted to evoke the corpus of stories, memories, and songs about Ezili as an expansive gathering of the history of gender and sexually nonconforming people of African descent—an archive which, following Brent Hayes Edwards, we might understand not as a physical structure housing records but as "a discursive system that governs the possibilities, forms, appearance and regularity of particular statements, objects, and practices."[3] I wouldn't be looking to cast light on the (somewhat familiar) argument that this archive shows how spirituality allows trans* and queer people particular kinds of self-expression, sympathetic as I may be to such claims. My choice to follow the lwa instead would explore how a variety of engagements with

Ezili—songs, stories, spirit possessions, dream interpretations, prayer flags, paintings, speculative fiction, films, dance, poetry, novels—perform black feminist intellectual work: the work of *theorizing black Atlantic genders and sexualities*. This is the kind of theorizing Barbara Christian asked us to take seriously when she reminded feminist scholars "people of color have always theorized . . . and I am inclined to say that our theorizing (and I intentionally use the verb rather than the noun) is often in narrative forms, in the stories we create, in riddles and in proverbs, in the play with language, since dynamic rather than fixed ideas seem more to our liking."[4] Reflecting on Ezili's theorizing, then, I look to situate a discussion of black Atlantic genders and sexualities not primarily through queer studies, but rather within a lineage of black feminisms: a lineage which pushes me to ask what it would sound like if scholars were to speak of Ezili the way we often speak, say, of Judith Butler—if we gave the centuries-old corpus of texts engaging this lwa a similar explanatory power in understanding gender.

-❧❧-

Nwaye nape nwaye! Ezili, si o wè m'tombe nan dlo pranm non. Sove la vi zanfan yo. *Drowning, we are drowning! Ezili, if you see me falling in the water, please rescue me. Save the life of your children.*[5] The Ezili are watery spirits whose name derives from Lac Aziri in Benin, and are associated with seas, rivers, waterfalls, springs, and other bodies of fresh and saltwater in Haiti.[6] Yes, as you're certainly thinking, this association suggests a metaphoric connection between femininity and fluidity that scholars have aptly explored.[7] But as I began research on Ezili in the wake of the January 12, 2010, earthquake, watching media displays of the dispossessed and their search for uncontaminated water, I wondered uneasily: when Haitian servitors of Ezili think of water, how often do they think of "a river that empties into no known sea" (as Luce Irigaray describes feminine sexuality)[8]—and how often of the very real, very well-known spring or tap from which they draw their daily water? As of 2008, 10.7 percent of Haitians had access to piped water at home. Surface water drawn directly from springs or piped from rivers makes up the principal water supply in rural Haiti, while communal taps serve this purpose in Port-au-Prince.[9] (Cisgender) Men generally don't collect water since, as one interviewee told a researcher studying water quality, "It's a woman's concern because we don't cook, clean the house or wash clothes."[10] But women, masisi, and children walk long, sometimes dangerous distances to haul water home, where they disinfect it with bleach. They purify their daily haul because they know that, even when a spring runs clear, there's too much in the water they can't see: pollutants they understand to cause diarrhea, malaria, typhoid, cholera, dysentery, skin problems, colic, cancer, female genital infections, malaria, and more.[11] Connections between femininity—whether transfeminine or cisgender—and water—whether brought home by women or by masisi—are not only metaphoric here but concrete, quotidian, and life-or-death; and women's and masisi's desires to conjure the clean-running water that Ezili represents are not purely idealistic but eminently practical, literally down-to-earth.

Let me locate this water quality discussion for a moment in the northern coastal city of Gonaïves and the body of water it opens into, the Gulf of Gonâve. On September 18, 2004, Tropical Storm Jeanne devastated Gonaïves and surrounding areas. Flash floods killed 2,800 people, displaced thousands more, and damaged or destroyed 80 percent of the city. A water shortage ensued as the "previously limited municipal water supply was further compromised and other drinking water sources"—that is, rivers and springs—"were contaminated with cadavers, excrement, and debris."[12] For weeks afterward, while city residents vied for bottled water provided by nongovernmental organizations, people outside the city center traveled longer distances than usual to seek potable water from semifunctional wells or rivers they hoped to find still unpolluted. This extra work, undertaken while grieving people and homes lost, and the consequences of being unable to find clean water even after extended searches, disproportionately fell on Ezili's children—on women and masisi, Gonaïves's water carriers and purifiers. Ezili, rescue us from the waters; Ezili, save your children.

But women and masisi are not only, by necessity, water purifiers on the Gonâve coast. They are also, and also by necessity, water polluters. While contamination like that suffered after Tropical Storm Jeanne may be sporadic, the gulf is daily, visibly polluted by trash disposal in city neighborhoods unserved by sanitation services. "In these conditions, people perceive the sea and gullies as vacant spaces into which trash can be thrown," Michel Desse explains. "The first meters along the coast are covered with detritus."[13] Since women are routinely responsible for cooking and sanitation, many items choking the water must have been thrown from their hands: soiled food wrappers, used sanitary products, empty relaxer bottles, unlucky lottery tickets. And there must be other things, too, thrown by other hands. While this contamination does not show up in any official studies or reports, storytellers document it. Nice Rodriguez's short story "Throw It to the River" depicts an urban poor community on the banks of a river near Manila Bay, which, much like Haiti's west coast, jettisons its domestic refuse—pet carcasses, dirty diapers, old love letters—into the water flowing by their back doors. *"Throw, throw, throw. The river hauls it all,"* the story's narrator intones. This narrator is a butch lesbian named Tess, whose tale revolves around the last item she threw to the river: an uncomfortable, rough-edged dildo she bought to make love to Lucita, the femme lover who's just left her to marry a Filipino American man.[14] Like Tess, the Gulf of Gonâve's madivin and masisi must throw queer detritus to the river, too—must throw to the river parts of their experience that, like Tess and Lucita's dildo, are too uncomfortable, no longer fit, are not useful any more, have become painful. Documented or not, the effluvia and refuse of same-sex-loving, same-sex-fucking, gender-reworking, gender-reharmonizing bodies must be polluting these coastal waters, too. Drowning, we are drowning! Ezili, if you see me in the water, pick me up.

Water is the depths of winter, and a premonition of summer, too. In December 2011, two days after the winter solstice, my daughter, my husband, my cats, and I traveled to Austin, Texas. With a semester off from teaching before beginning a new job in the University of Texas's African and African Diaspora Studies Department, I planned to use this time to start writing my reflections on Ezili. The new year showered us with an unusually warm winter of unexpected thunderstorms, the beginning of an end to the drought that parched central Texas. On these wet nights, someone I never expected to see arrived to visit me in dreams. Marie Laveau, famed Vodou queen who presided over New Orleans for much of the nineteenth century, came gently and imperiously to command I include her in my book. On those nights and mornings after, I didn't understand what the connection between this queen and my project was, no, I certainly didn't. But I set out to make sense of it in any way I could— reading everything I could get my hands on about Marie Laveau, trying to listen to what I was being told.

That Marie Laveau continues to appear in New Orleans over a hundred years after her death, I knew. She regularly presents herself in businesses and tourist attractions that flank the French Quarter where she lived, showing up during readings by famed gay psychic Phillip Humphries at Marie Laveau's House of Voodoo and brushing past patrons at the Quarter's oldest and most haunted queer bar—Cafe Lafitte in Exile—where ghosts of Tennessee Williams and Truman Capote perch on bar stools and chat with patrons.[15] And in the days following Hurricane Katrina, passersby saw her sitting at the site of her former house on St. Ann Street, sobbing for the city she loved and loves. But as I started to read more about her, I learned that while I knew her as a still-present ancestor, Marie Laveau was undergoing what Caroline Morrow Long calls a "Vodou canonization"—the process of being elevated to the status of a lwa.[16] This canonization is galvanized by the leadership of New Orleans–based mambo Sally Ann Glassman, who calls Marie the "historical lwa of New Orleans" and, at the midsummer ritual she performs in her honor at St. John's Bayou, draws a vèvè for her that merges her initials with a curvilinear, snake-like cross.[17] In her beautiful *Vodou Visions*, Glassman describes this emerging lwa as a spirit who performs

> a primal seductive dance with history and race. . . . Marie Laveau operates on many levels, most of which are misinterpreted, and all of which cause her much pain. She used these misinterpretations on the secular level during her life to promote awareness of the Lwa. She is seemingly open, but actually she is intensely private internally. She is open to the core of the psyche, that dark, magical territory where she works creatively. . . . Hear her drum rhythms pulsing like blood. It is the ongoing passage of the bloodline in the eternal feminine.[18]

Much of this description echoes that of the Ezili, lwa of the feminine and of the inner depths of creativity, mistresses of the erotic and the esoteric. During her lifetime, Marie Laveau, like Ezili Freda, was known as the bride of Danbala. Does this make the lwa Marie Laveau—or, perhaps, the pantheon of Marie Laveau—sisters to the Ezili? Cousins? Lovers, or wives? And what to make of the queer connection that the Ezili and Mademoiselle Marie share? Is it just geographical accident that Marie appears with such regularity to gay psychics and bar patrons in New Orleans, or does she share with the Ezili a special relationship to same-sex-loving folk? As I was asking myself these questions, Madamoiselle Marie, perhaps dissatisfied with my progress, started to send messages into my husband's dream world. Marie Laveau's children, we were called in his dream, and invited to participate in a night of raucous sex on the beach, a black gay party to end all parties. What kind of Mother Marie was this, and what did she need me to know about her?

The first question I asked myself, as I approached this project: Why Vodou? Why would contemporary novelists, performers, and filmmakers—many of whom explicitly state they are *not* Vodou practitioners—choose to mediate their reflections on gender and sexuality through the epistemology of this spiritual practice? To trace my answers to this question, let me begin with the very briefest of sketches of what Vodou is. The Kreyòl word Vodou was transculturated from the Fon kingdom, where sacred energies were called *Vodun*. Haitian Vodou practitioners work to communicate with these sacred energies, here called lwa (from Yoruba, meaning "spirit master")—forces of nature including the ocean (Agwe), land/agriculture (Azaka), metals (Ogou), death (Gede)—in order to achieve personal harmony and fulfill their life purposes.

In its cosmology as well as its community formation, Vodou is radically inclusive of creative genders and sexualities. The Ezili are one of many pantheons of lwa who model and mentor the divinity of gender and sexual nonconformity. Yes, Danbala, the simultaneously male and female rainbow serpent; Gede, the hypersexual lwa of death and sex; and Nana Buruku, the primordial, androgynous moon-sun, all inspire and protect creative genders and sexualities. A significant number of people who serve these lwa are gender and sexually nonconforming, too. Straight-identified manbo (priestess) Jacqueline Epingle attests to the important role that straight and same-sex-loving women, as well as masisi—in fact, everyone *but* cishetero men—play in Vodou priesthood: "There are more women than men, more *manbo* than *houngan* [male priests] in Vodou. . . . The majority of *houngan* are either homosexuals or bisexuals. Men would rather not go into trance: male pride. Men do not like to lose control. Women are freer! The homosexual's spirituality directs him toward religion, and certainly toward the Vodou religion. Many manbo are bisexual or lesbians."[19]

Manbo Racine Sans Bout asserts that there is a "higher percentage of homosexuals at Vodou ceremonies, and in the priesthood, than in the general population" because gender and sexually complex Haitians are excluded from the priesthood and congregations of Catholic and Protestant churches, leaving Vodou the only spiritual community open to them.[20] In fact, *every* Vodou temple is understood to need gender nonconforming practitioners. Marilyn Houlberg reports that masisi "are important to guarantee the efficacy of a service; as I have seen, they often play a special role in ceremonies," facilitating the arrival of spirit presences through their expert dancing.[21] And some houses, in fact, need only the gender and sexually creative. Manbo Racine, Houngan Aboudja, and scholar Elizabeth McAlister report several temples "composed entirely of gay men, or of gay women," as Manbo Racine puts it.[22] None of this means that Vodou's current organization is not practically patriarchal. Indeed it is, with (often purportedly heterosexual) men occupying positions of greatest power from which they routinely exploit the labor of women and masisi. But this does mean that Vodou offers more conceptual and spiritual space for expansive gendered and sexual practices than western European epistemologies circulating in the Caribbean. And so, it offers a particularly open space from which contemporary black queer artists can imagine love and possibility.

In addition to this queer present, Vodou has (what I would call) a queer past. As any Caribbeanist will tell you, Vodou is literally revolutionary. The world's only successful slave revolution, when Haitians emancipated themselves and defeated Napoleon's army to form the first black republic, began during a Vodou ceremony at Bwa Kayiman on August 14, 1791. Historians usually narrate the revolution that erupted afterward as a series of events propelled by a cadre of hetero-cismasculine heroes, including Toussaint L'Ouverture, Jean-Jacques Dessalines, Alexandre Pétion, and Henry Christophe. Less often documented are the roles of feminine and gender-nonconforming leaders. Kate Ramsey records the leadership of an unnamed "old black woman" who assembled groups of rebels in the Cul-de-Sac plain; she also cites the case of Maman Dio, decried as a "witch" and leader of a "band of freedmen" in Le Cap, who was accused of "terrifying the weak minded and . . . propagating the type of fanaticism abused to lead into disorder all the Africans who allow themselves to be taken in by these hallucinations."[23] There's also the story of Romaine Rivière, the Léogâne landowner of color who assembled a following of thousands of rebels and, acting on instructions from his "godmother," the Virgin Mary, waged guerrilla warfare against planters and soldiers during the revolution's first year. He adopted the name Romaine la Prophetesse, choosing the feminine title of Prophetess rather than prophet for reasons which, according to Terry Rey, no one knows. No one knows, no; but his choice of this name suggests not only that Romaine had feminine identifications, but felt those feminine identifications led him to do divine battle.

I want to return to Bwa Kayiman, that primal moment of Vodou revolutionary impulse. Most historiographical accounts record early revolutionary leader Boukman Dutty as the ceremony's presiding houngan, then note he was assisted by a (often unidentified) manbo sometimes named as Cecile Fatima or, alternatively, Manbo Marinette. But while this priestess plays a supporting role in canonical histories, other sources suggest she may, in fact, have been the *sole* officiating priest. Ramsey explains: "Boukman, one of the most important figures of the first months of the revolution, may or may not have been a spiritual leader himself; the earliest accounts of Bwa Kayiman do not mention him, and even Céligny Ardouin's oral-historically informed description of the ceremony in which he does figure represents the ritual being led by a woman."[24] What remains consistent in stories of Bwa Kayiman is that the most important presence that night was not human at all. Rather, the Haitian Revolution began with the arrival of fierce, dagger-wielding Ezili Danto, who (through the medium of the manbo) killed a black pig, distributed its blood to participants, and sent them to fight.

Danto, whom Brown describes as a "hardworking, solitary, sometimes raging mother," is a warrior spirit who fights alongside the oppressed—particularly oppressed women.[25] "And," as devotee George René puts it, "there's one thing you should know. Dantò, she's a lesbian."[26] Manbo Racine explains: "Homosexual women are considered very often to be under the patronage of Ezili Dantò who, while heterosexual in the sense that she has a child, is a fierce and strong female image. Many people think of Dantò herself as a lesbian."[27] What would it mean if we listened to these testimonies as part of the story of Bwa Kayiman; if we took seriously that the Haitian Revolution was launched not by a man or even a woman, but by *the spirit of women who love women*?

Dark-skinned, hard-working, woman-loving Danto's power to start a revolution came from her position standing firm on what Sylvia Wynter terms *demonic ground*. Drawing on the language of Shakespeare's *The Tempest*, Wynter theorizes demonic ground as the conceptual space assigned to Enlightenment Man's sexual-racial other: the black woman, whose rational, nondemonic self-expression cannot even be imagined because such a radically different way of understanding the world would explode the master's discourse. What better way to electrify this demonic ground than a ceremony for Danto: not only the mother figure in a religion too often decried as satanic, not only the darkest of the Ezili pantheon, but, as "lesbian," (arguably) the most outside patriarchal dominance? And, as Katherine McKittrick puts it in her beautiful analysis of Wynter's concept, what better to force us to imagine "what would happen to our understanding and conception of race and humanness if black women legitimately inhabited our world and made their needs known? . . . What does her nondeterministic impossibility add to our conceptualization of humanness?"[28] Perhaps, then, in calling on Vodou and its revolutionary past and potential, the artists I'm looking at also explore ways to speak from demonic ground; also explore ways to upend a world that refuses to recognize how heavily its self-conceptualization rests on the backs of black women, madivin, and masisi.

❦

If Ezili *is* water, then you know she contains all kinds of trash: seen and unseen, organic and inorganic, from individuals, companies, natural disasters, unnatural histories. The trash that circulates in Ezili is not only a concrete collection of detritus but, literally and metaphorically, an istwa de fatra—that is, a (hi)story of remains. I take my understanding of this concept from Jani Scandura's incisive discussion of the myriad linkages between archives and dumps in *Down in the Dumps: Place, Modernity, American Depression*. Excavating the long academic history of garbage, Scandura opens a discussion of nineteenth-century German historian Johann Gustav Droysen's "theory of remains." Following Cornella Vismann, she explains how Droysen "distinguished between materials that had been intentionally preserved for posterity and those 'more truthful' fragments that had been accidentally or unconsciously preserved from the past . . . calling these remnants or 'remains' (Uberreste) rather than 'refuse' (Abfall)."[29] Of course, Haitians who use their rivers either as a source of household water or as a garbage dump occupy precarious social positions such that they rarely have the remnants of their lives preserved in traditional archives. But the waters, the Ezili, become a history of remains that at once archives their past and predicts their future. In serving as a waste receptacle they collect unclaimed cadavers, (literally) broken homes, household waste, shit, blood, and, why not, unwanted dildos—which, like all the Ezili and unlike most official histories, tell stories of women's, masisi's, madivin's, and poor people's lives. And, in serving as drinking water, they witness that it is possible for the remnants of the past to poison you, yes—but, if properly filtered, that same water can become the key to survival.

For 90 percent of Haitians—because of their multiply perilous positions relative to class, gender, sexuality—this water, this history has not been adequately processed, and so has the capacity to sicken and kill those who imbibe it. But if the water-bearers, if Ezili's children can process and filter this water/history themselves, with their own hands and resources, then this same substance has the capacity to sustain and heal those who cook, wash, pray with it. Because they are in a position where their history—like their reproductive and other labor—is considered trash, women, madivin, and masisi will be those most often charged with processing the figurative as well as literal remains circulating in Ezili's waters. And if they can strategize and learn how to keep themselves alive by finding nourishment in Ezili, in the istwa (histories and stories) that she gathers, in all the reflections and surfaces that she claims: well, then, this becomes the most defiant act of resistance possible in the interpenetrating conditions of classism, misogyny, homophobia, and transphobia in which we all live.

The very, very beautiful Marie Laveau was born a free woman of color in New Orleans in 1794, where she reigned as Vodou queen for nearly seventy years until her death in 1881. "Marie Laveau" was in fact plural—not one woman, but two: Marie I and Marie II, the latter perhaps the biological, perhaps the spiritual daughter of the first Voodoo queen, who continued to reign in her mother's name after her death.[30] Mam'zelle Marie, as she's called, lived through two major events in the history of New Orleans Vodou. The first began in 1809, when the port of New Orleans received almost ten thousand Haitian refugees, suddenly doubling the population of Orleans parish. Nearly twenty years before, these masters and slaves, whites, mulattoes, and blacks had fled revolutionary Haiti and settled in Cuba, until the Spanish—fearful of Napoleon's ongoing campaigns—began a crackdown on Frenchmen that forced Haitians there to seek refuge in Louisiana.[31] While elements of African-based religions had been practiced in Creole Louisiana prior to 1809, New Orleans's sudden

Haitianization sparked the systematization of Vodou (or, as it is often spelled in New Orleans, Voodoo) in the city where Marie Laveau was coming of age.

The second shift in New Orleans Vodou began in the 1850s, when local police undertook an unprecedented crackdown on practitioners. As Ina Fandrich puts it, "Until the middle of the nineteenth century, the New Orleans police force had been turning a blind eye on the Voodoo events mushrooming in the city. During the decade before the Civil War, however, the city's Voodoo practitioners increasingly came under attack. The aggression culminated in numerous spectacular Voodoo arrests in the 1850s and 1860s." She then adds: "Interestingly, all those arrested were women."[32] As the *Daily Delta* reported, these women were charged with engaging in "an unlawful assemblage . . . of white women, free women of color, and slaves."[33] While interracial gatherings had long been illegal, in the decade following successful slave resistance among the Black Seminoles and on the Louisiana-bound ship *Creole*, enslaved women mixing freely in Vodou ceremonies with their "superiors"—white and free women of color—was perceived as a mounting, doubled threat to social order: because of both the well-known ways that Vodou had sparked revolution in the not-too-distant Haitian past, and the ways that interracial collaborations were fomenting slave resistance in the contemporary U.S. South. "There can be no doubt of the vast injury [Vodou ceremonies] do to the slave population," the *Picayune* insisted with venomous concern. "Carried on in secret, they bring the slaves into contact with disorderly free negroes and mischievous whites. The police should have their attention continually alive to the importance of breaking up such unlawful practices."[34]

At the same time, it was no coincidence that all those arrested were women. This was doubtless in large part because New Orleans Vodou was overwhelmingly a women's tradition, including a vast majority of female leaders and practitioners. In fact, not just Vodou but the entirety of New Orleans's Creole of color society was dominated by women. Two-thirds of the free population of color was female, and free women wielded significant social and financial success as shopkeepers, hairdressers, cooks, small business owners, and real estate brokers. The woman of color–led, women-only Vodou gatherings that police interrupted, then, stood out as metonyms for a social order in which female and African social power insistently threw unnatural challenges at the white supremacist patriarchy on which chattel slavery was so precariously, irretrievably based.

Newspaper articles covering these Vodou arrests and ensuing trials suggested another disturbing, titillating element to these all-female gatherings: was *something erotic* part of these ceremonies? The *Daily Crescent* reported in 1860 that police raiding a Vodou ceremony found "six Negro women in a state of perfect nudity, dancing obscenely"; three years later the *Daily Picayune* noted that an officer investigating a suspicious meeting "found about forty naked women—all colored except two—who were dancing the Voudou."[35] High priestess Betsey Toledano, defending her right to religious assembly after her 1850 arrest, testified that "she frequently had meetings of women only, at her house, to go through certain feminine mysteries" and that "there were secrets connected with the society, which it was intended were not for the coarser eyes and ears of the body masculine."[36] What feminine mysteries, and what women's secrets might those have been? Descriptions of Vodou ceremonies as orgies of naked, writhing dancers were commonplace in nineteenth-century newspapers, and recent historians have reacted to these with well-founded outrage. They point out that "naked" might have meant anything less than fully dressed in the nineteenth century; and, more importantly, that reading the ceremonies' dances as hypersexual betrayed a racist misunderstanding of the embodied nature of Vodou worship.[37] I agree with both of these points—but neither means there was *not* anything erotic going on in ceremony. Precisely because Vodou understands the body as divine, practitioners have been known to make use of breaks in ceremony to have a variety of kinds of sex, and certainly many end up in someone else's bed afterward. Why gloss over the possibility that the women dancing naked and sharing the secrets of the female body at New Orleans Vodou ceremonies may have been loving those bodies, too? Then the threats to the social order going on behind these closed doors multiply again, as the police break in to find not only white, black, and of color mixing promiscuously; not only women taking care of each other without patriarchal help; but women finding a kind of pleasure in these comings-together that could only lead them to cry out from demonic ground.

—•—

The second question I asked myself, the question I've never, ever finished answering: why do these artists return over and over again to Ezili—not Danbala, not Gede, but always Ezili? I knew easy answers to this question.

One of Vodou's complexities is that though day-to-day practice of this religion is dominated by women and masisi, few of its lwa are feminine spirits. The pantheon of spirits known as Ezili is the richly, expansively, riverinely powerful exception to this rule: Gran Ezili, Ezili Freda, Ezili Danto, Ezili Je Wouj, Ezili Taureau, Lasirenn, and others are immensely influential for all those practitioners who embody and/or desire femininity. Ezili's most prominent paths include Ezili Freda, the luxurious mulatta who loves perfume, music, flowers, sweets, and laughter but always leaves in tears; the fierce protectress Danto; and Lasirenn, a mermaid who swims lakes and rivers where she invites women passersby to join her and initiates them into mystical (erotic?) knowledge.[38] Indeed, no other lwa maps and mirrors queer femininity and womanness in the way Ezili does.

Because of this prominent, unique femininity, Ezili is also, as Colin Dayan notes, the lwa who most often appears in Caribbean literature, and her faces prominently mark work by Haitian women novelists from Marie Chauvet to Edwidge Danticat.[39] In anthropology as well, Elizabeth McAlister claims, "most fieldwork and writing on gender and sexuality in Vodou focuses on the spirit or goddess Èzili."[40] Building on these literary and anthropological writings, key theoretical texts in Caribbean gender studies often take Ezili as their focal point. The most foundational of these is Dayan's "Erzulie: A Women's History of Haiti." Her fiercely insightful, unrelentingly iconoclastic essay argues that the pantheon of Ezili, with their intimate, obscured connections to enslavement and emancipation, offer a more complex way of knowing Haitian womanhood than hegemonic feminism can produce— one that preserves "histories ignored, denigrated, or exoticized" by standard historiography, and "tells a story of women's lives that has not been told."[41] This is a story that complicates feminine sexuality, for "though a woman, Erzulie vacillates between her attraction for the two sexes."[42] And, though artistically, gloriously feminine, Ezili also quite spectacularly explodes gender binaries: "She is not androgynous, for she deliberately encases herself in the trappings of what has been constituted in a social world (especially that of Frenchified elites) as femininity. . . . She takes on the garb of femininity—and even speaks excellent French—in order to confound and discard the culturally defined roles of men and women."[43] Dayan opens academic space—or better, academic demonic ground—to think of Ezili as both sexually and gender queer, but never develops this possibility. She instead goes on to analyze novels in which the lwa appear in resolutely heterocentric plots. The novels, films, and performances I turn to here enter intertextual conversations with many of these earlier texts—novels, ethnographies, theories—but, rather than keeping the Ezilian sexual creativity they find in the margins, open directly *there*, moving deeper into where other possibilities for gender and sexuality break open in Ezili's arms. And I, in turn, try to follow.

But there was also a less straightforward, more sinuous answer that inspired me as I began this project. In her watershed study *Divine Horsemen: The Living Gods of Haiti*, Maya Deren writes of Ezili as "that which distinguishes humans from all other forms: their capacity to conceive beyond reality, to desire beyond adequacy, to create beyond need. . . . In her character is reflected all the élan, all the excessive pitch with which the dreams of men soar, when, momentarily, they can shake loose the flat weight, the dreary, reiterative demands of necessity."[44] In other words, Ezili is the lwa who exemplifies imagination. And the work of imagination is, as other scholars have already beautifully stated, a central practice of black feminism—indeed, it remains a black feminist necessity to explicate, develop, and dwell in the demonic grounds of realities other than the secular Western empiricisms that deny black women's importance in knowing, making, and transforming the world. As Saidiya Hartman writes, the deepest, most pathbreaking black feminist scholarship around sex and sexuality may be to imagine new possibilities for black women's bodies, stories, desires: "to imagine what cannot be verified . . . to reckon with the precarious lives which are visible only in the moment of their disappearance."[45] Reaching even more broadly, Grace Hong asserts, "Calling for a black feminist criticism is to do nothing less than to imagine another system of value, one in which black women have value."[46] As a principle of both femininity and imagination, Ezili calls out a submerged epistemology that has *always* imagined that black masisi and madivin as well as black ciswomen *create our own value* through concrete, unruly linkages forged around pleasure, adornment, competition, kinship, denial, illness, shared loss, travel, work, patronage, and material support. So in addition to engaging Ezili to enter conversations with well-known literary and academic texts, I see queer artists turning to her as the figure of a submerged, black feminist epistemology: one that, like their own work, testifies to the important antiracist, antiheteropatriarchal work that imagination can do, when it creates mirrors in which the impossible becomes possible.

⊰⊱

Manman mwen, manman mwen kote ou ye? Nou tande nan dlo. Kote ou ye, manman mwen? *My mother, my mother where are you? We're waiting in the water. Where are you, my mother?* Yes, the Ezili are water. And every summer, to remind themselves of and immerse themselves in the power of this, thousands of her servitors make pilgrimages to bodies of water all over Haiti. During the last week of July, pilgrims pay homage to the patron saint of pilgrimages, St. Philomene—who doubles as the mermaid lwa Lasirenn, known as the Ezili of the waters—at the northern seaside town of Limonade. Not surprisingly, foreign observers register as much shock at what they understand to be the dirtiness of this annual pilgrimage as they do over the region's poor water quality. Wade Davis, in his controversial *The Serpent and the Rainbow*, reports his frank disgust at seeing the invalids who arrive to seek healing and appear to him "the most diseased and wretched display imaginable."[47] In August 2003, ostensibly to reflect on Jean-Bertrand's historic recognition of Vodou as one of Haiti's national religions earlier that year, the BBC published an article about the Plaine-du-Nord and Limonade pilgrimages titled "Voodoo's Spell over Haiti." Reporter Nick Caistor notes that pilgrims arrive in Limonade at dawn to cleanse themselves after visiting the sacred spring and mud baths at Plaine-du-Nord, where the lwa Ogou (syncretized with St. James) is honored, and where a black pig is sacrificed and "thrown into a pool of brown, bubbling mud. Many of the blue and red-robed believers jump into the pond as well."[48] He does not note any echo between this ritual and the events of Bwa Kayiman, but instead encourages another reading of the black pig by citing the disapproval of Catholic priest Adonais Jean-Juste, who complains, "The Bible tells us we are made in the image of God. But these people who bathe in mud are behaving like pigs—they're the animals who like to roll in mud. These voodoo believers need to be made clean by being baptised in Christ."[49]

Those who make this pilgrimage, of course, have a very different understanding of what it means to find springs and seasides full of so much more than just water. Yes, there's something in the water there—and that something is the lwa they've come in search of. Daniel Cosentino explains the mud baths that raised Caistor's eyebrows are understood by servitors as "St. James' own pond, known as the Trou Sen Jak. Its celestial sludge . . . mark[s] the emergence point for a saint who is a generalissimo of a military family of spirits named Ogou."[50] And though at the sea baths of Limonade which follow the next day, observers like Caistor or Davis might not be able to see anything clouding the waters, the servitors there also experience it infused with invisible power—the power of the invisibles, as lwa are also called in Haiti. Pilgrims bathe in the sea not to be cleansed so they can prepare to meet Lasirenn, no, but so that they can meet, commune with, and become Lasirenn as she exists in those waters: as she penetrates their eyes and mouths, washes in rivulets down their chests, fills the space between their legs, reshapes the skin of their feet, softly, forcefully, and irresistibly.

And the pilgrims know that she's there because as they bathe, Lasirenn mounts—that is, possesses—one after another after another, leaves them temporarily moving, seeing, and speaking as Lasirenn. Just as I believe it's important to take seriously that the Ezili *are* water in its most concrete form, I find it crucial to take seriously that, in moments of possession, these servitors *are* the Ezili of the waters. Because, as Roberto Strongman so beautifully puts it in his description of what it means to witness a possession by Lasirenn, taking this seriously is part of the psychic and corporeal decolonization that Vodou challenges us to undertake: "You have plunged into her watery domain, and as any uninitiated European or North American visitor to a Haitian Vodou ceremony, you find yourself having to reappraise Western notions of selfhood in order to understand the complex interactions between the practitioners and their gods in this religious community. What enables the initiates to go into trance for these deities? . . . And you dive deeper into the waters when you ask yourself, how is the Vodou concept of the body different from your own?"[51] Part of the differing body concept that Strongman references is an understanding that, in moments of possession, not only practitioners' souls but their bodies are activated by Lasirenn. So now regardless of skin color, age, genitalia, or ability, when the servitors enter into trance, their body *is* temporarily that of the lwa.

You might think this means that this seaside full of Lasirenn is now a space of all women, all women who passionately love women, all Lasirenn who passionately love Lasirenn. This is true, but something else is, too. When you are Lasirenn, you are never purely woman. Half fish and half human, Lasirenn is never one, but more: two races—black and white; two sexes—male and female; two sexualities—straight and same-sex loving. Practitioners understand that while her upper body is generous-breasted, her body below the water can by itself change into either a penis or vagina depending on the lovers she takes, so that everyone s/he makes love to finds whatever, whoever they most desire. This seashore full of Lasirenns, then, is full of bodies that are endlessly gender-mutable, a space where everyone experiences their divine capacity for gender and sexual creativity: that invisible power that, like the lwa herself, is part of the unseen *something* that charges the waters full of seminude, semimermaid bathers. Yes, the water in Haiti is contaminated with things you can't see, and this constricts the lives, bodies, and possibilities of those who live there. And yes, the water in Haiti is full of powers you can't see, and this endlessly expands the lives, bodies, and possibilities of those who immerse themselves there. Lasirenn, Labalen, Chapo m tonbe nan lanmè. M ap fe kares pou Lasirenn, Chapo m tonbe nan lanmè. *Lasirenn, Labalen, my hat falls into the sea. I caress Lasirenn, my hat falls into the sea.*

Mam'zelle Marie, fe chauffez. Mam'zelle Marie, chauffez ça. *Mademoiselle Marie, make it hot. Turn up the heat, feel the power.*[52] Police raids never touched Marie Laveau, who apparently knew very well how to surround herself with political as well as spiritual protection. And this protection served her well despite the fact that so much of her work took place just feet from the center of police intervention, at her house on St. Ann Street. The house was shielded from street gazes by a large front yard with a garden of fruits, vegetables, and flowers— pomegranate and fig trees, banana plants and honeysuckle vines.[53] During the day the yard was full of Marie's biological and adopted children, of female visitors and relatives crossing in and out of her doors, and of Indian women who, in town from the country by the river and the gulf to sell wares at market, slept in her yard and left baskets and vegetables in return.[54] Beyond the endless mix of sounds, smells, and sights in this teeming exterior, Marie received a steady stream of clients of all races, classes, and genders who came for consultations inside her personal altar room. And Friday nights she presided over well-attended ceremonies that often spilled from the altar room into the fenced backyard, where, not surprisingly, voyeurs reported seeing participants dance naked while Marie stood regally clothed, crowned by her signature tignon and glinting gold at her ears and wrists.[55]

C'est l'amour, oui Mam'zelle, c'est l'amour. *This is love, yes girl, this is love.*[56] When Marie moved into this house she shared it with her white cismale lover,

Christophe Glapion, with whom she had seven biological children and infor-
mally adopted several "young orphans whom no one else laid claim to," as the
Picayune Guide to New Orleans put it.[57] Her partnership with Glapion was part
of a dual marriage system well known throughout Caribbean societies: proper-
tied white men were given social sanction to form two conjugal households at
the same time, one with a legally wed white wife and another with a mistress
of color. In New Orleans, the colored lover was often, like Marie, maintained
in a house in the French Quarter, where she would doubtless have come into
contact with men involved in another kind of conjugal arrangement. This is
what one interviewee calls the "uptown marriage," in which "you live with your
wife and children uptown and you keep a boy in the Quarter. In the last century
the Creoles kept mistresses in the Quarter, and more than one kept a boy—it's
a very old custom."[58] No doubt some of these boys were clients who came to
Marie for readings, dancers who filled her yard on Friday nights.

Mam'zelle Marie, fe chauffez. Mam'zelle Marie, chauffez ça. After the Civil
War, as emancipation led to a Jim Crow hardening of the color line and police
tracking Vodou intensified once more, Marie Laveau moved her Friday night
ceremonies to Bayou St. John on Lake Pontchartrain. On June 23, she continued
to hold the most famous of all New Orleans Vodou ceremonies at this bayou:
the midsummer celebration of St. John the Baptist. "Like so much in the life
of Marie the Second," as Martha Ward writes, this ceremony "was about water
and the flow of spirits . . . history through a woman's body."[59] Marie made a
dramatic, watery entrance recounted by Zora Neale Hurston in *Mules and Men*:
"Nobody see Marie Laveau for nine days before the feast. But when the great
crowd of people at the feast call upon her, she would rise out of the waters of
the lake with a great communion candle burning upon her head and another
in each one of her hands. She walked upon the waters to the shore."[60] There,
she ordered a huge fire lit, began dancing, and, at midnight, led followers to
bathe in the waters.

C'est l'amour, oui Mam'zelle, c'est l'amour. Veiled suggestions, as well as
outright accusations of scandalous sexual practices, surrounded these ceremonies. There were the usual intimations of interracial and group sex: a white
woman who lived on Lake Pontchartrain complained, "On St. John's Eve this
whole section was looking like a scene in hell. . . . Can you imagine all them
people, white and colored, dancing around like devils, and all of them naked
as jaybirds?"[61] Demonic grounds and demonic waters, too. Marie was known
to consort with sex workers and was accused of running a house of prostitution

at a nearby cottage; "to her influence may be attributed the fall of many a virtuous woman," the *New Orleans Democrat* moralized in her obituary.[62] While men were certainly present at these ceremonies, there were also suggestions that most of the devilish dancing—and other lewd acts—took place among women, since, as one *Times* reporter bemoaned, of the participants "two-thirds were females of the lowest order."[63] Was this, I began to wonder, the night of debaucherous black queer sex on the beach that my husband had been told about in his dreams? Were some of the few men there boys from the Quarter, too? Certainly, the celebrations at Bayou St. John seemed queer in that they offered a promiscuous meeting point for what Cathy Cohen describes as "relationships which have been prohibited, stigmatized, and generally repressed" and that trace "spaces of shared or similar oppression and resistance."[64] Oui mademoiselle, this, *all* this, is love.

———

But the question that I struggled with by far the longest before I could sit down to write a word of this book, the question I truly feared I'd never find an answer to, was *how* to write about Ezili. I was clear from the beginning that I wanted to write this as a serious, quite literal response to M. Jacqui Alexander's call "to move beyond the more dominant understanding of African spiritual practice as cultural retention and survival, to get inside the meaning of the spiritual as epistemological, that is, to pry open the terms, symbols, and organizational codes that the Bantu-Kongo people used to make sense of the world."[65] But if I wanted to, really wanted to, write of Vodou and Ezili as epistemology, to engage the religion and pantheon not just as subject matter but as a way of knowing that counters Enlightenment rationality, would standard academic discourse—the Enlightenment-inspired literary theory I'd been so well trained to produce—suffice? That was one way of reflecting on Ezili, certainly, but if I mirrored it back as the *only* way, I knew I'd be playing it too safe, refusing to tread the demonic ground I was praising from afar.

At first, I thought I might write each chapter in two voices: one which drew on my training as a priestess to reflect different manifestations of Ezili, and another which drew on my training as a literary critic to elaborate textual readings. In this way, I wanted to present the stories of Ezili as theorizing, but not in the way of a theory applied to a text. Rather, both Ezilian theory and fictional text would occupy the common space of the page in such a way as to interact in your reading, producing meaning somewhere between theorizing and imagining. It sounded like a good idea—at least for a few weeks. But I quickly realized that *two* voices was the wrong number. Vodou epistemology understands that one plus one equals (not two, but) three. And Vodou conceptions of human sentience work with the understanding that we come to konesans (knowledge) through the knowledge of the intellect (which I wanted to index by academic prose) and spirit (which I wanted to index by my explorations of Ezili), yes, but also by that of our ancestors, who continue to live in our cells, psyches, and imaginations. So, adding one and one, I came to the decision that I needed to add a third section to each chapter, one exploring the life and lessons of intellectual, spiritual, and biological ancestors who reflect into Ezili's mirrors.

Interspersing these voices on the page, then, is my gesture toward honoring Vodou's way of knowing the world. My deliberate heaping of disparate things together also honors the logic and aesthetic of an altar to Ezili, where you might find stacked together, say, a statue of the Virgin and Child draped in beads, a family picture, plastic dolls with hand-sewn clothes, rolled Vodou flags in red and blue, and Kongo packets doing work.[66] As Daniel Cosentino describes in his landmark *Sacred Arts of Haitian Vodou*, the sections "jostle one another like objects on a Vodou altar. In the manner of disparate votive objects, they are arranged according to an aesthetic first described by Heraclitus two and a half millennia ago, 'a heap of rubble, piled up at random, is the fairest universe'; and refined for our time by Charles Simic, 'You don't make art, you find it. You accept everything as its materials.' "[67] The disjunctures between sections in *Ezili's Mirrors* similarly challenge Enlightenment concepts of order and sense to reach for the other, black Atlantic senses that Alexander points toward. So when fonts change and you read the ruptures, breaks, breakdowns between sections and think, rightly, *this doesn't make sense to me*—please know this is because I'm reaching for that other kind of sense. And while, like Ezili Freda, I dream of perfection . . . I often create most through imperfection. Written in a language of gaps, fissures, and queer assemblage, *Ezili's Mirrors* is a difficult text. And while black women are often discouraged from claiming our right to be difficult, I'm asking you to wade through this recalcitrant disjointedness to bear witness to the difficulty of piecing together divinity from fragments of black queer life.

❧

In the sea at Limonade, servitors can so easily become water because they already are just that—because 70 percent of their bodies are water, and they're only connecting to what is so ever-present to them. And they can so easily become Ezili, too, because they already are; because like all ancestors she (they understand) is in their genetic code, and when she enters them in trance they're only bringing to the surface one of the many parts that make them who they are. Lwa are not gods. Like Catholic saints or bodhisattvas, they're elevated ancestors: humans who once lived and whose experiences so exemplified a force of nature that they merge with that force after death. As real people whose lives never disappear but are continually available to the living, the Ezili act as what Keith McNeal discusses as "mythistorical archives"—sources of information about the past that "activate the past by accessing a kind of memory not much given to everyday consciousness, at least not explicitly so."[68] Ezilian songs, dances, stories, and spirit possessions form a mythical archive of stories lost to the official record but that servitors not only refuse to forget but in fact bring into their very bodies.

McNeal's work focuses on how Afro-Caribbean Orisha worship and Indo-Caribbean Shakti puja in Trinidad and Tobago record histories of slavery and immigration that "offer imaginative truths in relation to which people make sense and compete over life; apprehend the present, past, and future; work out complex identifications and relations among self and other; legitimate or mystify social relationships and inequities of power; and seek self-transformation or greater forms of collective change."[69] *Ezili's Mirrors* focuses on how Vodou also preserves istwa (stories/histories) like that of woman-loving Danto and gender-shifting Lasirenn, stories of gender and sexual creativity that are also mythistoric records of slavery and revolution. Much immensely powerful work has already explicated how ungendering—particularly defeminization—became a crucial component of the systematic dehumanization strategized under conditions of enslavement. I want to add to this discussion a consideration of how the ongoing, unending development and archiving of creative genders and femininities also enacts resistance to slavery and its aftermath. As Matt Richardson so beautifully puts it, "For Black people to claim gender at all is brave given the array of violences done physically and epistemologically to strip us from gendered being. However, to claim such an assemblage of creative interpretations of the self is dangerous in its dizzying audacity and flagrant noncompliance with the terms of our dehumanization."[70] And as her servitors sway, turn, and fall into the arms of the lwa, the Ezili are an archive of this dizzying audacity, and a beautiful one.

As I worked through my first reflections on Marie Laveau, I sent my early writing to Manbo Sallie Ann Glassman along with a series of questions that I was puzzling through on the connections between my project and Mam'zelle Marie, and she immediately, very generously responded to each and every question. She explained something of how and why Marie Laveau is becoming a lwa at the turn of the millennium: "She fulfills many of the prerequisites of becoming a lwa: as living memory of the person dies out, some stories are forgotten; some are embellished or maybe made up, or maybe two people's stories get mixed up until an archetypal force emerges. People continue to go to Marie for help, healing, insight, empowerment, guidance. As we struggle to bring balance to forms of leadership—i.e. to balance male-oriented, competitive, top-down, command and control leadership with more feminine modes: bottom up, consensus-driven, collaborative, intuitive—Marie becomes increasingly important."[71] Ms. Glassman made clear to me why the emergence of Marie Laveau as lwa would be important to the people I've been writing about in this introduction, to Cecile Fatima and Romaine la Prophetesse, women and masisi who draw water and pollute it: glinting with gold and crowned with cloth, Mam'zelle comes to push us to imagine what it will be like when Ezili's children—the water carriers and the revolutionaries—lead their own worlds. And in a lighting-flash moment, Ms. Glassman also made clear for me why it is that Marie Laveau has come to be part of this project; and it was, of course, not *at all* for the reasons I had imagined on my own.

What kind of work do you do with Marie Laveau? I asked Ms. Glassman. As part of her answer to this, she told me, "I find her especially empowering to women, who lack confidence or are fearful. Like John the Conqueror, she helps people overcome their perceived limitations."[72] *She helps people overcome their perceived limitations, unlimiting their perceptions.* These people could be a collective, I understood from Ms. Glassman; could be the work of a society shifting its perceptions around gender and sexuality, or the work of gender and sexually creative communities as they respond to the tremors these shifts engender. Because, as Marie Laveau told Ms. Glassman: "Sexual backlash (against gay marriage, for instance) is part of the healing process. As the world shifts and becomes more tolerant and accepting, the repressive forces act out and get more judgmental than ever. Soon this too will be a thing of the past."[73] The people could also be individuals, female and transfeminine people doing the black feminist work commanded by the Ezili—yes, the work of expanding our imaginations. We are empowered to begin this work as Marie Laveau "helps women especially, overcome emotional enslavement" so that, as Audre Lorde wrote in "The Uses of the Erotic: The Erotic as Power," "we begin to give up, of necessity, being satisfied with suffering, and self-negation, and with the numbness which so often seems like the only alternative in our society. Our acts against oppression become integral with self, motivated and empowered from within."[74]

And the people could also be me, just me, a black feminist scholar struggling with a second book she felt too small to hold but who was told by a manbo years ago in a reading, "You were born to lead, but you stay behind." Yes, this message was for me, too; Marie Laveau was here, in this imagination and on these pages, because she was telling me to finally, *finally* let go of the limitations I wrapped myself in like a cocoon and realize that even as I doubted that I could find the way and the words to tell these stories, I could. I could, and I must, and I am, and, even where my words and I fall short, I try in the hopes of opening space for those who come after. And so now, I knew: I'm writing this introduction, this book *for the love of Marie Laveau*. For the love of Laveau, love that expands the dark spaces in us like a rain-swollen bayou; pushes the barriers of the world we know like a hurricane unleashed; and heals what has been unloved like the flow of a river. Love that joins Haiti and New Orleans, Ezili and Mam'zelle, demonic and divine, history and istwa de fatra, archives and bodies, women and masisi, my readers and me.

There's another beginning to this book, a story I haven't told yet. My first trip to Haiti, in August 1998, I never went to a Vodou ceremony. But on August 15, the Feast of the Assumption and of Ezili Danto, I did something I've never done before or since. Wandering off from Aux Cayes in midday heat,

I left my wrinkled summer dress on the shore and went swimming naked in a pond, laughing and drawing the women friends I had come with into the water with me. And she didn't claim me then, in daylight, but that night I learned a lesson I never expected from Ezili. Yes, that night when I went to listen to drumming on the beach, something happened that I couldn't explain. All I knew was that it felt like the first time I kissed a woman—like my body was not mine, and my body was made for this. And in the space of a moment, in one movement of my hand, the safe fences that I'd drawn around my research and myself—here is Afro-Caribbean religion as I study it in a book, here is desire as another someone theorized it, here is what I know and here is what I feel—they all collapsed, torrentially, and still I am swirling. Still, there are no words for this and still, I search to learn them.

PHOTO BY CINDY ELIZABETH

A BLACK
CISFEMME IS
A BEAUTIFUL
THING

Black cisfemme sisters, are we real? Every time I think I catch a glimpse of one of us in the public eye . . . she disappears. There was Trinidadian Black Barbie Nicki Minaj, who wore iridescent pink leggings & promised she stopped for bad, bad lesbians, signed fans' titties—then with her first studio album told Black Men Magazine she doesn't sleep with women.[1] No homo, Nicki said. And Louisiana daughter Raven-Symoné, who started posting pics of herself in fabulous makeup & pastel extensions cuddled up to fine-ass butch AzMarie Livingston, but told Oprah she isn't any kind of a gay (let alone a femme).[2] She's a human who loves humans, she declared as she tossed violet, aqua, & silver hair & batted her eyelashes. Then Dominican York Internet diva Cardi B brandished blue and silver nails while she talked about sleeping with females, but clarified her only deep feelings are for people with penises.[3] She a ho but no homo, just like Nicki.

Kanye West said it: Girls kissin' girls, cause it's hot right? But unless they use a strap-on then they not dykes.[4] If you're femme on the streets & femme between the sheets, girl, you aren't actually a femme—you're a straight woman in disguise. Black nonbinary crippled femme shark Cyree Jarelle Jackson said it better: "The idea of cisfemmes passing for straight and receiving straight privilege ignores the fact that to patriarchy inside every lesbian lies a straight woman. Straight people don't see anything but straight."[5] Black cisfemme sisters, we aren't real to anyone but ourselves. If you're queer then you must be a stud, if you're fish then you must be straight.

Cisfemmes & transfemmes are sisters, not twins. Julia Serano speaks truth: "My very different trans history has led me to having a very different perspective on femininity and femme identity than that held by many of my cis femme sisters."[6] All African-descended femmes face challenges to our femme-ininity. But, black cister femmes, our continuing disappearance is particular to our cisness, one way cis privilege works for & against us at the same time. If we don't stop to think about how being Nicki Minaj & being Laverne Cox is different, well, we're missing a lot about how black queer gender—how black femme realness—does, & doesn't work.

Black cisfemme sisters, I've dressed for, preened for, lived for being a black cisfemme for over twenty years. Nicki femmes may disappear, ladies, but some of us just keep dressing in brighter pinks. I'm still here, & I've come to say: Look, Mamas, a black cisfemme is a beautiful thing.

Look at the next pages & see these fierce black cisfemmes, watch them dance with knowledge incarnadine. See MilDred Gerestant, who shows her tits & jock & insists on being femme & stud at the same time, what? Look for Ezili Freda, who makes impossible black cisfemmeness possible & regal too. Watch Janet Collins, trying to dance her way into black cisfemininity until she falls.

Then sing it with me, sisters: a black cisfemme is a beautiful thing. **Yes.**

ONE

TO TRANSCENDER TRANSGENDER

Ase! Welcome to Brooklyn, New York, on the Saturday night of October 9, 2010. Adia Whitaker, artistic director of Afro-Haitian dance company Ase, is hosting a dance class and release party for her video "Ezili," a fund-raiser toward Ase's next evening-length concert.[1] Set to Whitaker's vocal styling of "Lay Down Body," the video opens like many visits from Metres Manbo Ezili Freda Daome do—with an artistic, fantastic, glitter- and pink-infused toilette. In *Divine Horsemen*, Maya Deren describes Freda's toilette as a "process of creative transformation" that begins with washing her hands and face in a perfect enamel bowl, combing her hair at the mirror, arranging a rose-colored scarf around her hair, anointing herself with perfume, and bejeweling her neck with gold and pearl necklaces.[2] Whitaker's video cuts between two contemporary, African/ Haitian American versions of this toilette. One centers Whitaker at the mirror transforming herself into a very recognizable, but very twenty-first-century Freda: wrapping a long pink scarf around her neck, cinching her waist in a corset, ringing her eyes with sparkling pink shadow, layering strands of light- and hot-pink plastic beads and a large costume gold heart around her neck. The second features the company preparing for the video shoot: warming up, putting on pink T-shirts, lining up to braid hair and spray it pink, cinching rose-colored belts over their shirts. Both—the folkloric toilette, the urban fashion warm-up—represent what it means to Whitaker to embody Ezili Freda. As she says at the end of the video: "Folklore and fishnets, everybody, that's what it's about—because we can't just be walking around with all these skirts and headwraps on all the time! Because it falls off: wrap attacks, and bra straps, and all the things. Come on, now, we can do better. It does *not* always have to be . . . and sometimes you have to wear the frock, like, respect to tradition. But folklore and fishnets, dog, folklore and fishnets; like, that's really what it is, folklore and fishnets. Yes!"[3]

Sparkling through transparent pinks, Ezili's twin stylings make you see Freda for who she never wants you to forget she is, ladies: a spectacular force of gender creativity. As she works grown blackwoman magic through the glint of gold necklaces, Metres showcases herself as the only lwa with power to "transform the female into the feminine" (in Deren's words)—to activate gender as a creative process as elaborately, artistically played out as her exacting toilette, yes, or Whitaker's choreography. Always perfecting her magic, Freda's gender creativity (in stories I've heard) inevitably centers prismatic expressions of fem(me)ininity. Lasirenn morphs between dick and pussy; Danto comes as bull dagger as well as fierce femme: so why does Freda only arrive in pink and perfume? Deren describes Freda as "the divinity of the dream," and Mambo Vye Zo Komande LaMenfo explains her demands for the elaborate and pristine—particularly in Haiti, where neither is in the grasp of most servitors—as exemplifying the divine power of *demanding the impossible*. "Her energy," she writes, "is the solo pursuit of that which is unattainable." And maybe this is her connection to black fem(me)ininity: for hasn't flawless femininity been imperially imagined as *impossible* for people of African descent?

In her beautiful *The Witch's Flight: The Cinematic, the Black Femme, and the Image of Common Sense*, Kara Keeling puts forth: "The sedimentation of notions of femininity into common sense over time . . . has tended toward the exclusion of its accrual to black female bodies. It cannot be assumed that 'black woman' appears within the dictates of 'femininity.'"[4] Black queer women's exclusion from femininity is doubled, as black lesbians are always already assumed butch by virtue of their race *and* sexuality. Defying this violent common sense of black (queer) women's inexorable unfemininity, Keeling spotlights the *black femme function*: a concept that positions the black femme's cinematic appearance not just as a representation of particular lived experiences but as "a portal through which present (im)possibilities might appear."[5] Black queer fem(me)ininity demands viewers unmake and remake constricted constructions of racialized gender in creative ways. "The black femme is 'black' . . . AND 'woman' . . . AND 'lesbian,'" Keeling rhythmically emphasizes. "And she is each of these in such a way that each category's claim to be an expression of her identity is exploded by the effort required to maintain the validity of that claim. In each case, the black femme urges the project expressed by the category to recognize an alternative potential within it."[6] Creating fem(me) ininity where it didn't exist before her arrival and projecting it onto her mirror, Metres Manbo Ezili Freda is, she *is* the lwa of the black femme function. Lover of butches, artist of gender, and undoer of any common sense that refuses her expressions of full fabulousness, she theorizes the difference a black femme in fishnets can make.

Kara knows. When *The Witch's Flight* came out, I thanked her for what remains (a decade later) the only book-length text centering black cisfemmes, the only one celebrating the transgressive spectacularity of our queer genders. And while Freda's patronage of transfemmes and femme gay men is legendary, this chapter follows Keeling's lead by focusing on black cisfemmes and our complex relationship to fem(me)ininity. This focus is less about starting this book where and how I live than about taking seriously Julia Serano's contention that acknowledging the different social situations of cis- and transfemmes is crucial to enunciating an expansive femme-inism. Commonsense expectations of butchness for black queer ciswomen are *not the same* as commonsense expectations of heteromasculinity for black folk assigned male at birth, and black cisfemme-ininity and transfemininity resist gender conformity in different, complementary ways. In a dialogue with Janet Mock, bell hooks suggests that given black ciswomen's persistent masculinization, *all* black women should be understood as queer or trans—and "rather than seeing ourselves as . . . outside the dialogue of queerness and trans I think that we need to place ourselves as black females at the core of the dialogue."[7] I don't agree black cisfemmes need to place ourselves at the core of black transfeminist conversations—no, Metres. But we do need to talk about ourselves: practicing "black trans-cis-terhood"— to use black transfeminist theorist Dora Santana's felicitous phrase—means understanding black queer cisfemininity on its own terms.[8] Just as watching Ezili's different toilettes expands our vision of what divine black femme power looks like, carefully considering the different challenges leveled against black cis- and transfemmes' genders opens possibilities for more nuanced critiques of white supremacist heteropatriarchy.

Like Whitaker's toilettes, Ezili as black femme function doesn't look like commonsense versions of "high" fem(me)ininity. Folklore and fishnets, she models an expression of black cisfemme like Atlanta performer Vagina Jenkins: "I'm femme like my mother and my grandmother are—hardworking, handywomen who repair a leaky faucet or change the spark plug in a car, who curse like sailors, who get dressed up for church, who can cook like gourmets when moved to do so and order pizza when they aren't."[9] Wi maman, Ezili Freda's gender expressions are specific to African diaspora histories, where womanness doesn't always desire to match ideals of normative (white) femininity or go by the same names. Like any twirling, skirt-spreading Freda, black cisfemmeness is a dancer: a mistress (Metres) of invented gestures, steps, and repetitions with a difference, an archive of embodied knowledge whose beauty is in its self-conscious artifice, neither natural nor fragile nor durable. Black cisfemme-inity refuses to play black swan to white femme-ininity or dying swan to black masculinity, dances in an ensemble where she touches, pushes away, circles, leaps over a gamut of genders as she pleases. So let the show begin, black femme cisters, unleash your pinks and let the show begin!

———

Welcome, welcome back: this is the East Village, New York, 1999. A longtime crowd favorite, super-smooth, superfly, super-tailored drag king Dréd glides onstage at Club Casanova amidst hollers and cheers, peering at the audience from behind her silver-rimmed shades.[10] MilDred "Dréd" Gerestant is a "multi-spirited, Haitian-American, gender-illusioning, black, shaved, different, God/dess, anti-oppression, open, non-traditional, self-expressed, blessed, gender bending, drag-kinging, fluid, ancestor supported and after all that—non-labelling woMan" whose drag star shot heavenward when she was crowned 1996 Drag King of Manhattan at the fabulously chocolate, largely black and Latina HerShe Bar.[11] She quickly went on to become one the few black performers to cross over into largely white drag king counterculture blossoming in the city in the mid-1990s, parading her smooth mackdaddy, 1970s-inspired act five or six nights a week. Tonight—working it black funk-style—she emerges with her back to the audience, then confidently turns to slick back the hood of her old-school black track jacket and pump her ringed, braceleted hands to the beat of the Sugarhill Gang. As the rap progresses, she strips off her black suit to reveal another suit of silky black men's pyjamas . . . then—deftly as the ladies' man Dréd is—

unbuttons her Hugh Hefner pyjamas to unleash a red bikini, black patent miniskirt, and bulging, well-packed red jock, revelations punctuated by a jutting chin nod. The audience coos and shouts in appreciation of the attitude, the package, the king.

"I like all kinds of music; I'm versatile in a lot of things," Dréd tells interviewers Sarah Chinn and Kris Kranklin. "But one thing definitely is that I like the traditional old funky disco. I've always liked classics like 'Disco Inferno,' 'Shaft,' 'Superfly.' . . . I saw some of those movies when I was a kid, and when I was older, I was like 'Gee, I wish I lived in that era.' In a way now, when I dress up, I'm living, you know, in my own way, in that era."[12] In her lucid analysis of Dréd's soul/funk drag king act, Jana Evans Braziel argues that the artist's performance of hit songs and singers she loved as a child at once offers audiences an homage and a parody: an homage to black men she admires, and a parody of the overwhelmingly white audience's stereotypes of mackdaddy and superfly. "It is, I argue, the cultural gaze of the audience that Dréd parodies, and not the black male performers that the performance artist appropriates," she writes. "Dréd's king performances parody racist and racialized sociocultural constructions of black masculinity and the circulation of stereotypes in the American cultural imaginary . . ."[13] But even while executing this complex dance around mackdaddyness, the gender possibilities of Dréd's performance stumble when she tries to entice her audience into taking in her bra and her jock, her skirt and her beard at the same time. The final striptease reveals the softness of breasts without necessarily softening her act into femininity in her audience's eyes. The confident nod of her chin, the set of her eyebrows, the squaring of her shoulders all continue to register more Shaft than Foxy Brown . . . and the crowd cheers more loudly at her crotch-grab than her cleavage-reveal.

But what lesbian doesn't love big black dildo, and didn't Foxy Brown (or Pam Grier) end up as the straight sister on The L Word? Or, in other words: while the mackdaddy, the stud, the aggressive have been widely eroticized in (white) lesbian communities, the lingeried, lipsticked black cisfemme has all too often been treated as a tenuous apparition, barely visible. Dréd herself, for example, appeared on an episode of the Maury Povich show dedicated to drag; rather than kinging, here she dressed as a drag queen. During the show she was one of the performers who removed her wig (a classic drag queen flourish) to reveal the self under the clothes. When confronted with her shaved head, the audience took this as proof that Dréd must be male: that is, they were quite vocally willing to accept only markers of white femininity—long hair—as evidence of womanness. Queer audiences aren't necessarily more adept at reading black cisfemmeness, either. Bajan/Canadian cisfemme TJ Bryan relates an incident when she came to a poetry slam dressed in heels, red lipstick, and skin-tight black dress, only to be written up in an article in "the city's queer community rag" accompanied by a picture of her face grafted onto the body of a black male boxer.[14] While this picture ostensibly extolled her champion-worthy performance, Bryan offered another interpretation. "We, Black femmes, can often be masculin(ized)—automatically viewed, treated, and cruised as butches," she writes. "And even if we are seen as Femmes, we can still be devalued or just plain not perceived as Femme(inine) in any sense but the sexual—not just in the larger world, but also inside of queer/Black/'colored' communities of supposed resistance."[15]

This persistent masculinization of black lesbians continues a long, violent history of colonial fictions that categorized black females as inherently, irretrievably mannish—a mark of primitive societies lacking the sophistication necessary to produce refined queens (in addition to virile chiefs). Writing on sexologists' dissection of black female bodies in the nineteenth century and what this means for the construction of black lesbian genders, Matt Richardson puts forth: "The Black becomes the aporia between sex and gender such that the two never meet in any fashion that would satisfy the dictates of normative heterosexuality. The supposed lack of physical distinction between the sexes was thought to indicate a low moral character and manifest in a morbid sexual appetite that included homosexual attraction. As Sharon Holland has observed: 'It appears that the words lesbian and black are forged in blood, in physiognomy, and ultimately in racist science.' "[16] Dréd's insistence on developing creative, pliable self-descriptors that trouble masculine/feminine, butch/femme, king/queen binaries—*fluid, nonlabeling, woMan, womb-man*—shouldn't sound like just a matter of personal self-expression, then. No, even as her language acts in fun, it enacts the importance of expressing a black femmeness, curviness, bejeweled-ness, open-thighed-ness that never has to be erased: oh, *no*, girl—*not even while working your daddy mack.*

The question, though, following MilDred around New York at the turn of the millennium: how to get her (largely white) queer audiences to *see* that, to see the African diaspora gender dance that she's choreographing? Black trans performer Storme Webber, in conversation with Dréd in the film *Venus Boyz*, puts forth: "I feel like we're very much in the tradition, too: because in African societies . . . there were always cross dressers, and there were always people who played both roles, both gender roles, a lot of times they were the people who were the spiritual people, who were the medicine people, who were the healers."[17] So, how could Dréd make visible that she performs *in the tradition*—in a black tradition of finding healing in expressing multiple ways of performing gender, desire, soul, music, me?

∽

Here you are, Miss Collins, where the Gulf of Mexico reaches up to meet you, storming and calm. On March 2, 1917, Janet Collins—who would become the United States' first black prima ballerina—was born "in a hurry" in New Orleans, Louisiana. Her birth certificate, which incorrectly moved her birthdate to March 7, noted her as the "lawful issue" of parents Ernest and Alma (nee de Lavallade) and, like them, "colored." While Miss Collins retained few memories of her first years in New Orleans, the opening page of her unfinished autobiography devotes a full paragraph to what otherwise might seem a small detail. "I remember one of the happiest moments of my childhood was when I was placed on a bed of many colors and patterns," she begins, and continues reminiscing:

> I remember also being near to a lady who loved me and was there with me in that quilted garden. Her name was Mrs. Cashmere. . . . She would place me on this bed with all these colors! It must have been one of those southern "crazy quilts," which was made up of all sorts of leftover scraps of colorful cloth. It was her love, colors, and comfort that soothed my baby heart. Years later as a dancer I used the crazy quilt in *Juba*—the skirt of the costume I designed was a crazy quilt![18]

At the height of her career, Miss Collins would wrap herself in this crazy quilt again as part of her work, yes, but also as a metaphor for that work: the dance of piecing and holding together an eclectic, vibrant collection of styles, compositions, and characters.

In 1941, the Collins and de Lavallade families followed an established pattern of Creole migration to Los Angeles. There, Janet received her first formal ballet training from Mrs. Louise Beverly, "a light-brown-skinned lady with a very dignified friendly face and manner."[19] But when she looked to expand her dance foundation as a high school student, no prominent ballet school would accept a black student. "The most prominent ones were not available to me when they learned I was 'colored,'" she recalls. "Classes were somehow all full. I knew what was going on. If they accepted me in the midst of all the white dancers, they were afraid they would have no classes."[20]

Miss Collins finally found a new teacher in Charlotte Tamon, who agreed to give her private lessons at a discount rate. One day (when she was probably seventeen), Janet's Aunt Adele pointed out that the Ballet Russe de Monte Carlo was in town holding auditions and encouraged her niece to try out. She auditioned with a piece titled "Anitra's Dance," the story of a girl who breaks free from the chains that bind her to find freedom in dance. When she finished, a burst of applause from company members surprised the young, now smiling dancer. Company choreographer and lead dancer Léonide Massine immediately offered her a place in the company—but with a caveat: "Looking into my upturned waiting eyes, he stated in both a kindly and realistic manner, 'In order to train you and take you into the company, I would have to put you onstage with the ballet corps first in performances—and I would have to paint you white.'"[21] Janet Collins immediately, politely declined his offer, changed back into street clothes, and, exiting the auditorium and sitting down in front of the Los Angeles Public Library, cried, and cried, and cried. Then she took a streetcar home and related what happened to her Aunt Adele. "Now, that is marvelous and this is only the beginning," her aunt replied enthusiastically. "You must not strive to be as good as they are—you have the talent to be better! Now, you get right back to the barre on Monday and keep right on working on your dancing!"[22] Of course, she did.

⊰✦⊱

Mistress Ezili, girl, yes—yes, she is. Once her toilette is complete, Whitaker's Ezili Freda faces the camera in a throne-like chair and fans herself rapidly with a lacy pink fan, presiding over a table magnificently crowded with pink and white feathers, bottles of champagne, silk roses, and a white cake crowned with Freda's vèvè in pink icing. Her pink headwrap rises high above her forehead then cascades down her back, as if imitating a head of long, straight hair; the tones of the wrap bring out those of Whitaker's light brown skin. This tableau mirrors the first reason you might be surprised to imagine Ezili Freda in the black femme function: because isn't she identified with the pale, with pink and white—doesn't she refuse to identify herself as black? Sometimes, yes, she does. Elizabeth McAlister describes her intimacy with whiteness as a legacy of how slavery racialized and sexualized women in colonial Haiti. "Ezili Freda is depicted as light-skinned, wealthy and dripping with gold . . ." she writes. "She is called 'the goddess of love' and is known as *Metrès* or 'Mistress,' a term that goes quite directly back to slavery days. Then, the mulatta creoles of Saint-Domingue formed a class apart of mistresses, concubines, and sex slaves of the wealthy white planter men. . . . Freda recalls these mulatta prostitutes, who were famous for their beauty and high style, and dressed in silks and laces in the competitive decadence of Saint-Domingue."[23] Mambo Vye Zo Komande LaMenfo has a more figurative interpretation of Freda's association with whiteness. She believes it links this lwa to the Kabbalah's Yesod, "the female prototype of Vodou who represents the moon for dreams of promises yet unfulfilled." Of course, these two interpretations of Freda's love of pallor are not only not mutually exclusive but perhaps related. Why wouldn't enslaved Africans associate whiteness with pure, unfulfillable potential? Why not, after centuries of pressure to assimilate, and the reality that no matter how completely they did they would always be almost the same, but not quite; "almost the same, but not white"?[24]

But Whitaker's pink-swathed Freda isn't the only face that marks Ezili. Most of Ase's dancers (all black women) have full head shots in the video, and the face of Erin Holmes—the most deep chocolate of the dancers, with the deepest, most shocking pink lipstick—dominates several shots. Whitaker's choices reflect the simple, crucial fact that everyone's Freda doesn't look the same: no, more and more Metres is imagined as richly, beautifully dark-skinned. Turn-of-the millennium paintings by Hërsza Barjon, Evelyn Alcide, Gerard Fortune, and Frohawk Two Feathers, for example, depict their spectacularly clothed, graceful Fredas in deep, earthy browns.[25] Freda's recent (and not so recent) darkening in her servitors' vision is part of what makes her especially interesting to me in the black femme function. As Keeling describes it, the black femme's blackness (like her womanness, her queerness) hovers tenuously between the invisible and visible, retreating and advancing, ebbing and flowing. Her moments of racial and sexual invisibility mark her existence *inside* social climates of racism and misogyny that simultaneously denigrate and erase black women, rather than in some mythical outside. But in those moments when her black queer womanness moves into our frame of vision—moments when the palest of lwa manifests beauty and power by darkening—Freda and/as the black femme function beautifully disrupt the histories of enslavement, colorism, and coerced sexual contact from which they come. Dance, Ezili-Erin, dance your way across the frame!

And now, cut back to the table. In her pink-kerchiefed manifestation of Freda, Whitaker sits alone as queen of the table, carving and eating huge pieces of sugary, pink-and-white cake by herself, smearing frosting across her face. No other members of Ase—no other black women—share this sweetness with her. And this image, now, brings us to the second reason you might be surprised to think of Freda in the black femme function: she's not always been known to love women. McAlister calls her a "fiercely heterosexual femme" and Mambo Vye Zo Komande LaMenfo notes that she often ignores women present when she arrives or offers them only her pinky finger in greeting.[26] But in both these descriptions, the writers' understanding of "women" seems focused on commonsense versions of "normal" womanness: that is, cisgender and heterosexual. Because Freda is closely aligned with male femmes, with masisi and transwomen whose gender expressions she nurtures and enjoys; and she's also known to display generous, loving attention to those females who, as Zora Neale Hurston put it, "tend toward the hermaphrodite"—that is, madivin and (particularly butch) lesbians.[27] So is this Ezili Freda as "fiercely heterosexual" as all that? Like femininity/masculinity, heterosexual/homosexual seems a binary that falls short of capturing the complexity of how Freda and other lwa express pleasures and desires. This, too, reads as part of Freda's work in the black femme function. Because we might understand the femme, too— that queer female often accused of not *really* being lesbian, and of being too girly to be gender queer—as fundamentally troubling binaries of gender and sexuality. As Lisa Duggan and Kathleen McHugh put it in their "Fem(me)inist Manifesto": "Fem(me) is not an identity, not a history, not a location on the map of desire. The fem(me) body is an anti(identity) body, a queer body in fem(me)inine drag. . . . Fem(me) is *la je ne sais quoi* of desiring difference prior to any determination of sexual preference or gender identity."[28] And in the group scenes of "Ezili," when a kerchief- and corset-free Whitaker joins other dancers in using a chair as a platform on which black women roll playfully, forcefully over one another, you have to wonder: is what her Freda desires really the absence of other women—or the presence of those who come ready to make gender into a spectacle, a choreography, an expression of endless, sparkling creativity?

"Ezili is a higher functioning energy, but she is often set too low in our expectations," Mambo Vye Zo Komande LaMenfo meditates.[29] And when we think of her only as the mulatta mistress—as the femme who loves whiteness and men—we certainly expect too little of her and fail to take in too much of her. Or, as Colin Dayan describes Ezili's endless complication of gendered and sexual identity: "'Ezili o! Pa Ezili sa!' Someone calls her name, thinking they have defined her person, and she responds, 'That's not me.'"[30] We could call her white or black, cisfemme or transfemme, straight or queer, but to fit her into any of those binaries would be too limiting—would be so much more constricting, so much less pleasurable than a corset and fishnets. So isn't it best just to call her Manbo Metres Ezili Freda Daome, and to try to understand all the complexities that entails? Isn't it best just to name the video "Ezili," then show all the colors, pleasures, and dances that can inspire?

———————

Bonswa: this is Haiti's Tenth Department, New York Dyaspora, 1998. The landmark exhibition *The Sacred Arts of Vodou* is electrifying the American Museum of Natural History, and an outburst of Haitian dance surrounds the event. While Jean Léon Destiné's dance company and the Ibo Dancers give talks at the exhibit, the Alvin Ailey revival of Geoffrey Holder's Vodou-inspired dance drama *The Prodigal Prince* draws audiences intrigued by sacred arts encountered in the museum. Unlike drag king shows, Haitian dance concerts are a well-known phenomenon in Manhattan. The 1970s wave of Haitian migrants included a number of folkloric dancers and choreographers; and in the 1980s, when La Troupe Makandal began staging Vodou dans (ceremonies for lwa) as concert dance, other companies followed suit. The explicit goal of such performances was to render Vodou more respectable in dyaspora. Makandal's mission statement puts forth: "Part of the company's repertory derives from the rituals of Vodou, widely known and disparaged in the United States as 'voodoo.' The Troupe's performances repudiate racist stereotypes while keeping the magic alive. In other words, La Troupe Makandal uses music and dance to represent a Haiti that is beautiful, dignified, and true."[31]

Neither femininity nor female sexuality are excised from this "beautiful, dignified" representation, but are enacted as intensely, unerringly cis- and hetero. *The Prodigal Prince*, for example, climaxes in stylized sex between the female lead—Ezili Freda herself—and the titular prince, based on renowned Haitian painter Hector Hyppolite. Paired center-stage, these characters eroticize their sharp gender contrast: the suppleness of Freda's flowing, heart-embroidered blue robes and flower-crowned headdress face Hyppolite's arrow-tight, ringing-red costume and unadorned, shaved head. Celia Weiss Bambara describes their love scene: "Each bends his/her knees and begins to circle his/her hips while facing each other. They circle their hips and then throw their pelvises forward . . ." Unlike descriptions of drag kings, the split pronoun "his/her" here indicates not that each performer explores gender nonconformity, but that dancers of "opposite" sexes meet to charge the show with heterosexuality. And, indeed, enacting this heart/arrow, blue/red gender contrast becomes part of representing Haiti's beauty and dignity on stage, of visualizing conformity to imperial epistemologies that read gender differentiation as proof of civilization.

In this same city, these same years, MilDred—transitioning from her drag king repertoire to new kinds of performance art—is piecing together a very different picture of Vodou dans. Kirsty MacDonald's short film about her work contains a long scene in which MilDred—clad in a man's black button-down shirt and suede blazer, offset by heavy hoop earrings and black lipstick—stands on a New York street and speaks into the camera about her relationship to Vodou. She starts with a formulation not unlike La Troupe Makandal's: "It's interesting because in Haiti there's a lot of Voodoo, Vodou—and it's gotten a bad name as black magic. I don't believe that Vodou is black magic; I don't practice it but I've read about it and seen videos on it. And what it is is a rich . . . umm . . . experience of the *divine*, you know, of the ancestors, following and appreciating the spirits that guide and protect you."[32] But she continues more queerly:

> And I've seen some videos where people practicing rituals, in Vodou rituals, like, they would be possessed by another spirit, but sometimes that spirit would be the opposite gender. So if a man, for instance, was possessed by a female lwa (they call it), or spirit, he would take on the characteristics of that spirit and dress up like her and move like her. And

there are women who have been possessed by male spirits, and they would take on the mannerisms of umm, those male spirits. And that's how I felt about my show, when I would be Dréd: that this male energy was so intense that I would be taken over sometimes by the spirit, but in a safe way.[33]

MilDred's deceptively simple discussion of Vodou gives words—and her own radiant style—to a submerged epistemology of gender variance that recasts dominant white and North American queer understandings, say, of butch-femme. She smiles and puts forth that all people have the possibility to be simultaneously man and woman, Shaft and Foxy Brown, packing and lacy—but not because gender is constructed, or performative, or any other queer theoretical word. No, because they're always surrounded by multiple, multiply gendered spirits and may temporarily *become* any of these spirits at any time. She goes on to give her listeners a literally and figuratively Kreyòl formulation of queer gender as she intones with the cadence and animation of a prose poem: "Mwen gen yon gason andedan mwen: *I have a man in me.* Mwen gen yon *fanm* andedan mwen: *I have a woman inside of me.* Mwen gen *tou le de* andedan mwen: *I have both in me.* Nou tout gen tou le de andedan nou: *We all have both in us.* Se yon benediksyon Bondye ba nou. *It's a blessing that God has given us.* Renmen tout moun. *Love everyone.*"[34] This moment literalizes the work MilDred looks to take on in her art: the work of translating to her fellow New Yorkers a Kreyòl understanding of gender in which gason and fanm expressions refuse binarization, and all aspects of mwen can be loved and embraced vigorously. Kreyòl is her first language, MilDred also tells viewers in this scene. And—unlike relentlessly gendered French—this is a language in which nouns, adjectives, and pronouns are never gender-inflected, with a single third-person singular pronoun, li, to communicate s/he, his/her without the divisive backslash. This gender undividedness, too, is what MilDred's performance looks to translate.

Her bilingual poem here also calls out the gender (and other) queerness inherent in Vodou's understanding of benediksyon—blessing—that is, the intimacy between human and divine. If everyone could simultaneously have Ogu and Ezili Freda, Danbala and Ezili Danto guiding them, protecting them, moving their bodies, spirits, and thoughts, then doesn't everyone at some time—depending on which lwa comes into their body, when—have the potential to consider themselves "fluid," as MilDred prefers to call herself? *The Prodigal Prince*'s climactic scene between Ezili Freda and Hyppolite is based on a dream recounted by the painter, when Freda appeared and guided him to become an artist by gifting him with visions of the humans and lwa he was to paint. But what if rather than interpreting this as a dream where Freda seduces Hyppolite, we visualize it as a moment when Hyppolite becomes Freda: when he begins to see with her eyes, paint with her hands, bring her into the world through his body? What if the man fully realizes himself only by listening to the woman in him? And what if he danced so the audience could see him transition to "his/her," simultaneously a cismale dancer and an arch-feminine lwa? Maybe this would be just what it takes to transition from endlessly looped performances of the black gender stereotypes that we all know and can't escape, into *something else*—into the kind of gender expression Rinaldo Walcott heralds as "modes of self-fashioning that allow for a reconstruction of black manhood from the place of incoherence and femininity which might be best exemplified, or at least typified, in recent representations of and by black trans-cultures."[35]

The possibility of this kind of gender choreography is what Dréd's new-millennial performance art—a series of pieces that combine Haitian dance, music, and original poetry—explores. As she puts it in her description for the 2010 debut of *I Transcender: The Gender Expression of Haitian Gods and Goddesses*, this work "is a mix of dance, poetry and music experiencing the spiritual dance expressions of the fabulous Haitian God/desses: sexy Danbala, cross dressing Baron Samedi and beautiful Erzulie."[36] In dancing gods and goddesses into god/desses, MilDred does for Danbala, Baron Samedi, and Ezili something similar to what her drag act did for Shaft and Superfly. She at once pays homage to the characters she portrays and troubles the gaze of audiences who come with black-and-white, predefined notions of these characters' pleasures and dangers. Yes, she challenges both North American–centric understandings of gender queerness, and the heterocentric gaze of those who come to watch Haitian dance with expectations that certain roles are for cismale dancers and others for cisfemale dancers, and that boy will always meet girl—but somewhere other than in the movement of a single performer. Dressing Bawon Sanmdi in a skirt and Freda in a beard, MilDred reflects queerness directly into Ezili's mirror and beckons to her audience *to look differently*, to gaze on all the possibilities that the divine can offer them.

∞

The Pacific, now: the Pacific is not pacific but the largest ocean in the world and yes, Miss Collins, watch it open to embrace you, all of you. On November 3, 1947, Janet Collins's first solo concert debuted at Los Angeles's Las Palmas Theater to rave reviews. The concert had been three years in the making, two of these funded by a Julius Rosenwald fellowship. Ralph Ellison received this fellowship the same year Miss Collins did, and past recipients Katherine Dunham and Pearl Primus used its support for dance research in the Caribbean and Africa, respectively. But, as Collins's biographer Yael Tamar Lewin notes, "While she received a Rosenwald Fellowship just as Dunham and Primus had, there the similarity ends—Collins valued her heritage, but her interest was not anthropological."[37] Rather than traveling to study dance elsewhere, she used these years of funding to develop her own, elaborating the majority of her signature repertoire.

"If dance has ever peopled your nocturnal dreams, then you can achieve a fairly good idea of how Janet Collins looks on stage," critic Doris Hering greeted her debut. "For dream dancing is often fantastically rapid. Just as you focus upon the dancer in one part of the stage, she is no longer there, but is in a distant spot, and you're not quite sure how she got there."[38] And yes, in this concert, Miss Collins bridged a lot of ground as if effortlessly—she brought together elements that audiences expected to be kept distant from each other and did so with a great deal of charm. Prior to setting her own work, Collins received significant training as a modern dancer, including two years with Katherine Dunham's company. The chosen eclecticism of her dance background was highlighted and appreciated in her solo debut, with *Dance Magazine* noting that this "Creole beauty . . . is a dancer whose astonishing range encompasses the modern dance, the essence of a fluid classicism in ballet, a sure acquaintance with ethnic and other dance forms, a quick ear and sympathy with music."[39]

With such a range of technique—especially unusual for black dancers of the era, who were often unable and/or unwilling to build on classical training—Collins put together a crazy quilt of a solo concert. Her repertoire mixed not only modern and classical dance, but "black" and "white" music and themes. She opened in a classical European vein, with *Blackamoor*—in which Collins performed "neatly styled 17th century court dances" satirized by her character, one of "those little black boys all dressed up in the elaborate and colorful costumes from the French courts" of Louis XIV—and the "Rondo" and "Romanza" from Mozart's *Eine Kleine Nachtmusik*.[40] From there, Collins moved into what would become her signature piece, *Spirituals*, danced to "Nobody Knows the Trouble I've Seen" and "Didn't the Lord Deliver Daniel." After an intermission and a musical suite featuring the music of Bach, she danced a folk music suite that drew on her Creole heritage. "The Young Fishwife," "La Creole," and "Apre le Mardi Gras" were all choreographed to Louisiana Creole music, representing Creole women characters in vibrant costumes and (sometimes improvised) dances. This broadly ranging repertoire immediately made clear that, as Lewin writes, it would become "impossible to neatly fit Collins into any particular dance camp, to view her as anything but an uncategorizable individual."[41] Rather than attempting to wrap the categories modern/classical, black/white dance around her choreography, Lewin insists: "Truly, when we consider the combination of her diverse creative offerings, classical technique, and enthusiastic reception in what was still a predominantly white modern dance scene, a tantalizing theory is yielded—that Collins was the first transitional black choreographer in the concert dance world."[42] Or you might say, too: that night, she danced like Metres Manbo Ezili Freda Daome—like a black femme who could make her blackness and whiteness, her womanness and otherness both visible and invisible.

Over the course of this program, Miss Collins would also move in another way—between performing several racialized genders, from the blackamoor to the Mozart hero to the Creole quadroon. Strikingly, the European-influenced opening pieces were the only ones that introduced masculine personae. *Blackamoor*, one of her best-received and most comical pieces, was a satire not entirely unlike the work of Dréd's drag king act. Portraying a young African court page imitating "these strange people: old men who couldn't dance—they ached all the time when they were trying to be young," Miss Collins's opening piece at once poked fun at the pompous masculinity of Louis XIV's courtiers and prodded the audience to question any tendency to imagine the blackamoors of classical European portraiture as marginal, easily dismissed personages, without their own critical view of the kings, dukes, and marquises they came to wait on.[43]

In counterpoint, the Creole "Folk Music" suite dealt exclusively with representations of African American womanhood. Here Miss Collins introduced her audience to a "tough, haggling" marketwoman in "The Young Fishwife"; a hilariously intoxicated, exuberantly leaping and spinning reveler in "Apre le Mardi Gras"; and a young girl dreaming of her first dance in "La Creole." These are light, comedic, celebratory pieces, whose attitude (literal and figurative) is best captured for me in a photograph of Collins in "La Creole." Here, with hair in a long braid that hangs well past her waist on the left side, she bends forward and kicks her right leg up in an attitude in arabesque; gazing over her shoulder at her perfectly pointed, bare foot, her painted mouth smiles openly as if in delighted midlaugh. Her ears are ringed in gold, her midriff bared under a lacy bodice, and her flounced, layered skirts fly upward to reveal petticoats decorated with large, cut-out cloth flowers that seem to reflect the playful emergence of this Creole's sexuality and pleasure.[44] The carefree nature of Miss Collins's representations of black womanhood might reflect the strategically insouciant attitudes about Creoles and women that she remembers being raised with: "My people thought they were the greatest things in the world, and they taught us that we weren't allowed to grow up with an inferiority complex. We were in a society that looked down upon women and blacks as inferiors, and we were both. And so we decided that we were going to forget about that."[45] Tottering and smiling, lounging and dreaming, these characters certainly seem to have forgotten, too.

But Miss Collins never meant for this program to be an extended meditation on black gender, and it never looks like one. Creole womanhood is less the subject of commentary here than the taking-off point for her creativity, and viewers also noted the superficiality of her Creole characterizations. Though the titles and songs of the folk music suite are in Louisiana Creole, the choreographer herself didn't speak that language. Her mother and grandmother did, but deliberately neglected to teach Janet and her siblings so they couldn't understand grown folks' talk. The surface nature of her understanding of Creole language and culture becomes most apparent in "La Creole," whose subtitle on this program is "Dreams of the Quadroon Ball." Fellow choreographer Lester Horton criticized the piece to her, telling her "quadroon ball was a scandal—it was a ball when the girls came down, and the men came to choose mistresses." She added, "I didn't know that. I took it very innocently."[46] Alerted to this history of sexuality and power that she unwittingly conjured up, she subsequently removed the subtitle of "La Creole." But I can't help but wonder what might have happened if, rather than excising "Dreams of a Quadroon Ball," she had rechoreographed the piece to explore her unintentionally provocative subtitle. Quadroon balls, now, what space could be more evocative of the "class apart of mistresses, concubines, and sex slaves of the wealthy white planter men" that, according to McAlister, Ezili Freda recalls?[47] And what would it look like if Miss Collins had worked to imagine another way of understanding and embodying the fictions of black womanness generated by that space, just as she choreographed a new persona for the blackamoor? Could her otherly imagined "La Creole" have offered a black femme choreography: one in which she challenged her viewers to see a Freda-like sensuality as something not to be auctioned off at a ball, but summoned for Miss Collins's own pleasure?

❧

You know a black femme is fabulous, now, by her shoes. Yes, from the half-shadowed spaces where she hovers gracefully, they might be the first things to catch your eye. When Whitaker's Freda has finished the last slice of her spectacularly sugary cake, the camera pans down to focus on her feet: bathed in clear water then slipped into glinting slippers generously, ostentatiously covered in plastic, pale pink diamonds. Ezili Freda, Zora Neale Hurston tells us, is the lwa with pretty, flowery toes.[48] And a cisfemme, Duggan and McHugh muse, is a woman who, finding in androgyny "too much loss, too little pleasure, and ugly shoes . . . takes from the feminine a wardrobe, a walk, a wink, then moves on."[49] But for a black cisfemme, parading fabulous footwear is a much more charged proposition. Remember TJ Bryan, the black cisfemme who showed up to a poetry slam in stilettos only to have her face pasted on the body of a black male boxer in the next day's newspapers. Beginning with this anecdote, she goes on to explain what her selection of footwear that night signifies: a choice to walk on a path of racialized gender she knows was never meant for her, but that she insists on forcefully reshaping through her footsteps. "My understanding of African-descended wimmin's existence in the west mediates my experience as a dyke and as a Femme . . . not because it has to, but because I've decided it will," she writes. "My Black consciousness combined with a belief in the validity of my perceptions and love of my Femme self gives me space to say: IT TAKES BALLS TO WALK IN THESE SHOES."[50] Or, Freda's mincing steps in Whitaker's video suggest: it takes power so great you could call it divine.

Footwear has been a highly regulated commodity for women of African descent in the Americas. Saint-Domingue was one of many Caribbean colonies that passed sumptuary laws forbidding women of color to wear shoes in the late eighteenth century. But stories remember that, with Freda's creativity, women of color instead strode out at public events with diamonds adorning their toes, enraging white women who hoped this law would distinguish their racialized gender from mulattas' in a way that was to the latter's detriment.[51] With emancipation the ban on shoes was lifted, but black women's fitness to wear them remained a subject of concern—especially when their shoes were pretty, delicate ones. Charles Day complained in *Five Years Residence in the British West Indies*: "Those ladies who aimed at the superior civilization of shoes and stockings, invariably clothed their pedal extremities in pink silk stockings and blue, white, or yellow kid shoes, sandaled up their sturdy legs."[52] During the trial of Duchess, an emancipated Barbadian woman accused of stealing money from her former master to buy fine apparel, judge John Colthurst appraised her Freda-like ensemble with disdain: "She had bought wearing apparel fine enough for a Princess. Their colours vied with those of the rainbow, first a flaming bright yellow bonnet, flashy dresses without number, necklaces and earrings without end, rose colored silk stockings and two pairs of pink satin shoes."[53] He fretted that those satin shoes looked ridiculous on black female "hoofs" and ordered her to put on her two pairs at trial, one over the other, to prove their absurdity.[54] The pink silk femininity layered on brown legs meant for labor, these men suggest, represented an excessive imitation of European ladyness—in excess of the markers of sexual difference that the black body was able to bear. Traces of concern over black women's shoes persist in the twentieth-century world of concert dance and particularly ballet where, as Brenda Dixon Gottschild documents, black dancers' feet were long considered congenitally bad and unfit for pointe work. *Those* satin shoes were still deemed inappropriate for black women well into the last quarter of the century.[55]

So what does it mean to dance as the lwa of beautiful, flowery toes, the lwa in pink diamond shoes? Whitaker's "Ezili" suggests it means being uncomfortable in those shoes, sometimes; and then learning to be creative from this space of discomfort. When Whitaker's Freda spins in her sparkling shoes, her dancing is markedly different from Ase's group choreography. The shoes mince in small circles, first one direction then the other, dancing but going nowhere, beautifully. But when the video cuts back to Ase's group choreography something else happens, again. These dancers wear sparkling shoes, too, but theirs are shimmering gold Ugg boots, easy to dance in. Their movements are large, round-house kicks and leaps over one another, sending golden feet flying. In one shot Erin Holmes falls to her right into the arms of another dancer, who supports her while she opens her boots into an airborne split; in the next we see pink-clad, gold-shod legs (Holmes's, seemingly) walking and dancing on a pink-graffited wall—yes, walking with her body parallel to the earth—as other dancers carry her. These group shots visualize for me what else it can mean to walk in gilded shoes: when choreographed in concert with other black (cis)femmes, it can pres-ent an opportunity to make an art—and a graffiti art, at that—out of inhab-iting and reshaping colonial legacies. You can put those shoes on and, with support of other black women, change the orientation of your world; you can change the grounds on which you choreography your gender, your race, your *whatever*, as Rinaldo Walcott would say, creating identities that leave "room for surprise, disappointment, and pleasure." Yes, with the right shoes, you can change how you see and are seen, if only for a moment.

———

March 11, 2010: at the WOW Café Theatre in New York's East Village, three one-wo/man shows are premiering to a sold-out house. "Get three new shows for the price of one each night! Come Experience MilDred's NEW Show: 'I Transcender: The Gender Expression of Haitian Gods and God-desses,' choreographed by the fabulous and talented Sokhna Heathyre Mabin. Tantra Zawadi presents 'Soldier Blues,' an exploration through word, music, and movement of the battlefield of the soul and heart. And also introducing a new performance by Sokhna Heathyre Mabin!!!"[56] Par-tial benefits will go to survivors of Haiti's January 12 earthquake, and some directly to support members of MilDred's family left homeless or injured. MilDred is the star act, the first name on the playbill. Costumed in flow-ing white robes, she begins her performance dancing the lwa she calls "the sexy Danbala," a serpentine spirit whom one houngan describes as "a bi-sexual entity containing both the male and the female . . . a unified force of sexuality."[57] Stage lights dim, bringing into relief the candles on the altar that stands at the back of her set, and MilDred transitions into her dance as Bawon Sanmdi, lwa of death and rebirth.

For audience members who've seen her drag for years, her next costume may offer a surprise: because who knew they'd been seeing her perform

Bawon for over a decade? Dréd often paraded her superfly smoothness in black suits topped with shades and a black hat or hood, including one particularly memorable and jaunty top hat.[58] This is Sanmdi's signature costume reappropriated, macked out: his top hat, sunglasses, and black frock coat in dyaspora. When Sanmdi came dressed in Dréd's drag, the artist's embodiment of this lwa was all about performing black (female) masculinity. But tonight MilDred recostumes and regenders Bawon. Still shielded behind black shades, she unbuttons her jacket to reveal the contours of breasts; she replaces black pants with a swirling skirt, men's shoes with heels, and dances in full energy recolored by a red light. Sanmdi, and MilDred, have danced their way from Bawon to Baron/Baroness, from drag king to drag king/queen.

Now, this costume change evokes another variation of Bawon Sanmdi's dress: he sometimes pairs his frock coat with a raffia skirt. In a radio interview with Victoria Gaither, MilDred says: "Through my research I'm finding out some amazing things about these god/desses. For example one of the goddesses and gods that I'm going to be portraying, on stage through dance, ritual, poetry, and music is Bawon Sanmdi, and he, he's the lwa of the dead, and he's also lwa of sex and resurrection. . . . But also, interestingly enough, he's . . . depicted as a figure who crosses traditional gender boundaries through cross-dressing or expressing bisexuality."[59] The Sanmdi she reads about in a raffia skirt, along with the Sanmdi she portrays in cloth skirt and platform heels, perform culturally specific choreographies of the masisi as well as the gwo nèg (big man)—or, in MilDred's case, of movements where the masisi meets the gwo nèg.[60] McAlister writes of the Gede, the pantheon of death spirits headed by Bawon Sanmdi: "The ultimate destabilizers, Gede mediate yet disrupt dichotomies. . . . Androgynous yet vulgar, they perform an ambiguous gender scheme where both femininity and masculinity are parodied and ridiculed."[61] While Gede and Bawon are phallic spirits who love to sing about their big dicks, McAlister underscores their simultaneous "effeminacy" and specifically links them to transfemininity as she claims: "Very like drag queens in the United States, the Gede are brilliant social critics of gender . . . and are capable of a quick 'read' of the politics of either domestic or national power."[62]

But MilDred's "Transcender" Bawon isn't exactly the spirit McAlister describes. Oh, no—it only takes one look to see how this performer not only self-consciously queers Sanmdi, but dyasporizes his/her style. Her jacket is not a frock coat but a blazer reminiscent of Richard Roundtree's John Shaft; his skirt is not raffia but the kind of cotton boho chic skirt Beyoncé was wearing that year in her turn to 1970s styles. And how many black drag kings perform as Shaft, or black drag queens as Beyoncé? MilDred's distinctly African North American styling of Bawon Sanmdi suggests that when her audiences witness black queer and trans/gender performance, they may want look for models not (only) in white kinging and queening, but in African diaspora performance traditions—in transcender as well as in transgender. And then, a more sustained gaze at MilDred's dance reveals other dyasporic twists to her version of Sanmdi, too. Instead of straight-up gender satire, MilDred performs transcendering as a supplement to—and comment on—the dips and sways of normative black genders.

Look closely at her from the waist up, first, and see that there's a hint of the her in his dress. The choker that accessorizes Sanmdi's blazer expresses what Dréd's drag collaborator Shon calls *smoothness*: an expression of black queer man(ish)ness which produces itself through loving relationship to women and womanness, "showing men and women how women should be treated" by honoring the woman within the man as well as the woman beside the man.[63] The smoothness MilDred brings to her blazer tonight asks: Butches, brothers, studs, why not share a necklace with your woman? Why not share a string of connections with your woman? But look down now, and you'll see something more dramatic. Her peasant skirt and platforms flare out, highlighting the fanm *literally* beneath the gason, the high heels beneath the blazer. And as she dances, it is her woman "half" that literally holds up the man, that at once stabilizes the entirety of Sanmdi's incoherent gender just enough so s/he doesn't fall over . . . and shakes it up to keep it continually moving, dancing, transcendering. This gender *métissage* isn't the striptease, the surprising finale, as it was in her drag; no, it's the whole dance. Now make no mistake, the heels she dances in are an important addition to Sanmdi's costume. While a skirted Haitian Sanmdi might dance barefoot, MilDred comes out more than than well-heeled, masterfully balanced in Foxy Brown–height shoes that visualize black femmeininity's ability to rise. Describing learning to love feet that she never felt were pretty enough, MilDred writes that she came to understand them as "powerful roots to our Haitian culture—our Haitian ancestors."[64] And oh, the ancestors—the funny ones, the sissy ones, the ones who insisted on being womanish when everyone told them they couldn't—they are riding high on those shoes tonight.

☙

And now the Atlantic, the black Atlantic reaches out to you, Miss Collins, folding you into her constellations like all the rest. In 1948, Janet Collins bought a train ticket to New York and arrived in Manhattan with trunks full of costumes, eager to make a name for herself. In April 1949 she revived her solo concert at the 92nd Street Y to rave reviews and was named "Most Outstanding Debutante of the Season" by *Dance Magazine*. Then, in 1951, "the planets must have been exceptionally aligned . . . for Collins because in that year, it seemed as though her personal star could only rise," biographer Lewin notes.[65] While she was making conversation during the intermission of a Balanchine dance concert with Zachary Solov—the Metropolitan Opera's new choreographer and ballet master, and an admirer of her solo concert—Solov spontaneously asked: "Janet, would you like to dance at the Met?" Initially skeptical of this invitation, she was soon contacted by Met general manager Rudolf Bing, who offered her the position of prima ballerina for the upcoming season. Not only did this make her the Met's first contracted black performer, breaking the color line three years before Marian Anderson sang at the opera, it made her the first black prima ballerina of any major U.S. dance company. "In the 68-year history of the Met, Premiere Danseuse Collins is the first Negro to become a member of the regular company," *Time* noted, and Miss Collins told *Opera News*: "I am extremely proud to be a Negro."[66]

But what would the Met *do* with this proud Negro dancer; how would they make black femininity not only legible to its audience but beautiful? The Met opened that year with a production of *Aida* in which Miss Collins—in bare feet, dramatic jewelry, and gold-studded bra and panties—danced the part of an Ethiopian slave. But while this role might seem to play on the prima's history as a descendant of enslaved Africans, her major scene elided her blackness. The entire cast wore brown makeup as they portrayed Egyptian characters; but Miss Collins, whose natural skin shade was somewhat lighter than their makeup, did not. She was partnered with Loren Hightower and Socrates Birsky, who, in contrast to petite, light-skinned Miss Collins, were costumed as huge, overly blackened Watusi warriors. Hightower remembers: "We were a ridiculous black. We were burnt-cork black," but the prima ballerina was "*not* painted dark. Absolutely not. She was her natural skin tone."[67] So in her first stage appearance, the

Met's first black performer appeared significantly less black than those white dancers surrounding her, and much, much lighter than her male partners. Her comparative fairness leaves open the possibility of her being more easily read as feminine to Hightower's masculine than she would have been otherwise—while not white, she remains whiter than those around her. Almost the same as white femininity, but not quite; almost the same, but not white.

Next season, Solov's choreography for Miss Collins in *La Gioconda* took another approach to staging her blackness. Rather than attempting minimize her darkness, this production metaphorized it: Miss Collins appeared as Queen of the Night to Hightower's King of the Day. Once the ballerina's blackness was rendered metaphorical she would be costumed like a traditional ballerina, donning a classical tutu (which Collins disliked—"you can't really see your legs. . . . It's the strangest feeling") and dancing on pointe.[68] For decades to come, black ballet dancers would remember these stage appearances in which Miss Collins danced on pointe as personal turning points. In an era when choreographers considered black feet innately unsuited to pointe work, her performance was a resonant inspiration. Rising high on these shoes, Collins's Queen of the Night enters into a balletic duel with Hightower's King of the Day and, after much spectacular dancing, loses to her opponent and is carried out upside down. In the New York of 1952, it seems, a black woman—even a prima ballerina—had to submit to a white man's show of dominance to garner applause. The production drew stellar reviews.

Despite and because of such success, this was a physically and emotionally taxing period for Miss Collins. Her intensive rehearsal schedule left her without time or energy to develop her own repertoire, though she continued to perform earlier choreography. And her intensive touring schedule exposed her to blunt racism. Miss Collins wasn't allowed to perform in Atlanta, Birmingham, Dallas, Houston, Memphis, Oklahoma City, and Richmond; she stayed in her hotel while an understudy went on in her place. Who can wonder, then, that when she abruptly resigned from her position with the company in 1954, she was spent; who can be surprised if, literally and figuratively, she needed a crazy quilt to wrap herself in once more?

⊰⧱⧱⊱

I know her dancing shoes are dazzling, oh, I know, but look up, too: look at what crowns this Freda. When you see how a black femme's done her hair for a dance, you know it means *something*. Reflecting on her conversations with fellow black cisfemmes, TJ Bryan proclaims: "We've talked that hair shit to DEATH! Wanting to love it, color it, cut it, fry it, locks it, grow it, hide it, politicize it, ignore it, or just plain pull it out from the roots in big, kinky handfullz! Notions of blackness and womanly beauty converge on top of my head."[69] In the opening frames of "Ezili," we see Whitaker's Freda, too, asking us to witness multiple visions of beauty converging on her head. She cuts between two ways of fabricating a pinkly feminine and flashy "hair"style for her Ezili—neither of which involves her own (or anyone else's) hair, but experiments with inventing other eye-catching headdresses for herself. In one shot, she carefully ties a pink headwrap in the mirror until it rises off her forehead and cascades down her back. In another, she pulls the hood of a clear pink plastic raincoat on and off her shaved head, dancing her way in and out of material that imitates the cascade of straight hair from her crown to her shoulders. In both headdresses, she reinvents hair itself—reinvents this contested marker of race and gender and keeps reinventing it.

Now, Whitaker's Freda could have donned a wig or braids, too, to approximate the long head of hair this lwa is credited for. But the choice of two kinds of headwrap speaks to a history of black women's headdresses that's every bit as contested as the backstory of her shoes. Literally crowning black womanhood, the art of head covering has long carried complex meanings that Caribbean women passed between themselves. Building on Yoruba and other West African traditions of expressive headwrapping, elaborate patterns for tying head cloths were a means of both adornment and communication throughout the eighteenth and nineteenth centuries. Yes, a beautifully tied headwrap might be an expression of a woman's individual creativity. But it also might express the creativity of Afro-Caribbean women as a group, their ability to invent coded systems of communication. Steeve Buckridge notes that in Haiti, Martinique, Guadeloupe, Suriname, St. Lucia, and St. Vincent, "the way the fabric was tied and how it was styled on the head conveyed specific messages or meanings" about women's occupations, marital status, religious affiliations, and other things.[70]

In particular, carefully arranged head ties often said something about sex. They were a way of inviting or foreclosing flirtation, of letting observers know whether wearers were single or attached, closed or receptive to new lovers. And more than this, headwrapping publicized many high-flying black female desires far outside heterosexual monogamy. Buckridge notes that Martinican and Surinamese styles could mean: I'm not single, but if I'm intrigued enough I might just sleep with you; I'm going to meet my lover on the corner; I'll conduct my erotic life as I please, talk about me all you like.[71] Gloria Wekker reminds us that in Suriname, Afro-Creole women developed special ways of arranging head ties to court other females, too, letting womenfolk know: I'm in search of a mati (female) lover; are you?[72] Headdresses like these, then, communicated a radically different conceptualization than the European not only of what went with your best dress, but of what could go on under it—of what kind of sexuality was fitting for ideal womanhood. Wordlessly communicating what intentions the black woman had for her sexual body, headwraps let other black Caribbeans know that those intentions were rarely to remain the domain of one, or any, man. No, honey, how creative women could be with their headwraps reflected how creative they could be with their sexuality—how many ways they could walk in the world as femmes, and how many ways they could dance as Freda.

But in "Ezili," Whitaker doesn't just do, redo, and reinvent her own hair. We also see her in Ase's group effort to sculpture one another's hair for the dance. Whitaker sprays pink designs onto one woman's halo of natural hair and swiftly weaves braids into another's, then a dancer blows glitter onto Whitaker's shaved crown. Lay down, body, lay down, little while . . . trouble soon be over, lay down, little while, the soundtrack sings to their hairstylings. And of course, of course. Listen and see the music, the hair doing, are both slave songs—both ways black women conjured their creativity in order to survive enslavement. Wekker cites a beautiful, wrenching account of a slave ship's arrival in Paramaribo, when an eyewitness noted that the female enslaved "had marked each others' heads with different designs, suns, half moons, without the help of a razor, without even soap, only with a piece of glass." She meditates: "The cultural vitality expressed in these images, amidst the horror, fixing each other's hair . . . and making the unbearable bearable by way of creatively expressing themselves, is as impressive as it is shattering. Apparently, these shipmates, with their diverse places of origin, languages, and backgrounds, had already been able to find a common idiom with which to encourage themselves and each other. It is worth noting that part of the performance of their subjectivity was beautification . . ."[73] And even as they beautified each other in the belly of the ship, women loving each other in those sex-segregated slave holds was also part of how they survived and remade themselves in the Atlantic crossing. Wekker strongly argues that the present-day Sranan term "mati"—which Creole women use to mean my mate, my girl, my same-sex lover or partner—derives from the African diasporic concept of the shipmate, and from words the enslaved used to refer to those who survived the Middle Passage with them. Hair sculptures—the work of beautification—and erotic touch—the mati work—she suggests, were intertwined ways that women rescripted what their commodified bodies were supposed to mean. Lay down, body, lay down, little while . . .

So look, now, making yourself into a black cisfemme—making yourself beautiful, and doing it to light another woman's fire—isn't just a frivolous Saturday afternoon. For a long, long time, it's been an act of resistance and rebirth. Listen again to the song Whitaker remixes. "Lay Down, Body" is a shout song from the Georgia coast: that is, it's part of the Gullah tradition of ring shout, in which call-and-response music, dance (counterclockwise, in a circle), and bodily percussion (stamping feet, clapping hands) come together as spiritual practice. The art of embodying Ezili, the art of performing the black femme function, are like a ring shout, too. They're about activating your body to save your soul; and they're about doing your dance, your hair, and your soul with creativity—by creolizing the languages, musics, styles you're given so as to make them into a kind of beauty you were never supposed to believe was yours. Never, my love, never is not for Ezili Freda. Oh, no, lanmou mwen, look in the mirror and you'll see something else; look, and you'll see the endless *mise-en-abyme* of black cisfemmes' possibility.

———

Lanmou mwen, vini, an nou danse; lanmou mwen, you're here, you came back. As MilDred's Bawon Sanmdi exits the stage, the final character of her Haitian God/dess performance emerges: the beautiful, endlessly desirable, divinely insatiable Ezili Freda. Metres Ezili Freda Daome, we know that you've arrived when Sanmdi raises a hand mirror to his/her face, slowly, lovingly removes his/her hat and beard, paints her lips in tantalizingly kissable black lipstick, and changes into a flowing top that matches her newly flowing, feminine dance. Full moon on my back, I do not lack, MilDred's Freda tells us, smiling and dancing. Now, this lovely moment may usher in a new surprise for those of MilDred's faithful audience members who didn't yet know who Ezili was: because how were they to know that they'd been watching Freda for years, too? At the end of her drag king act, Dréd peered into just this kind of hand mirror to remove her beard—then, to her audience's delight, reached into her well-packed jock to reveal the apple lodged inside, raising it to her mouth and taking a loud, tempting bite.[74] But where this drag finale was focused on the apple, consciously and humorously rescripting the biblical story of Eve, I Transcender focuses on the power of the mirror and its link to another understanding of the relationship between women and divinity. Both the apple and the mirror, Vodou practitioners know, are symbols of Ezili Freda: who, when she arrives in ceremony, is immediately handed a mirror to gaze into and "dream of perfection," as Sallie Ann Glassman puts it.[75]

When MilDred transitions from Sanmdi to Freda, she begins the final act of her show with a dance that seems, at first glance, to have moved beyond her act's earlier embrace of gender incoherence to end up luxuriating in the girly, womanly lace and roses that Metres Freda can command. But if you look closely into Ezili's mirror here, another, more complicated reflection emerges. Mildred's mirror-framed debearding and lipsticking is an act that makes visible what cisfemme activists have begun to call ftoF, or female to femme transition. Meaning, as cisfemme writer and filmmaker Elizabeth Stark says, that—like mtf transitions—ciswomen's coming into queer femininity is neither natural nor default, but an intentionally orchestrated process: "My sexuality and desires, my sensibility and my gender expression are all going against the grain of the expected female. In fact, becoming a femme in a world that insists on a certain femininity . . . without taking on that enforced femininity is a delicate, powerful move; a transition indeed, that is under-investigated and overlooked."[76] But MilDred, of course, is not rescripting what this white cisfemme experiences as "enforced femininity." No, she's movingly, seductively, powerfully embodying a kind of luxurious, champagne-kissed, sugar-coated womanness that, as a queer black female, she was never supposed to claim—let alone dance and be applauded for.

Stark also celebrates femme-ininity in terms that mirror MilDred's act more closely. "Femmes," she says, "know how to fail and succeed at femininity at the same time. We use our flaws, our fat, our hairiness, our loud mouths, our oversized brains and our excessive accessorizing to celebrate ourselves and those we love."[77] MilDred's transition to Freda doesn't fail and succeed at femininity at the same time, though, so much as it embodies and disidentifies with Freda at the same time. Her movement into this character both echoes and refuses Alfred Metraux's striking description of Ezili Freda's arrival in his classic Voodoo in Haiti: "At last, in the full glory of her seductiveness, with hair unbound to make her look like a long haired half-caste, Ezili makes her entrance. . . . She walks slowly, swinging her hips," and demands to be clothed in pink and white.[78] But while MilDred's Freda enters slowly, swinging her hips, and while she, too, uncovers her head, she refuses to become this long-haired, fair-cheeked mulatresse. Instead, she bares the glory of her perfectly shaved head and, rouging her lips, bypasses Freda's signature pink in favor of a rich black. Yes, these choices in self-aestheticizing consciously blacken Freda when black is supposed to be neither beautiful nor Ezili-like. For part of MilDred's difficulty in performing the fanm in her, she states, comes from the necessity of transitioning her own internalized standards for ideal womanhood from blonde-loving to Afro-positive. "Growing up," she writes, "I was constantly teased for the same things I once hated about myself, but now through the power of self-transformation and self-love, love about myself. 'Tar baby' becomes beautiful dark cocoa skin; nappy hair becomes perfectly shaped shaved head; four eyes . . . a mystical clairvoyance through almond shaped eyes."[79] In other words: white viewers aren't the only New Yorkers in need of unlearning that blackness and femininity are discordant, and when MilDred blackens Freda she publicly performs an act of emancipation from mental slavery for this largely African-descended audience. An nou danse, my cocoa-skinned Freda, dance for Haiti tonight!

And just as much as MilDred's hair and makeup beautify blackness, they queer Ezili-ness, too. This is absolutely not *The Prodigal Prince*'s Ezili. She dons no headdress here, nor does she drape herself in Madonna blue. Instead, this Freda's well-lit, perfectly shaped shaved head looks "visibly queer," as black femme Marla Stewart puts it.[80] And her black lipstick—the only makeup she wears, notice—reflects the queer Afro-punk subculture rocking Brooklyn in the 2010s. If you met Ezili Freda at a black lesbian club in Brooklyn in 2010, now, this is what she would look like; this is how she would dance with the femmes, butches, and aggressives who, starstruck, can't help but approach her.

The Atlantic and then the Pacific again but colder, yes, in a year of storms. Now without the physical, emotional, and time demands of a prima ballerina, Miss Collins returned to finish a biblical piece, *Genesis*, which she'd begun while choreographing her solo concert over a decade earlier. She performed this piece only once, at Marymount Manhattan College in 1965, and it was never reviewed.

As Miss Collins's argument for the piece describes it, *Genesis* danced a creative interpretation of the creation story in which an unnamed, gender-unspecified first human (Miss Collins) moves from embryonic form, to awareness of his/her own body, to a frustrated "aspiration to transcend earth," and finally comes into consciousness of the power of creation itself, reaching heavenward for divine warmth and inspiration.[81] Lewin suggests that this interpretation of the Bible opens space for multiple figurative readings. Perhaps "Collins," she speculates, "unfolding and evolving onstage, represented the shaping of not the first man in the Bible but, rather, an everyman/everywoman. The nontraditional casting, in which the female choreographer herself performed the part of the first man, could have reinforced this, too—turning Adam into a figure of indeterminate gender, even androgyny."[82] I imagine *Genesis* also acted as a ritual of detoxification for Collins, an opportunity to move her way out of the mythologies of racialized gender—from blackamoor to Creole, Egyptian slave to Queen of the Night—which she had had set on her body for decades. Reaching upward and outward, straining toward the light, she compels her audience to view her not as the creature of demonic ground but as a body, *the* body capable of generating the conditions of possibility for humanity. She—a black woman—dances the beginning of humanity and the genesis of creativity itself.

Genesis was evidently a difficult piece for Collins to choreograph. Gerald Gordon, one of her students, remembers that working on it pushed her to moments of breakdown: "One day she looked at me and the tears were rolling down her cheeks, and she said, 'I'm empty, I can't think of anything' . . . and she picked up the phonograph and threw it across the room."[83] Gordon, along with many close friends and family, began to be concerned about the dancer's mental health. She'd been hospitalized for depression in 1940, and the illness now returned and deepened. Alvin Ailey, who worked briefly with the choreographer during these years, called her one of his "crazy black ladies" and wrote in his autobiography: "She was a fantastic artist . . . but she had psychological problems that later drove her to extremes and out of the dance world."[84] Miss Collins's cousin-in-law, *Prodigal Prince* choreographer Geoffrey Holder, chalked her illness up to professional strain. "Depression—we naturally all in show business go through that," he opined. "And to be a soloist, doing a one-woman show—which she really was, was not very easy."[85] On January 31, 1968, Janet's mother died in Los Angeles. Now sick herself in and of New York, Miss Collins returned to California. She only stayed a few years before heading north to Washington in 1979, retreating from public life and residing with the Sisters of the Visitation in Federal Way, then moving to a Seattle nursing home.

In January 2000, the *Seattle Times* Sunday newspaper featured a lifestyle article about this color line–breaking star now living quietly in a high-rise, low-rent apartment in West Seattle. The article opens with a description of the toll age had taken on the dancer: "Arthritis has turned her fingers into lightning-bolt zigzags, and two years ago, after one toe folded like a crossed leg over its neighbor, she had it surgically removed. More recently, she fell and broke her hip. Then doctors told her she'd need cataract surgery, one for each eye, and sometimes, Janet Collins doesn't know whether to laugh or cry."[86] *Whatever happened to Janet Collins?*, author Marc Ramirez goes on to ask readers, and, reminding readers how she once styled in furs and updos, describes her coiffure—"a fluffy white wig hides her smooth gray head"—as a sign of her decline and virtual disappearance. After describing her ascent in the dance worlds of Los Angeles and New York, he brings readers back to her recent trials in Seattle:

> After she lost her toe in 1998, she grew short-tempered. She could do nothing but lie in bed. As each physical ailment limited her artistry, she grew withdrawn and lonely. Her mind raced with vivid imagery, radiant with joy, gloomy with misery.
>
> She checked into the hospital, where she was diagnosed with bipolar disorder and a chemical imbalance. Now it made sense, why friends would tell her: "Janet, you're the only person I know who can go from laughter to tears."[87]

Miss Collins communicated her experience of bipolar disorder through a dramatic, dancerly gesture: " 'Your dreams are like this,' she explains, spreading her arms. 'Then, when you realize you can't do them, you become depressed.' "[88]

The causes of bipolar disorder remain imperfectly understood. The disease runs in families and can be triggered by physical, emotional, and social stressors. I found no extensive research focused on black women and bipolar disorder. But more general studies of black women's mental health suggest that living out creative black genders—the very kind I've been celebrating in these pages—can involve social and emotional stressors that bring on mental illness. Beverly Greene's research on lesbian and bisexual women, for example, traces how black lesbians who read as masculine can experience a gender-specific form of internalized racism—that is, a wrestling with their own stereotypes of black female masculinity as inherent and pathological—that impacts their mental health.[89] But don't black cisfemmes experience gender-specific forms of internalized racism, too? If it's difficult, heart-shattering to embody a black female masculinity imagined to be inescapable and deviant, isn't it just as shattering to embody a black cisfem(me)ininity that's supposed to remain an impossible desire—isn't it hard to continually fail and succeed at, identify with and disidentify from normative femininity? Wouldn't lacking the resources to develop La Creole, and being pulled between the roles of pale Ethiopian slave and Queen of the Night, drive you crazy, too? *Crazy* can be a quilt to wrap yourself in in a lot of different ways; in a lot of different ways, it can represent something you inherit from a black woman elder to insulate yourself when you need it.

I began this chapter rehearsing how Ezili Freda arrives at a ceremony, and now I want you to remember how she leaves. Entering in a dazzling cloud of creativity, perfume, and laughter, Metres Manbo Ezili Freda Daome always departs in tears. Like Janet Collins, she emerges with dreams of limitless possibilities, limitless creativities: but then, faced with the limits contained in the world around her—the world of servitors, not lwa—she collapses, begins to weep, and cannot stay. Mambo Vye Zo Komande LaMenfo describes this element of Freda in terms of bipolarity: "Perfection has its darker side. The hunt for Perfection can degenerate into compulsion, obsession, or delusion. This bi-polar analogy is the place that Erzulie straddles."[90] Ezili Freda demonstrates for us that it's important to begin celebrating cisfemme queenness, to understand the history, power, and generative capacity this gender expression brings to the mix of African diaspora experience. But having done that, black high cisfemme-ininity can't move through without leaving us to remember that being as womanly as you can be also invites pain, stabbing your breast. Being a black ciswoman is a high-risk vocation, one that brings physical, social, economic, sexual, emotional, and other kinds of vulnerabilities. It can mean being brought to trial for having too colorful clothing and too many shoes, if you're Duchess in nineteenth-century Barbados. It can mean being harassed walking in the street in a dress in a way you never are when you wear men's clothing, if you're MilDred. And, as Whitaker sings before her Ezili descends into sorrow, it can mean, "I got no soap for my water / no honey for my bee / no bread for my butter / no sugar for my tea." Once we understand where the black cisfemme comes from—from a place of resistance and creativity, rather than failure or frivolity—we're left with the responsibility to figure out what it would take to make the Bridgetowns, New Yorks, Port-au-Princes, and Los Angeleses where she emerges safer places for her to stay . . . places with fewer tears. O Metres Ezili Freda, o, lanmou mwen, I so, so want you to be able to stay.

PHOTO BY CINDY ELIZABETH

PHOTO BY CINDY ELIZABETH

bridge

SISSY WERK

I love me some Big Freedia. LOVE. *Homegrown New Orleans sissy from Josephine Street & Queen of Bounce, you already know: after Miley Cyrus's infamous performance at the Video Music Awards in 2013, Freedia generously offered the "Blurred Lines" singer twerking lessons.*[1] *Freedia could teach her something, too. Not just technique—twerk's contractions, isolations, & circular rhythms—but something more. Its roots in the Mapouka that Ivoirienne women dance in circles, its predecessors in African American black bottom,* DJ *Jubilee's first recorded use of the word "twerk" in 1993. She's studied it all, (t)werked it all out, earned her title as Big Freedia,*

Queen Diva. Her voice-over in Beyonce's "Formation" warns you: "I did not come to play."[2]

No, Big Freedia came to work. "I've been steadily working my ass off," Freedia told an interviewer who asked about her rise to fame. "It's taken me 15 years to get here. When I decided this was gonna be my full time career, I went all in."[3] Fans look at her colorful extensions, her on-point makeup, her love of sequins & accessories & if they don't know, maybe they see a black queer femininity that's about show. They see glowing performance, but Freedia talks about sweaty labor. The Queen Diva has been working to make ends meet since she took a job at Burger King in high school: "From Burger King to Bounce Queen, who knew?"[4] And she & her mother bonded as black feminine folks not through shared love of hairstyles or men, but through shared relationships to work. "She was always proud of my work ethic," Freedia remembers. " 'You're like your mother,' she'd say. 'Always gotta work.' "[5]

From work to work, Carole Boyce Davies describes the circularity of black women's lives and movements. Concentrated in sectors like health support, fast food, & retail sales, black women in the Americas work more, differently, & less profitably than black men or white women, Boyce Davies reminds us.[6] Yes, people's gender heavy-handedly shapes their work possibilities & realities—but just as much, their work realities shape their gender. Born Freddie Ross Jr., Freedia became Freedia by work-ing like her mother: by always working more & differently than if she'd grown up to be a straight black cisman like Freddie Ross Sr. Listening to work histories like hers—histories of sissy work—pushes us outside ciscentric conversations about black women's labor that assume (in Saidiya Hartman's words) "the material relations of sexuality and reproduction [that] defined black women's historical relationships as laborers" are always about common sexual/reproductive biology.[7] Conversations that imagine pussy & vagina are always the same thing, or that "partus sequitur ventrum" is a curse leveled only at black folks with a uterus. After all, Freedia's gay daughters work just like she does, just like she works hard as her mother Miss Vera.

Please take my advice: if you haven't already, watch all of Freedia's reality show Big Freedia: Queen of Bounce. Watch it alongside sissy/masisi work stories told in the documentaries I look at in these next pages: Masisi Innocente pressing hair & performing ceremony in "Of Men and Gods," Ezili Danto working hard as Big Freedia & Miss Vera rolled together in Poto Mitan, Angie Xtravaganza slaying on the floor & ruling her house in Paris Is Burning. They'll all tell you: they did not come to play with you—they came to slay.

TWO

MACHE ANSANM

Girl, you know we're all in this together: ansanm nou fanm, ansanm nou fo. On March 22, 2003—the first day of spring in a city that really, really needed it—Dwa Fanm, a newly formed Brooklyn-based women's rights group, hosted a benefit and celebratory event titled Voices of Women. "Voices of Women is our third event," Dwa Fanm's board chair Carolle Charles explained. "This event is to amplify women's voices, promote women's work, and acknowledge their activism, their struggles, and their achievements."[1] Along with a reception, live performances by Haitian jazz artists, and raffles, the documentary *Of Men and Gods*—winner of Festival Dwa Fanm's 2003 Voices of Women Trophy for Activism, Courage, and Achievement in Film—was presented by director Laurence Magloire. An exploration of gender-variant practitioners in Vodou, this innovative film (billed as "a frank look at a largely unexplored area") traveled widely to LGBT and African diaspora film festivals in the Caribbean, North America, Europe, Asia, and the Pacific.[2] "Countering misperceptions about the voodoo religion, 'Of Men and Gods' succinctly illustrates through the examples of several gay male practitioners in Haiti that the faith is progressive, rather than exclusionary and backwards," Robert Koehler summed up in his *Variety* review. "Fests should scamper for such a rarity."[3]

The film was the result of years of work by Magloire and her codirector, anthropologist Anne Lescot. Born in France to a Haitian father and Italian mother, Lescot settled in Haiti in 1997 to complete doctoral research on constructions of femininity and masculinity in Vodoun. When an interviewer asked her how this segued into a film on "gay men," she explained:

> I used to go to a lot of ceremonies, as much as I could, actually, because it was so much fun. And at this same time, what I noticed was that in the ceremonies there were a lot of gays—men and women, you know—that expressed themselves, that seemed to be quite comfortable expressing their, their sexuality. And I was very much surprised because I didn't see that in the civilian society. It seemed like it was totally taboo, you would never hear anything about that, there were no gay bars, no discos, no magazines, no papers, nothing. But in Vodou ceremonies they became like people who were very much respected, and actually, a Vodou ceremony with gay people was a very successful ceremony.[4]

So instead of documenting normative expressions of femininity or masculinity, she came to focus on how gay practitioners—far from appearing as aberrations—become representative of Vodou's complex gender system, a system where womanness is understood to be mediated by divine as well as social forces. Lescot began filming interviews as ethnographic practice; but when she lost her entire dissertation along with her computer, she salvaged her work by using this footage to begin *Of Men and Gods*. Bringing together many different kinds of work and questions, the film follows a cast of sevite to markets, salons, churches, Vodou temples, living rooms, nightclubs, and pilgrimages, recording their thoughts on how gender and religion weave through their daily lives.

Magloire and Lescot's documentary was chosen for Dwa Fanm's Voices of Women because of its directors' gender; but when it screened at the Brooklyn event, it amplified women's voices through its interviews, too. Because despite *Of Men and Gods'* title, many of its interviewees refer to themselves not as gay or *any* kind of men but as masisi: a Kreyòl word that references the fem(me)ininity or womanness of someone assigned male at birth, and/or their desire for male lovers—and over the course of the documentary, many of the masisi tell viewers they, too, are women. The term describes a spectrum of transfemininity that could include those labeled "feminine gay men" in the United States as well as those identified as "transgender women"—a distinction which isn't made by the film's interviewees, who all place themselves in the category masisi. While the word may be related to Kreyol *sé* (sister), Roberto Strongman speculates it's in fact derived from

Fon *mamisisi*, the word for devotees of Mami Wata (African counterpart of Lasyrenn); mamisisi are either cisgender women or males who dress and braid their hair like—or perhaps, *as*—women.[5] As evocative as this African connection is, though, I'd also like to think of the term in relationship to its cognate, African American *sissy*. Masisi and black rural sissies are similar formations in many ways, as Roderick Ferguson describes the latter in his beautiful essay "Sissies at the Picnic." Like masisi, the sissies Ferguson grew up with "ran the gamut of gender styles": some "were limp-wristed and sachayed when they walked; others, like my literature instructor, were straight-laced and masculine; others displayed a fondness for perms and relaxers."[6] And, like the masisi in *Of Men and Gods*, while they endured jeers, they were also recognized for performing crucial work in their communities: the work of hair stylists, diction coaches, teachers, as well as cultural and artistic work. Most importantly, maybe, both gender/sexual formations suggest crucial contours of the world understandings of Africans across the waters: suggest everyday ways that things the West binarizes—male/female, traditional/modern, sacred/profane—can, do flow in and out of each other.

Not really all about men, *Of Men and Gods* isn't about gods, either. The film is about lwa, about how they show up in practitioners' way of being in the world; and most especially, it's about Ezili Danto. Because while Freda is the spirit generally associated with masisi, one of the particularities of the interviewees gathered in this film is that they identify as Danto's children. Several explain they became masisi because as children Ezili Danto "gate-m" ("spoiled me"). As in English or French, that *spoiled* could mean marred, ruined; but it could also mean endulged, showered with gifts, loved too much. The confluence of Danto's very beloved children in Lescot's interviews is just coincidence, maybe. But this confluence certainly suggests something important about black queer gender: namely, that while we often talk about gender creativity through language of expression and performance (Freda's realms), we might also do well to talk about it as labor. Ezili Danto is a fierce lwa, a woman-loving lwa, and, above all, what you call a working lwa—one who answers her sevites' calls swiftly and thoroughly. And her masisi daughters in this film are very much working women, too; are women who invent their womanness through their labor, through intertwining remunerative, spiritual, and community work. In return for their mother's gifts and endless love, Danto's masisi children have to work for and *like* their mother: have to become her daughters by learning the work of being black women. Ansanm nou fanm, ansanm nou fo—and we work at it, too.

–◈–

On April 2, 2009, in honor of Haiti's National Women's Day, Dwa Fanm joined a cadre of activist groups assembled at the Medgar Evers College auditorium to comment on the New York premiere of Tèt Ansanm Productions' documentary *Poto Mitan: Haitian Women, Pillars of the Global Economy*. Told through the narratives of five women workers in Port-au-Prince, the film tracks intersecting stories of gendered violence, feminized poverty, interrupted education, passionate mothering, union organizing, and antiviolence work in Haiti's capital. The project's genesis came through the work of Santa Barbara graduate student Mark Schuller, who, while in Haiti researching the effects of globalization, encountered women workers who asked him to make a film about their lives. "These factory workers and street merchants are savvy about geopolitics and what scholars call 'globalization,'" Schuller notes. "They know the power of video to move people, and wanted to engage the people who buy the fruits of their labor, people whose governments are shaping daily life in Haiti. . . . Since they can't have U.S. visas to visit us in person, producing a documentary was the next best thing."[7] The documentary literally focuses on the hardships and importance of Haitian women workers whose labor has long been rendered invisible. Far from a marginal workforce, Solange, Marie-Jeanne, Frisline, Hélène, and Thérèse—the principal interviewees—emerge as "five brave poto mitan who requested to have their stories told."[8] The explanation of this titular phrase, "poto mitan," comes as a voice-over: "In the Vodoun religion, there is a poto mitan, a temple center post around which everything happens, all ceremonies. That's why we call women 'poto mitan,' because everything revolves around women."[9] Or, as Minister of Women's Condition and Rights Marie Laurence Jocelyn Lassègue puts it, "It's women's labor that keeps the country from going under."[10]

In spring 2013, I showed this film to my senior seminar in African and African Diaspora Studies at the University of Texas, Austin. We'd been reading Karen McCarthy Brown's work on Ezili in *Mama Lola: A Vodou Priestess in Brooklyn*, and students were puzzled as to why Haitians would have such a complicated, imperfect, imperious spirit force. Especially troubling to them was Ezili Danto, whom Brown describes as a "solitary, hard-working, sometimes raging mother" and also a lesbian—descriptions many Christian students found incompatible with divinity.[11] I screened this film for the class to help them make sense of Danto: to help them see how most Haitian women's lives revolve around work, and why they would need celestial support from a lwa whose power also revolves around work. This divine laborer is Danto, who, as the single (lesbian) mother of the Haitian pantheon, is (not surprisingly) known as the hardest working of all the lwa. Travay, travay-o! "She love to work," Mama Lola says of the lwa she calls "Mother," and Mambo Vye Zo Komande LaMenfo, extolling "her holy sweat," explains: "When Dantor comes in ritual, she is ready to work. She rolls up her sleeves in digs in . . . with both hands to help her children," mixing medicine, offering advice, granting petitions, and "encouraging us to work harder, faster, and put more of ourselves into [our] work."[12]

Like the labor explored in *Poto Mitan*, Danto's endless labor is not that of a transhistorical woman-as-worker archetype. Rather, it emerges as a reflection of a very specific intersection of geopolitics, global economics, and feminized poverty that runs through Haiti. Mambo Vye Zo Komande LaMenfo very eloquently paints Danto's connections to women's role in the Haitian economy:

> It is not uncommon in Haiti to find a single middle age woman, tilling land, washing clothes, preparing meals and tending small children and elderly parents. Along with all this "domestic" work, comes the harvesting and selling of goods to feed these people. The country women walk long miles every day to the Carrefour (the crossroads), carrying their baskets of fruit, produce and herbs on their heads. They get up before sunrise, to make a meal for the family, before walking the long dirt roads, so they can get a good place in the market. After toiling in the sun all day, they then walk the miles home, not to rest, but to cook, clean, and get ready for the next day.[13]

Sick, tired, and angry from this endless, wringing work, these women, she imagines, find "a thoughtform emerges, taking over, giving you the strength to carry on. Erzulie Dantor comes into being out of the thoughts of all of those market women."[14]

Danto comes not to accept these women's labor conditions, though, but to transform them. Like *Poto Mitan*'s interviewees, she's a merciless warrior in service of social justice; never forget, Mama Danto is the lwa who appeared at Bwa Kayiman and demanded that her servitors end slavery's murderous labor conditions. And this revolutionary lwa—this manly black superwoman who arrives dressed in royal blue,robes and carrying double-edged daggers—comes to her children not only in order to transform women's work, but to transform what it means to be a woman in the first place. Danto demands: what if woman-ness doesn't mean being expected to be a docile worker until five o'clock, then everyone's caretaker after? What if it doesn't mean bearing children, or being able to bear children, or taking care of lovers who act like children? *What if?* Then, the idea of woman-as-poto mitan can be recarved into something that Haitian women can actually lean on; then we could reimagine womanness as activism, forceful action, active loving, active imaginations, electrical activity. This kind of reconstructing womanhood is what the film *Poto Mitan* is about, what Ezili Danto's power is all about, and, in the end, what this chapter will be about.

∞

Listen, now, listen to Junior Vasquez: *You know I want you, you know I love you— but you're just like a QUEEN.*[15] Yes, Mother Angie, yes you are! On July 22, 2012, New York's House of Xtravaganza—founded in 1982 by Father Hector and Mother Angie Xtravaganza—hosted a lavish thirtieth anniversary ball at XL, a "slicker than vinyl club" near Times Square.[16] Divinely titled Wrath of the Gods and Goddesses, the ball was moved from usual sites in Harlem or the South Bronx to Manhattan, where it drew a crowd of hundreds. Before participants took the runway to walk categories like "Amazon Warrior," "Men of Sparta," "Diana of Paradise Island," and "Hermaphroditus," the lights were dimmed to screen a video tribute to founding Mother Angie, who died from AIDS-related liver disease in 1993. "To the Xtravaganza gods & goddesses who are no longer here on earth with us, this evening your powerful presence is felt," proclaimed current father Jose. "Tonight I, Father Jose Xtravaganza full of loyalty and pride for this House, humbly bow and kneel before all the Xtravagant gods & god-desses. I ask you to join us in this celebration—our celebration of 30 years serving. 30 years of this iconic family that you, Mother Angie, and our brothers and sisters created so long ago."[17]

The following week, the *New York Times* ran a "Fashion and Style" article on the ball titled "Paris Is Still Burning."[18] This title nostalgically refers readers back to an earlier tribute to Angie Xtravaganza's mothering: the scenes dedi-cated to her in Jennie Livingston's *Paris Is Burning*, the iconic documentary that followed New York's ball scene in the late 1980s. Angie's first appearance in

Paris introduces her as the quintessence of house motherhood as, wearing a sparkling gown and brandishing an open fan, she elegantly names herself for the camera: "I am Angie Xtravaganza, and I am the mother of the House of Xtravaganza."[19] Seated by a statue of Hindu deity Ganesh and already the Xtravagant goddess son Jose will later declare her to be, Angie goes on to describe, in a measured, melodious voice, the many ways she cares for her children. The film then cuts from her voice-over to a scene of Angie laughing on a city street with three of her sons, who trill for the camera: "Xtrrraavagaanza Power!!!" "I bought her her tits," one son proclaims, pointing toward her chest. "I paid for them." Angie lifts a soft brown breast out of her shirt and affirms: "He paid for them, my tits." The sons continue: "I gave my mother her tits. Shake those tits, mami. Shake those tits, mama." After a rousing chorus of "All she wants for Christmas is her two front tits, her two front tits . . ." one son takes her breast in his hands and covers the nipple with his mouth. The film then abruptly cuts to a black screen with the word MOTHER written across it in white capital letters. As we cut back to the street scene, Angie's son laughs lovingly: "Our mother even nurses us. She's a good woman. She nourishes us."[20] The scene ends with Angie in profile, smiling, a gold necklace glinting at her throat.

Reflecting on this memorable moment in *Paris Is Burning*, Barbara Browning searches for a way to make sense of its image of a brown woman nursing adult sons. Is she a queer version of the mass-produced images of nursing black mothers circulated in public service campaigns: another kind of ad for the way that mother's milk does a body good? Is she an ironic commentary on the lack of resources available to black mothers, who offer breasts even though they're empty? "Angie Xtravaganza," Browning concludes, "is both of these and neither. She is 'Ezili Danto, the solitary, hard-working, sometimes raging mother . . .'"[21] And of course, she is. She is the wrathful goddess her son will later name the Xtravaganza anniversary ball after, the tough-love mother who can walk the street right beside you and tell you what you need to know, the fiercely generous mother who loves her children so hard she could will an empty breast to give milk. She is the Black Madonna who once met another Madonna and came away looking divine. In his memories of Mother Angie shared at the thirtieth anniversary ball, Jose Xtravaganza includes introducing his mother to Madonna at the Love Ball II in 1991. He recalls: "After being introduced Madonna leaned into Angie and said, 'Your boys are amazing!' Angie being the proud mother answered ever so graciously, 'Thank you—aren't they!' It was and is still one of the proudest moments of my life. I was just as proud to be your son that night all those years ago, as I am today to be here to celebrate you Mother Angie."[22] Yes, to celebrate her just like a queen.

O girl, o girl, no woman's work is ever done: gason konn bouke, men pa fanm. Opening with handheld camera shots whose jarringness marks the labor of the filmmakers themselves, *Of Men and Gods* begins on the way to many kinds of women's work. The film opens in silence, as the camera unsteadily follows—but never quite catches—the straight, willowy back of Blondine as she makes her way through an early morning Port-au-Prince open-air market, looking for a spot to sell snuff. As the camera moves over Blondine's shoulder to focus on her face, her voice-over offers the film's first words: "If I can't be who I am in Haiti I'd rather die, or go live in the Dominican Republic."[23] Blondine, we see right away, works from daylean to dayclean to be able to be who she is in Haiti. Immediately following the title screen, viewers start a workday with her. Once arrived at her stall, Blondine pulls a flowered vest over her clothes, opens a black plastic bag of snuff, and starts pouring it into a large red basin. "Right now I'm in Port-au-Prince to make a living," her voice-over explains. "I'm not ashamed of who I am. I'm a street vendor, I sell snuff in open air markets."[24] The camera focuses on Blondine's hands as she mixes and kneads the snuff, then pans outward to show her whole working body leaning into her task with concentration and attentiveness. "I like my work," she says. "It helps me a lot. Even if I sell snuff for a few bucks, I'm satisfied because I didn't have them before."[25] This opening sequence about Blondine's work ends in a lovingly shot moment that showcases the dignity and pleasure she feels in her work: slow-motion of her walking regally between stalls, tilting a carefully coiffed head, raising pencil-thin eyebrows, and curving pink lips into a flirtatious, haughty smile.

This dignity is something she works hard for. Fellow vendors launch taunts across her snuff, one woman needling: "Hey! How many men do you do a day?"[26] But whether it makes her friends or not, Blondine's konmès (business) places her squarely in a larger community of Haitian women workers: machann (market vendors) whose work, as Karen McCarthy Brown notes, "both in the countryside and in Port-au-Prince, [is] almost exclusively the province of women," and whose earning power gives the machann "what leverage she has in otherwise male-dominated families."[27] Blondine's profits support her womanness, giving her the money to "buy clothes and shoes to go out."[28] She also expresses pride that her konmès not only allows her to take care of herself, but to provide for other women in her family. "When my mother died, it helped me bury her, my konmès did," she says, lifting her head.[29] Blondine, we see, is doing well for herself: much better, she scoffs, than the vendors and customers who jeer at her—and better, apparently, than elder male relatives who didn't have money to bury her mother.

Blondine's work not only makes her money, but makes her into the kind of woman her sister-friends might call a fanm/gason. Literally a woman/man, the fanm/gason is, Carolle Charles writes, "a very paradoxical Haitian way of describing independent women."[30] This creative gender is not necessarily one North Americans would call queer: "Though the paradox rests upon a traditional gender binary, the label does not necessarily convey a sexual meaning. My mother was a *fanm/gason,* wearing the man's pants in her negotiation of gender relations and prescriptions within Haitian society."[31] The fanm/gason whom Charles describes are activists organizing around domestic workers' rights, women who leave husbands and find a way to support daughters on their own, midwives who attend women in their communities—women who make it on their own and help other women do the same. But what does it mean for a masisi to be a fanm-gason? Dan Irving writes that when theorizing transness, scholars and activists need to think not only in terms of how trans folk fit into (or trouble) gender binaries, but how they fit into labor markets. He argues that working- and middle-class FTMs, in particular, attempt to authenticate their manness by doing "real men's" work, "aspiring to and performing hegemonic 'business-class' masculinities."[32] Blondine is also making herself into a recognizable gender through work, but hers is something quite other than hegemonic. Selling its realness in a market woman's flowered vest, her masisi fanm/gasonness taps into a resistant gender formation through which Haitian women strategize ways to act as what Charles calls "machanns ak machandiz" (merchants as well as commodities): that is, she joins all kinds of women who step outside gender prescriptions in order to make their lives work for them as best they can, becoming agents even when they also can't help being treated as objects.[33] Ignoring taunts that suggest her sex is for sale while very profitably marketing something else her clients can put in their mouths, Blondine works at her fanm/gasonness with a grace that earns her *Of Men and Gods*' slow-motion admiration.

Of Men and Gods' second sequence takes viewers to another women's workplace, one much more intimate, more relaxed, more—well, more pleasurable than Blondine's: the brightly painted, single-room, multiply mirrored salon whose sign reads Femme Ideale Studio de Beaute Chez Marceline (Marceline's Ideal Woman Beauty Salon). The camera leaves Blondine walking out of frame in the marketplace and cuts to Innocente strolling smilingly into frame as she opens the salon's green door, greets sister-friend stylist Jean Marcel with a kiss, and sits in front of a full-length mirror to apply pink lipstick. This salon is, we soon see, the space where most of the film's interviewees hang out, beautify, and/or work together. The camera returns to follow the two masisi exiting the shop, Innocente smoking a cigarette and dancing down the street to a konpa as they meet other girlfriends relaxing between two trees. One of these friends, Madsen, runs Chez Marceline. The next shot shows Madsen styling a fanm whose hair is set in rollers, her voice-over explaining how she became a very successful, very hard-working masisi stylist in Cabaret: "When there are weddings, parties, funerals, I can have up to ten customers. If I weren't from this town I'd have problems. But they accept me for who I am."[34]

Like Blondine's work sequence, the scene in which Madsen, Innocente, Jean Marcel, and Flanise gather between the trees ends with a slow-motion shot—but, rather than framing any one of the girlfriends, this shot foregrounds the trees themselves. A visual echo of this image later returns in the Cabaret peristyle where Innocente, Jean Marcel, Blondine, and others serve the lwa, as the camera again lingers on another tree—the poto mitan the sevites dance around. This shot visually suggests that the beauty shop, too, offers a poto mitan, a pillar around which community congregates. Madsen tells us that Chez Marceline is a touchstone for Cabaret's ciswomen, a place they count on to prepare them for landmark events in their lives like weddings, baptisms, funerals. And it is quite a bit more central to the daily lives of the film's masisi. This is where some work, and where others hang out because they have no work; where all create new hairstyles and makeup, where they meet friends to talk about their days and lives. As Willi Coleman describes black women's beauty shops, Madsen's is "a place where extraordinary cultural, political and economic business [gets] taken care of":

Ya could meet
A whole lot of other women
Sittin there . . .
Lots more got taken care of
than hair . . .
we came together
under the hot comb
to share
and share
and
share.[35]

The image of Madsen styling hair quickly cuts to a second shot of her
in the salon, and to a moment of such sharing: a conversation between
Madsen, Jean Marcel, and Innocente about their early experiences of gender. Standing in the doorway, Madsen says: "Since I was small, I knew. I've
never lived with my father. Only my mother." Jean Marcel breaks in: "I was
six years old when I started feeling that I was a girl." And Innocente adds
thoughtfully, smiling in her pink lipstick: "I was born a girl and I feel like
a woman. I was born a girl and I feel like a woman, for real. I stand like a
woman, I walk like a woman, I feel like a woman." Jean Marcel punctuates:
"That's it!"[36] Jean Marcel and Innocente are doubled in mirrors as they
speak, framing the beauty shop as a site of literal and figurative reflections
of masisi womanhood and masisi community.

You might say these reflections are what happens during breaks from
work; but you also might say they're an intimate part of the work that goes
on in the salon. Hairstyling is an attractive profession (literally and figuratively) for people like Madsen because, like Blondine's konmès, it's a business
with low startup costs where a masisi's skill set and gender presentation are
provided their own material space—the salon—to develop and flourish. In
the "beauty shop, with the physical space it plots out and the social relationships it contains,"[37] along with the manipulation of women's bodies (cis-
and masisi alike), Madsen and Jean Marcel are performing the cultural and
conceptual work of *working through* womanhood, exploring what it can mean
to themselves and their sister-friends. What Ginetta Candelario writes of
Dominican beauty salons in Washington Heights also rings true for Chez
Marceline: "And while beauty regimes are not empowering [for women of

African descent], the community that is developed around beauty practices often is. Small revolutions ferment in the beauty shop daily when Dominican women confront oppressive conditions generated by government offices, hospitals, schools, employers, husbands, and lovers, with the support and assistance of beauty shop kin."[38] Madsen and Jean Marcel are not paid to be either (queer) gender theorists or group counselors; but because they are paid to style hair, they have the space and community to perform this work—the space, aptly named Ideal Woman Beauty Salon.

⸙

"Bourik travay, chwal garyonen," Frisline proclaims in *Poto Mitan*—poor folk work like donkeys so the rich can gallop like horses.[39] In a voice-over that accompanies a shot of her braiding her long, black hair, Frisline introduces herself to viewers by telling the story of how her parents sent her to Potoprens when they couldn't support their children in the countryside any longer. Funneled into a shantytown, Frisline went to work manufacturing T-shirts in U.S.-owned factories in the state-run industrial park, SONAPI. There she worked like a donkey so rich companies could run away with profits like horses; there she worked hard, and there she lost her jobs. First, when she went back to the countryside to tend to her dying mother, she returned to find herself replaced at the factory. At her next position, she was fired for organizing a union; and though she and other women workers mounted a successful lawsuit, they were forced to pay their winnings to male lawyers and union leaders. "I won't say that unions aren't good, but after what they did to me, I won't ever join a union again," Frisline concludes.[40] Frisline's story underscores the multiplied forms of labor she performs on top of her factory work: the daughter's work of providing health care and other services that the government cannot subsidize, the woman worker's travail of having to deal with patriarchal harassment from male bosses and (supposed) male advocates alike.

Now, *this* kind of work—gendered labor imposed on women who have too much to do already—risks making Danto very, very angry. Though she's syncretized with the Black Madonna who carries an infant at her left breast, Danto is not a long-suffering, mild-virginal kind of mother. Known for her passionate mothering, one of her motherly passions is her blinding, world-splitting rage at injustices leveled against her children. Disrespect of the bond between mothers and daughters can bring out the force of a thunderstorm from her. Karen McCarthy Brown explains: "In woman-headed Haitian households, the bond between mother and daughter is the most charged and the most enduring. Women and their daughters form three- and sometimes four-generation networks in which gifts and services circulate according to needs and abilities. . . . The strength of the mother-daughter bond is one explanation of why Haitians identify the child in Ezili Danto's arms as a daughter. And the importance and precariousness of that bond add meaning to Danto's fiery temper."[41] Yes, the importance of the mother-daughter bond adds to her temper, sparked when people don't respect the work that it takes for women like Frisline to care for their mothers when they already have to work to make their quota at the factory, find enough food and gas to make a meal, make space to use the neighborhood's communal shower, and pick through garbage on their way to and from the factory. And the precariousness of that bond fires her temper, too, when women who labor so hard have no one and nothing else to depend on than their overworked daughters.

Danto also has no tolerance for unequal treatment of men and women workers. This mother does every kind of work that any male lwa or human man can, and demands respect for that equity on the human as well as the extrahuman plane. One practitioner expresses: "Ezili Danto is a powerful spirit and she empowers me when she descends. . . . She is a revolutionary woman and she can fight alongside men, as an equal to men. She doesn't buy into the ideals of femininity or heterosexuality."[42] So what would she have to say to male union bosses who take the money that women like Frisline organized for—what would she have to say about this kind of unequal work for unequal pay, even among those who are supposed to be comrades? You see all the reasons that Danto has for making the angry black woman into a divine figure: when you work that hard, you *know* you deserve respect and you want to model for your daughters how to demand it, too.

Frisline's story is one of remaking her own working conditions so she can garner that kind of respect. After losing her last factory job, she manages to open her own konmès out of her one-room, blue-painted house by borrowing money from friends and saving. This home business affords her both better work conditions and higher earnings than her SONAPI positions. "This last year, I've been doing commerce, and I live better," her voice-over tells us as an image of her selling bread to a young woman plays on screen. "In the factory,

I only saw a penny every two weeks. This little pittance didn't do anything for me. Now, every day, I earn some money. I get money and invest it here."[43] Figuratively and perhaps literally too, opening this konmès comes as Frisline's gift from Danto, the hard worker who is also the most gifted businesswoman of the lwa. As Houngan Hector remarks: "I love Mama [Danto], she is such a hard worker. When she agree to help someone, I know they are in good hands, that they will get what they want. She is a pig seller in the market, you know? She is a good business lady."[44] Doyenne of the market, Danto reflects for her children what empowering work looks like: it may not be glamorous and it may be hard, but it's work that affords women both dignity and self-reliance. Yes, Mama Danto models and mirrors this kind of meaningful, sustainable work as Haitian women's right.

Junior Vasquez tells the story again: *work this—work this—work this pussy!*[45] Work, yes, work is what pussy does. Angie Xtravaganza's past is difficult to uncover; she worked hard to keep it that way. "She believed in her ability to eradicate the past, to be renowned simply and purely for what she had made of herself," Michael Cunningham reflects. Angie "refused to talk about her childhood, to anyone. She'd never been . . . one of 13 children, most of whom had different fathers. She wasn't the son of an abusive Puerto Rican woman in the South Bronx. She hadn't had a rotten, violent childhood haunted by Catholicism. She was and had always been triumphant, dazzling, the fiercest thing in high heels."[46] At age fourteen Angie began transitioning—from the South Bronx to the Village, from boy to girl. Evenings she snuck out of her mother's house with girls' clothes and makeup hidden in a shopping bag, then rode the subway to join friends on the Christopher Street piers. There she worked nightly to present as woman: slipping into dresses, applying makeup, and, at fifteen, beginning hormone shots to change the shape of her face and encourage the breasts her children would later nurse from. According to Cunningham, Angie obtained hormones in clubs where they were sold by a doctor called Jimmy Treetop, "who would sell you a syringe full of female hormones and vitamin B-12 for $15, or a kit of six shots for $60. Angie, like most of the other queens, bolstered the hormones with estrogen and progesterone, which she took in the form of birth control pills."[47] Transition—from getting yourself new clothes, removing facial hair, and perfecting eye makeup, to honing your gestures, to changing your walk, and taking shots every week—is a lot of work; and this was work that Angie undertook with resolve and precision.

To fund this unpaid labor, Angie had to find paying work. This she did, turning tricks at the Hotel Christopher, a pay-by-the-hour hotel located upstairs from a gay bar called The Cock Ring. According to former patrons' memories of this bar/disco/sex club, there was a lot of sex work to be done there. "The Cock Ring was dark, cruisey, **and always hot**," Will Kohler recalls.

> It was the at the center of the gay universe in the mid 70's and anyone that was anyone in the village went there; though not everyone admitted it. . . . Upstairs The Hotel Christopher, had to be one of the sleaziest hotels in the 1970's in New York City. . . . On Sundays during the height of the unofficial cruise party it wasn't uncommon to see half naked men beckoning to men below to come up and have sex or to witness sex acts going on in broad daylight in front of windows to cheers from the crowd below.[48]

These Sunday night crowds were swelled by middle-class, white, cisgender "uptown gays" looking for a downtown vacation, which they paid brown transwomen like Angie to provide.

If Angie's earnings as a sex worker helped make her a woman—by generating the cash necessary to buy clothes, makeup, and hormones—they also helped her become a mother. Hector Xtravaganza remembers that by fifteen, young Angie was already making herself into Mother Angie. At thirteen Hector was living on the piers where, night after night, Angie invited him to put his head on her lap so she could watch over him while he slept. One afternoon the older girl found him looking melancholy and asked, "What's the matter? Where's your mother?" When Hector answered that she was probably at work, Angie corrected him: "You don't know where your mother is? Your mother's right next to you. . . . I'm your mother."[49] Soon after, Angie and Father Founder Hector Xtravaganza (father to the Hector narrating these stories) began the House of Xtravaganza as what Hector Jr. calls a "street family" or "a loving gay street gang." Emerging as the first primarily Latino house, the Xtravaganza family took its place in the "gay" kinship structure that Marlon Bailey describes as being one of the most important features of Ballroom culture: "In Ballroom culture, houses are kinship structures that are configured socially rather than biologically. Although houses are mostly social configurations, at times, they serve as literal homes or gathering places for their members. . . . These alternative families, as it were, are led by 'mothers' and 'fathers,' house parents who provide guidance for their 'children' of various ages, race and ethnic groups (usually Black and Latino/as), and genders and sexualities . . ."[50] The House of Xtravaganza was initially composed of Hector and other gay and transgender pier children—many of whom, like Angie, were Puerto Rican and/or (light-skinned) Afro-Latino—"adopted" by Mother Angie and Father Hector. While she couldn't provide a physical structure to house them, Angie reportedly used her sex work earnings to feed children (including Hector Jr.) who otherwise wouldn't get enough to eat.

She also used her experience turning tricks to help protect daughters who engaged in sex work. Though many were chronologically older than she, hookers often sought her out as a mother because of the advice and care she reserved for them. In fact, sex work was for Angie a double labor: the labor of prostitution itself and the labor of protecting herself and her daughters from the danger this work entailed. Angie gives insight into this aspect of her mothering at the end of *Paris Is Burning*, when she talks about her relationship with her "main daughter" Venus, whose body Angie had to identify after Venus was strangled by a john. She had worked hard to counsel Venus on how and where to work as safely as possible: "I always used to tell her Venus, you take too many chances, you're too wild with people in the streets, something is going to happen to you. But that was Venus. She always took a chance, she always went into strangers' cars, she always did what she wanted to get what she wanted."[51] Also part of this aspect of Angie's work is the emotional labor of grieving those dangers she cannot protect her daughters from. "I miss her, every time I go anywhere I miss her. That was my main, the main daughter of my house, in other words," Angie says of Venus. "But that's part of life, that's part of being a transsexual in New York City and surviving."[52]

———

O girl raise a hymn, sing it now, mmm: si se Bondye ki voye, li peya fre ou. As the title suggests, *Of Men and Gods* focuses most closely on masisi's loving, continual spiritual work, labor as necessary to them as any other. Keeping on the path of women's work, the opening sequence cuts from the Femme Ideale beauty salon to Denis in denim overalls and white hat, walking into a church with a white candle in her left hand and a bundle of herbs in her right. The camera later returns to her in her house, wearing a black-and-white print dress and matching headwrap, seated between the images of Our Lady of Sorrows (Freda) and the Black Madonna of Czestochowa (Danto) adorning her green walls. She begins describing her spiritual practice: "I give myself to Jesus, God first and the lwa after. I depend on them. My mother was in Vodou and I grew up in it."[53] The camera pans to her praying in front of a candle on Danto's altar as her voice-over continues: "I want to serve the spirits even if they don't help me. I can't abandon them. I must be faithful to them and when things change for me, I'll have a ceremony for them and they'll be satisfied and they'll help me in return."[54] Denis understands her spiritual work as a central force in her temple's successful functioning. She later puts forth evenly and emphatically: "When the drum starts beating and a masisi or madivin starts dancing, you can't stop them or you stop the celebration. . . . That's why a houngan has to love masisi, why a mambo has to love masisi."[55] As she speaks, the scene cuts to Blondine, Innocente, and Denis dancing together in ceremony. The medium close-up of their dance underscores that this is really, *really* work, focusing on the physical labor involved in ceremony: Blondine and Innocente with knees parallel and deeply bent as they wind hips, roll shoulders, and circle arms simultaneously, working out a fast-tempered, polycentric and polyrhythmic dance in the hot sun. Blondine later describes what this dance feels like, the weight it puts in her head, arms, and legs, and uses verbs like *kraze* (crush) and *chaje* (load) to recall the toll on her body: words that evoke the labor, fatigue, and physical charge involved in serving the lwa.[56]

For some, this hard work becomes paying work. As Judi Moore Latta writes of African American spiritual workers, masisi who take the ason (become priests) are "women who are not legitimized by patriarchy and whose principal work is considered outside the orthodox work force. Their authority to be bold in what they do comes from . . . the Eternal."[57] Reflecting the glow of this authority, one of the film's most beautiful shots centers Innocente reclining beneath a tree by a calm river, eyebrows coiffed, lips rouged, and eyes serene and glowing, describing her work as a priest. She reports that becoming a houngan has earned her a lot of respect—and cash—she didn't previously have access to: "They used to call me masisi, masisi, masisi. They made fun of my clothes and my hair. Since I've become a houngan, they've stopped. Now they come knocking on my door, asking me to call the lwa, to give them a remedy for this and that."[58] And paying for those remedies, of course. But the most important asset that spiritual works brings, she later comments, is a network of friends. She reflects that through serving the lwa she's able to "make friends, friends who are like me," other masisi, "and also serious people, like engineers, lawyers, doctors and nurses who also serve the spirits. The lwa give me all I have."[59] Like her good friend Jean Marcel's, Innocente's work allows her to fashion a financial and social support system for herself—her work becomes a pillar that holds her up, much like the thick-trunked tree she leans against as she talks or the poto mitan she dances around with Blondine.

Like Innocente, many of the film's interviewees count on to spiritual work to bring them not only spiritual harmony but worldly security. Flanise, the most direct about her economic desires, holds up a prayer card of the Virgin syncretized with Danto and addresses it spiritedly, tapping the Madonna vigorously with her long nails: "This is the lwa who brings us luck, and who made us masisi. She has to give us work. Ezili Danto, give us money, give us money!"[60] Though shots of the masisi's homes show that most are not members of the elite, the film is careful not to reproduce clichés about Haitian poverty. Still, moments like these make clear that material gain is a substantial part of what masisi seek through Vodou devotion. Even interviewees who don't make money directly as priests find that serving Ezili remunerates them indirectly. Blondine (who goes to ceremonies in a Danto-blue headscarf) is emphatic that her faithful attention to the lwa has kept her from suffering spells, beatings, or anything else that would interfere with her work. "I love the lwa, they protect me," she states.[61] Such material concerns are especially important for these practitioners, given how gendered as well as classed division of labor limits their economic opportunities. Denis, who's been unsuccessfully looking for work throughout the film, finally explains that she's limited because she can only look for "travay fanm" (women's work),[62] that she has gender-specific employment needs she's been praying for at shrines visited throughout the film: "If I had to leave the country to work elsewhere, I wouldn't be able to hold a man's job. The only work I can do is for women: seamstress, hairdresser, manicure, or pedicure. Those are jobs I'm comfortable with."[63] Flanise's cry "Ezili, give us money!" reminds viewers that for these subjects, religious as well as gendered self-definition is not primarily a matter of "self-expression," as it might be for elites or Global Northern trans folk. Instead, it is part of strategizing for the greatest material advantage possible from the racialized, classed, and gendered positions they maneuver within. If you've sent us, Ezili Danto, pay our costs; Ezili Danto, o!

❧

"We need to go inside the factory to make our demands heard," proclaims Marie-Jeanne as she stands in front of the sagging chain-link, barbed-wire-crowned fence around her workplace, arching her eyebrows and cutting her eyes toward the other side of the fence as if to penetrate the factory with her gaze.[64] *Poto Mitan*'s first interviewee, Marie-Jeanne begins the film by speaking stories that factory owners want to keep silenced. "It's like washing your hands to wipe them on the ground," she says of her job, then tells viewers: "I want the authorities to look at what's going on in the factories."[65] She details the literal dirt that SONAPI works to hide: "The water they give us, we shouldn't even bathe with it. If we don't have 1 Goud to buy water, we'd rather die of thirst than drink the water because when we drink it, it makes us sick. And we have a single toilet for everyone who works in the factory. It often takes them 3 months to clean it. That's what we have to use every day. We go 3–4 days without using it because the toilet's in such bad condition."[66] When foreign inspectors visit, bosses temporarily improve the unsanitary conditions they otherwise care nothing about. "They fix things, get rid of garbage, and the day of the visit they sweep up the factory," she tells us. "But when foreigners don't come, they leave it for us to work in the dust, because to them we aren't human."[67] Marie-Jeanne publicly airs the factory's dirt even though she knows bosses fire women for complaining about these conditions to each other, let alone to an international viewing public. The youngest of eight children, Marie-Jeanne left school after third grade because her parents needed her to work to pay for her siblings' education. If she'd been a boy, she says, her parents wouldn't have made that choice. If she were a man, she knows, she wouldn't be working in this factory where she has to keep her mouth closed tight against thirst. At age thirty-two, after thirteen years employed here while her eldest brother works as an engineer, Marie-Jeanne speaks out with resolve and righteous anger.

Marie-Jeanne's speaking out is political work, yes, and it is also spiritual work. Both keeping and breaking silences are ways of serving Ezili Danto. One of Danto's most recognizable characteristics is that when she arrives in spirit possession, she comes without language: her horse is only able to utter "ke-ke-ke," the sound of an open throat clicking, and gesture to make her/himself understood. The traditional explanation for this speechlessness draws on stories of Danto's participation in the Haitian Revolution. "During these battles, **Ezili Danto decided to join her people** in war," opines Houngan Hector. "Her people feared that she would give away their secrets should she be captured, so—**her own people—cut out her tongue** rendering her mute."[68] Mambo Vye Zo, however, offers another explanation: "I suggest that her inability to speak comes from her exhaustion and fury at working so hard to feed her children and tend her land. It is the inevitable anger and frustration at having so little, despite great effort otherwise."[69] In other words, Danto's speechlessness is a reversible condition. If poor women's labor came to reward them more than washing their hands to wipe them on the ground, as Marie-Jeanne puts it, then the divine muteness that mirrors this disempowerment might shift. Breaking poor women's silence, then, is a ritual of speaking which translates the frustrated protest that Danto's *ke-ke-ke* represents, even as it imagines alternatives to its wordlessness.

In fact, though, it might be less accurate to say that this lwa doesn't speak at all than to say that in the present set of historical circumstances out of which she emerges, Danto only speaks collaboratively. She has a loyal interpreter in her youngest child, Anais, whom Mambo Vye Zo describes as "Dantor's greatest love . . . forever carried in her arms" and "the messenger of Dantor's true will."[70] Anais relays all messages to and from Danto, and sevite often address one lwa to reach the other. Channeling her voice through her daughter's in this way, Danto forces servitors to break what Linda Alcoff calls the "metaphysical illusion" that women's speech is ever their own property—that it can ever be disconnected from other women's conditions, experiences, and messages.[71] This is a disconnection that Marie-Jeanne also repudiates. "People overseas, foreigners, you need to take responsibility. Now you know we work for a low wage, you could make them raise our salaries," she rejoins in *Poto Mitan*'s concluding voice-over. "Even if we don't see the change, our children will."[72] As she makes this appeal, Marie-Jeanne performs Anais's spiritual work along with Danto's. Speaking for coworkers who can't speak for themselves for fear of losing their jobs, she acts as a "messenger" advocating for their collective needs. And speaking directly to viewers in the Global North, she asks us to acknowledge a metaphysics as well as an ethics of connection across space and time: to acknowledge both that what we do in New York affects how workers

live in Potoprens, and that how these women live will affect their daughters'
and their daughters' daughters' lives.

Now, close your eyes and listen to the beats building through Junior Vasquez's
remix of "Dream Drums" and tell me: are these the rhythms of the club or
of the toque, of the ball or of the ceremony—of all of these, or none?[73] How
can you tell? Bailey reminds us that there are lots of "similarities between [the]
ritualized performances engaged in vodou ceremonies and those at balls,"
including their use of music and dance to alter consciousness.[74] And in *this*
world of queer black and Latino ritual, there aren't many who would argue if
you said Mother Angie wasn't just a star of New York's Ballroom scene, but
one of its high priestesses. While creating kinship networks is one of Ballroom
culture's primary functions, its other is organizing and participating in ritualized events called balls: performances where contestants walk (compete)
and are judged on dance skills, fashion sense, physical appearance, gender
presentation, and style. Angie was a doyenne of the 1980s Ballroom scene
as both a competitor and a mother who successfully nurtured her children to
trophies. "Angie Xtravaganza was an upstart, the youngest of the legendary
mothers; from the moment she started walking balls, though, at the age of
sixteen, she was a star," Cunningham remembers. "She came up with a new
angle. If luminaries like Dorian and Pepper LaBeija relied on flash and audacity, Angie pushed her fashion sense."[75] Angie went on to gift her children with
this fashion sense as well. "When there's a ball I'm always doing something
for everybody in the house," she told Livingston proudly in *Paris Is Burning.* "I
do this one's hair, the other one's makeup, you know, choose their shoes, their
accessories. I always offer advice—as far as what I know, you know . . ."[76] Under
Angie's tutelage, the House of Xtravaganza rose to a stellar status from which
it has yet to fall: "The Xtravaganzas carry on Angie's two overriding fixations:
fashion and perfect performance. The balls are the family business, and the
Xtravaganzas are as serious about apparel and presentation as the De Beers
family is about diamonds."[77]

But much more than Angie's family business, Bailey reflects, balls are a
family spiritual practice—rituals that reward souls more lavishly than pocket-
books. "For Ballroom members, balls are akin to rituals in that these events

concretize and affirm values that strengthen and affirm this vulnerable community," he writes. "Yet, perhaps even more critically, the performances and other practices in which participants engage at balls bring the community together to enact a politics of social, cultural, and spiritual renewal."[78] This is a ritual that depends on gendered labor—on the labor of house mothers like Angie, who serve as the "primary organizers of all facets of the ball events."[79] Angie's organizational work, her children remember, began long before any ball was thrown. It started with recruiting and training protégés like Hector and Venus: approaching them at balls, clubs, or piers and asking them to walk for the Xtravaganzas in a chosen category, then orchestrating the combination of clothes, accessories, hairstyles, gestures, and dance moves she judged likely to bring home a trophy. And when the house was hosting a ball, Angie's work multiplied. After choosing a theme and securing a venue, it was her responsibility as house mother to transform that venue into ritualized ball space: procuring flowers, choosing tablecloths, assembling themed decorations, setting up a runway, renting judges' microphones, providing awards, and making space for the DJ booth all fell under her meticulous care. Last but never, ever least, Angie's stardom helped pack the now-transformed ballroom with spectators. *Paris Is Burning* reminds us of this as it pans in on a drawing of Mother Angie—complete with signature updo and dangling earrings—gracing a flyer for the House of Xtravaganza's Snow Ball 1988, which pictures her bust rising above the Manhattan skyline and a spectacular flash of light opening the sky behind her to draw viewers toward her brilliance.[80]

Angie's work at balls echoes the ritual work put in by another famous house mother: Alourdes Margaux, better known as famed Vodoun priestess Mama Lola. When Mama Lola hosts a ceremony at her Brooklyn house, her labor also begins months ahead of time with recruiting and training ritual participants: "An enormous amount of energy and anxiety is involved in building and maintaining the core group that attends these ceremonies," Karen McCarthy Brown notes.[81] Once this group is summoned by phone calls, personal reminders, and messages sent through friends and family, Mama Lola begins transforming her home into ritual space: obtaining food and drink, providing decorations for the lwa, setting up an altar, rearranging the family room to accommodate ceremony, providing musical accompaniment, and preparing ceremonial dishes and implements. And ultimately, it is her own star power—her reputation as a master healer—that draws people from Manhattan, Long Island, and the Bronx to attend these Brooklyn ceremonies. The ritual labor performed by

Mother Angie and Mama Lola is hard, never-ending work, requiring extended amounts of time, money, and energy that sometimes fall into short supply. But for both, it is fundamentally rewarding work; theirs are divine callings that earn these socially and economically marginal women of color a measure of power and respect they couldn't access any other way. As Willi Nija puts it in *Paris Is Burning*, "It's the mother that's the hardest worker, and the mother gets the most respect."[82] This respect still reverberates twenty years after her death, when Hector Xtravaganza builds the thirtieth anniversary ball as a tribute to Mother Angie rather than his namesake Father Hector. Like any other favored child, he worships his Ma in a special way.

Reprise, ladies: ansanm nou fanm, ansanm nou fo. But even after all that, please don't think the work of *Of Men and Gods'* interviewees ends when they leave the marketplace, hair salon, church, or peristyle. No, it just moves to the kitchen and the bedroom—where, they make clear, their sexual and social relationships require another kind of labor. The work of partnership, these masisi demonstrate, is less like romance and more like a concrete skill set to be learned. Blondine explains: "They always say that a masisi cooks very well. You understand? She's always trying to learn more. So, a guy who's with a girl who doesn't know how to cook goes to a masisi's house because he eats better there, sleeps better. So he usually ends up leaving the girl to stay with the masisi!"[83] She goes on to intimate that her reproductive skill set includes a lot about what Trinidadians call *wuk*—sex: "They also like us because they say we're tighter than girls. Some men would rather take a masisi than a girl."[84] Apparently Blondine and her friends have become so proficient at this work that all agree that lovers are eminently easy to come by. Just after Blondine's explication of her relationship skills, Jean Marcel remarks, "Men, there are lots of them," and Flanise confidently proclaims: "Ninety percent of Haitian men are homos."[85] In fact, the interviewees find this particular relationship work so easy to come by that while they enjoy it, they don't seem to particularly value it. As Flanise is making her proclamation, Innocente, seated to her far right, silently rises, crosses in front of the speakers, and goes to the mirror to redo her hair, as if the line of conversation has lost her interest. And with dramatic flair and raised eyebrows, Jean Marcel emphatically proclaims: "I would have to be really *crrrazy* to ask [the lwa] for a man. A man you can find in any garbage heap. . . . Ask for a man . . . never!"[86]

The more important work of connection for these masisi comes through the work of sisterhood—comes through the relationships they build and maintain with each other. After they dismiss the subject of men, Madsen, Jean Marcel, Innocente, and Flanise—leaning toward each other, in overlapping remarks—tell the interviewer, "We're girls, sisters . . ." and Flanise, facing the camera, adds, "Nou bien, nou mache ansanm [We're good with each other, we walk together]."[87] This joyful declaration of emotional intimacy is matched by playful physical intimacy, as Innocente leans against Jean Marcel's left breast and Flanise falls laughing into Innocente's lap, lovingly grazing those bodily sites most connected to femaleness. Now, perhaps this bodily contact suggests something queer in a sexual way. Later Blondine will explain that for her, being a woman includes the possibility of loving other women. "Mwen se masisi," she says flirtatiously—"I am masisi"—then follows with a hypothetical: "If I meet another masisi who I like, we'll get together and become madivin."[88] Sexually suggestive or not, though, certainly, Flanise, Innocente, and Jean Marcel are working out something queer in a social sense. Their working together—literally, as fellow hairstylists and priestesses, and figuratively, as *girls, sisters*—enables what Jasbir Puar calls a queer assemblage, "a series of dispersed but mutually implicated and messy networks . . . that merge and dissipate time, space, and body against linearity, coherency, and permanency."[89] Or, to borrow a phrase from Flanise, we might call this set of connections *mache ansanm*—forging commonality not through gender, sexuality, or other identities but through *walking together*, through shared activity, experience, and support.

This phrase echoes the opening of the most classic of Vodou documentaries, Maya Deren's *Divine Horsemen*. This film, a compilation of her Haitian footage assembled and released by her widower Teiji Ito almost twenty-five years after her death, opens in silence that frames a lone, unspeaking woman who, clad in white and balancing a basket on her head, walks a forested path toward the motionless camera, finally meeting the viewer with a smile. (The opening shot of Blondine walking to market recalls this moment, too.) As this lone woman is joined on her path by three other load-carrying women, the film's first voice-over proclaims: "There is a Kreyòl expression: *to walk together*. Where life is hard, people depend upon and help each other."[90] *Of Men and Gods'* portrait of masisi's many, complicated

intimacies with each other, and with the lwa, in many ways acts out an extended commentary on this famous opening. But it does so while troubling
the idea that mache ansam is something that Haitian sevite do only where
life is hard. Yes, here *girls, sisters* also walk together where *nou bien*, where
they're good, creative, prosperous, funny, sexy, loved. Ansanm nou fanm,
ansanm nou fo: together we're women, together we're strong, Flanise, Jean
Marcel, Innocente, and Madsen seem to tell us, laughing and nestling in
each other's laps.

❧

"We created a campaign against violence. Stop verbal violence, physical violence, psychological violence: any kind of violence against women," Hélène
tells interviewers as her fingers circle rapidly like a blessing, braiding the hair
of a girl seated in a chair before her.[91] So begins the concluding section of
Poto Mitan, its cameras literally focused on Hélène's grassroots organizing work
among girls and women in Potoprens's shantytowns. The camera cuts between
this shot of Hélène braiding hair and shots of her hanging banners and distrib-
uting flyers representing the work of Women in Action, the antiviolence organization she founded the year prior to the film's release. The group's foundation
was inspired by a particular act of violence—a spousal beating that left one of
Hélène's women friends nearly dead. Responding to a broader crisis, however,
Women in Action brings women together to address the brutal frequency of
relationship and stranger violence against female factory workers. In a voice-
over, Hélène explains the daily threat faced by women who walk to the factory
before sunrise because they can't afford a bus, risking robbery or rape in the
dark morning. And the risk of sexual assault doesn't end at the factory door.
Hélène herself was sexually harassed by a supervisor and quit her job rather
than accede to his demands. "Women have had enough of being victims. We're
fed up. Everyone should be equal. People should help each other. Support one
another. Women, when you hear of situations like this, please make women's
organizations aware of it," Hélène proclaims in front of a large black and red
banner demanding "Combat Violence against Women."[92] The camera pans to the
all-women audience, dressed in T-shirts that match the banners and clapping
and singing joyously: "Women aren't trash, tramps, or garbage dumps! Women
rule the world!"[93] At this last line a very young woman jumps, smiles, and points
two fingers at the camera, playful and triumphant.

Beating out rhythms, swaying to the beat of their own voices, singing shoulder to shoulder, these women raise the energy of a ceremony in honor of their own power. Describing how noninitiates can mount a service for Ezili Danto, Mambo Racine Sans Bout insists: "Dance vigorously! If you know Vodou songs about Dantor sing them, otherwise sing songs about strong women, broken hearts, and loving mothers."[94] Women in Action's meeting becomes a secular mirror of such a ceremony. Hélène's entreaty to bring stories of women's abuse to advocacy groups also echoes the instructions Mambo Racine includes for survivors of abuse who want to serve Danto: "Dantor is especially offended by domestic violence or sexual assault. If you have been a victim of these abuses, tell Dantor! She will come to you in dreams and embrace you, nurture you and heal you."[95] Fierce warrior that she is, Danto's advocacy includes turning perpetrators' violence against themselves; Mambo Racine reports that women who ask for Danto's protection may even see their attackers turn suicidal. And devoted mother that she is, Danto's intercession also promises to turn survivors toward more sustainable love—love for themselves and other women. Practitioners often describe Danto as madivin or lesbian, and she's known to make frequent spirit marriages with human women and female lwa. But in addition to nurturing sexual relationships between women, Ezili Danto gives divine sanction to the woman-woman love of mache ansanm. As one houngan puts it, Danto is a divine reflection of the peasant women who, left to provide for themselves and their families in harsh conditions, "are known to comfort each other, so [Danto] too is seen as having certain characteristics"—like building primary relationships with female friends rather than male lovers.[96] This kind of embodied, essential, nourishing love between women shines through as Women in Action dance together on screen, their bodies leaning into one another, making rhythm together, singing out women's strength in solidarity and catching their sister as she jumps for joy.

Women in Action in particular, and Hélène's organizing work in general, occupy an honored position in *Poto Mitan*, closing out this often bleak film on a note of hope. The film's website reflects this in its profile of Hélène, which concludes: "Even more than the others, Hélène reminds us that through collective action, change is possible, even in a place like Haiti."[97] Hélène's final voice-over accompanies a scene of another, much larger outdoor meeting where an educator speaks to a crowd (including a few men) about women's rights as human rights. The meeting ends with Ezili Danto–esque songs about strong women accompanied by rapid drumming, and the camera focuses in on a row of young women singing in full voice: "Women, if we don't speak up, no one will speak for us!"[98] The camera then pans into a tight shot of two women standing next to each other in this row. One woman is dressed in blue, the other in red: Danto's signature colors. As they sing together, both sway to the same beat but in opposite directions, so they first curve toward each other, then away, then back together. This lovely, gentle yet strong motion embodies the experiences of the women interviewed in *Poto Mitan*: an unyielding rhythm of life in which women have to do so much for themselves, but the time comes when they don't have to do it alone. There will always be another woman there for you, Danto lets poor women know, and don't forget: that woman may often be her, in all her dagger-wielding, heart-piercing, woman-loving ferocity.

In 1994, honorary Xtravaganza Junior Vasquez released a single dedicated to recently deceased Mother Angie Xtravaganza.[99] Simply titled "X," the song—which sampled Angie's sons trilling the word "Xtravaganza" in *Paris Is Burning*—immediately became a house music sensation. This celebration of Angie by her sons, which set the beat for dancing bodies in clubs throughout the country, memorializes the lasting work for which Angie perhaps had the greatest gift: the work of putting and keeping together the House of Xtravaganza, of nourishing *Xtravaganza Power* from her own brown breast. Bailey gives the name *housework* to this "kin labor . . . Ballroom members undertake to develop and maintain [the] familylike units" of their houses.[100] Like her runway walk, Angie's housework maintained a signature style: regal and spirited, exacting and protective, stern and loving.

Cunningham hears from Angie's children:

> Angie Xtravaganza was a loving mother, if a little peevish about expressing her softer emotions and remorseless in her enforcement of the rules. As the children clamored around her—as fifty-plus grown men called her Ma and vied for her attention—she sometimes lifted her face to the ceiling and hollered, "I should have had abortions." But she never lashed out at the kids with any real seriousness, and the kids knew never to let her get too angry. They teased her and, if teasing didn't work, they simply obeyed.[101]

She was the mother who, in the afternoon, might sit on the sofa and shout to her son, "Shut up, you damn butch queen, and get me a cup of coffee before

I get up from here and beat your ass"; then, that night, would stay up in the kitchen until dawn making chicken soup for her children after their long hours at the club.[102] One son remembers her intertwined generosity and prickliness in *Paris Is Burning*: "My birthday will come and I'll always get a birthday gift from Angie. I won't get one from my real mother. And when I got thrown out of my house, Angie let [me] stay with her till I got myself together and I got work, and she always fed me. She can be a pain in the ass sometimes, but I wouldn't trade her in for any other mother."[103] This kind of tough-love, endless-love caretaking was geared toward "keeping her children intact," as the judge praises Angie when she wins a Mother of the Year Award in *Paris Is Burning*: intact physically, intact psychologically, and intact as a family.[104] Her son sums up the sense of togetherness—of mache ansanm—that Angie fostered: "The House of Xtravaganza has done a lot. It's made me feel like I have a family. We're always together. We're always, if we're not together, we always speak on the phone."[105]

Angie's housework was based on a radical inclusivity that brought scores of children of different ages, genders, and backgrounds together around her skirts. At the same time, though, her house became a site of pointed exclusion—that is, it actively excluded dark-skinned and non-Latino blacks from membership. When Mother Angie and Father Hector founded the House of Xtravaganza in the early 1980s as the first primarily Latino house, they did so in part to counter anti-Latino bias they encountered in the Ballroom scene. Caught in the tense overlap between North American blacks and Puerto Ricans in New York, Angie's children often turned her house into a safe space to use antiblack racism to boost Latino pride. Arbert Evisu, founder of the House of Evisu, remembers: "The Xtravaganzas always were Spanish and Puerto Rican, but they held their own identity. And they make sure that they will stick together by their own identity. And they were racist against Blacks. And they were strong enough to call them Black monkeys and things like that. They were racist against Blacks."[106] Venus Xtravaganza, in her haughtily elegant "reading" of a member of another house in *Paris Is Burning*, plays up antiblack racist common sense that weds the black to the simian even as it divorces blackness from femininity when she quips: "What is wrong with you, Pedro, are you going through it? You're going through some kind of psychological change in your life? You went back to being a man? Touch this skin, darling, touch this skin honey, touch all of this skin! Okay? You just can't take it! You're just an overgrown orangutan!"[107]

Ever the beautiful lightning rod, Venus, in outtakes from *Paris Is Burning*, also calls attention to the Xtravaganzas' internal rifts. Walking together in balls might sometimes mean mache ansanm, Venus opines, but not always. In an interview with her reclining delicately on her bed, she complains that while houses might be good for cheering brothers and sisters on at balls or "showing off in the Village," her connection to Xtravaganza siblings often feels "not real" since they aren't there when she needs them outside the ballroom.[108] In another, more trenchant critique, Venus, standing by a table at a ball, calls Ballroom houses "bullshit" and "scandal," a system focused on a "bunch of stupid trophies" rather than the people who win them.[109] Venus's feeling of isolation is, of course, entirely her own, one no other Xtravaganza shares on screen; and certainly, her charged situation as Angie's main daughter may have contributed to the tension she experienced in the house. As in any family, the situation in Angie's appears to have been complex, a tangled mix of camaraderie and dissension. Sometimes the hard times these pier kids experienced brought out mache ansanm, and sometimes they did not. As important as it is to recognize the creative kinship that Angie's housework supported, it's just as important not to romanticize it—not to imagine these children's precarious social situation means that forming connections comes easier to them, or that these connections magically make up for everything else they lack. Mother Angie, we all still need your help.

———

"The message I want to send out is I think the girls need to come and work together and join each other in support and, you know, stop turning our backs on each other, you know. Let's get stronger, let's empower each other and get stronger and bring this community up. Let's fight, let's fight for our rights," Haitian American trans activist Tiffany Mathieu declares in her YouTube video "#GirlsLikeUs: WE NEED TO BE UNITED."[110] Born in Brooklyn to Haitian parents, Mathieu is the only black woman on the organizing team of Translatina Network, a New York–based organization "of latina transgender women whose main aim is to promote the healthy development of trans people through the delivery of a wide range of information, promotion, outreach in education and capacity-building, allowing the creation of a safe and productive environment for transgender women."[111] Mathieu came to her work as a public speaker and community organizer after surviving over one hundred assaults, some from clients (in her hustling days) and others from strangers—like the men who threw eggs and bottles at her and friends walking together on 125th Street in Harlem. Walking together, mache ansanm didn't keep her and her girls safe, but it did keep them safer; all survived to tell the tale. Now, like Danto, the very beautiful Mathieu carries a knife wherever she goes and is studying to become a social worker, hoping to help trans sisters transition to safe, legal employment.[112] "I'm so glad that you agreed to talk on camera, which is very important, you know, to have material, you know, and document our history," fellow trans (white) Latina activist Brooke Cerda reflects in her interview with Mathieu.[113] It's important to document the work of black transwomen, yes, to take in the endless labor that makes black woman-hood the volatile, dangerous, capacious, despairing, fiercely womanist way of walking in the world that Danto reflects.

PHOTO BY CINDY ELIZABETH

PHOTO BY CINDY ELIZABETH

bridge

MY FEMDOM, MY LOVE

Her name is love & black resistance: Venus X. Her love & resistance are both the hard kind, sometimes. Born Jazmin Venus Soto, this Harlem-bred Dominican came to radical political consciousness at seventeen while reading Assata Shakur & attending Black Panther meetings. Then her politics queered: "I got into feminism, gender politics, art history—understanding art as a means to address a wide variety of political topics . . . embedding that all into my work through nightlife."[1] In 2009, she founded legendary New York underground party GHE20GOTH1K. Held weekly in dark clubs where she DJs for crowds of hundreds, GHE20GOTH1K, she explains, is "all about doing the opposite of what the mainstream wants. Goth in the 90s alienated everyone, and its darker themes can be sexy, contrary to popular belief. Ghetto culture, although culturally accepted, is even darker when you think about the politics and poverty behind it all. Why pretend everything is a bed of flowers when it isn't?"[2] Black, Latinx, & queer, the space Venus X holds in these parties is kinky, too. "Choke me" projected on the wall, partiers in BDSM hoods, collars, & chains, femdom worship & satisfied slaves are part of the scene. "DJed a bdsm performance last night . . . slave was getting eaten out on stage while swinging from a crane in full bondage as I played," Venus X tweeted in February 2016, adding a purple devil emoji.[3]

Her name is love & violence, too. Roman goddess of love and beauty, Venus was a common name given enslaved African women. "Variously named Harriot, Phibba, Sara, Joanna, Rachel, Linda, and Sally, she is found everywhere in the Atlantic world," Saidiya Hartman proclaims in "Venus in Two Acts." "The barracoon, the hollow of the slave ship, the pest-house, the brothel, the cage, the surgeon's laboratory, the prison, the cane-field, the kitchen, the master's bedroom—turn out to be exactly the same place and in all of them she is called Venus."[4] But what difference does it make for a black woman to choose the name Venus, rather than bearing it forcibly? For a black woman to script BDSM scenes, rather than being conscripted into scenes of subjection? How can BDSM become "a critical site from which to reimagine the formative links between black female sexuality and violence," as Ariane Cruz puts it?[5]

Ask Venus X. In her post-Panther days, "all black everything" takes on new possibilities: "black bondage tie, black balloons, and black outs," as one of her event promos insists.[6] Ask Domina Erzulie, the Montreal-based dominatrix who rides into the next pages flanked by reimagined historical characters Jeanne Duval & Mary Ellen Pleasant. They can tell you how, in BDSM, "violence becomes not just a vehicle of pleasure but also a mode of accessing and critiquing power . . . a fertile site from which to consider the complexity and diverseness of Black women's sexual practice and the mutability of Black female sexuality."[7] Venus X, Venus uknowable; Venus X, Venus enchains.

THREE

RIDING THE RED

Red, beyond rouge. Red, brightened into scarlet: rouged red lips and scarlet letters ERZULIE blaze across the header of a website for Domina Erzulie, self-proclaimed "Goddess from the Antilles" and "Montreal's Best Black Domina." Red, yes, scarlet the latex that drips over her taut breasts in the photo gallery, red straining each side against her black bodice laces and cinched by reflections of a clear plastic belt as she pulls in her pale white slave, humble on his knees before her. Reined in by a leather collar and chain, he gazes obediently up at her as she—red-lipped and clear-eyed—turns imperiously toward the camera. "I'm a sadist, I'm a woman, I'm black . . . I'm a goddess desired by most men!" her blog promises. "I love to put you into bondage, I love to trample you, I love to whip you, I love to wrap my legs around your throat and squeeze. These turn me on . . ."[1]

Erzulie, scarlet. Written in the color of blood rising, Domina Erzulie's choice of a prodomme name can be neither a careless nor flippant one. "I have a deep interest in Voodoo," acknowledges her post titled "WHO I AM." "Its spiritual and ritualistic influence has added a unique and profound dimension to my craft."[2] But which Ezili is she claiming to represent, this universally desired black goddess/sadist who ties you up, whips you, sits on your face, constricts your breathing, and exacts tribute for it? Look hard at her forcing her slave's head toward her patent leather stiletto and I promise you, you'll see the lwa Edwidge Danticat evokes as the "hot-blooded Erzulie who feared no men but rather made them her slaves, raped *them*, and killed *them* . . . the only woman with that power":[3] Ezili Je Wouj, Ezili of the Red Eyes. Inhabiting the reverse side of Freda's perfumed dreams and the extreme expression of Danto's ferocity, Ezili Je Wouj is closely related to her sister Ezili—but less discussed than those more popular manifestations. Her descriptions tend to be brief yet ominous. Occult websites and scholarly texts alike style her the "red eyed militant of fury and vengeance"; "wild, feisty"; "abusive, quick to anger, and holds a grudge"; "very dangerous . . . histrionic and violent, enraged and full of sorrow."[4] When she arrives in possession, she feeds on servitors' pain. She digs fingernails into horses' flesh until blood surfaces, rubs red peppers into eyes until they stream with tears and "glow with a fiery scarlet."[5] Violently recoloring servitors' bodies if she needs to, turning their flesh inside out if she needs to, Ezili Je Wouj explodes into ceremony as the "cosmic rage" of the black woman distilled to its purest power;[6] and anyone unprepared to witness that powerful, passionate black womanhood, well, Je Wouj will burn their eyes until they only see her shades of red.

Descriptions like these are designed to make readers shake with fear, clearly. But couldn't they also evoke frissons of pleasure? All the Ezili manifest distinctive, forceful sexualities that are always instrumental, never incidental to their power. Much ink and fantasy has been spilled imagining the sexual powers of Freda and Danto but no parallel stories exist for Je Wouj. Why not? Why are we so afraid to call her what she always already has been, the cosmic dominatrix? If it's at all because BDSM is nasty, freaky, outside the divine realm—well, listen to Pat Califia's reminder in "The Dominant Woman as Priestess":

> Goddess mythology is full of examples of SM techniques being used for sacred purposes. Inanna's descent to the Underworld, where her sister Ereshkigal turned her into a corpse and hung her from a meat hook, is more severe than any consensual SM scene. When the galla, the emissaries of Ereshkigal, seize Inanna's consort Dumuzi so that he can take her place in the Underworld, it's no more or less rough than "The Surprise Party." These dramas were almost certainly reenacted annually in Sumeria. Bondage and sensory deprivation have been used crossculturally as aids to meditation, trancework, and shamanic journeying. . . . There ought to be nothing new or controversial about the idea that we can use our bodies' capacity for intense sensation to obtain consciousness of other realms.[7]

When Je Wouj comes and digs her nails into your flesh, it's not senselessly. It's to bring you into "consciousness of other realms," realms where the black woman transforms pain to her own uses, power, and pleasure. You *have* to be jolted out of comfort, normality, and impunity to go there. Are you going to tell me no one gets wet for that?

Domina Erzulie does. Proclaiming herself "a strict and firm dominant, a divine creature to be adored and worshipped,"[8] she explains in "What I Like about Being Dominant": "What you have to understand is that I love the sensation of dominating a man, to see him crawl at my feet and act for the sole purpose of pleasing me. . . . In short, I'm proud to be a woman, I feel great about who I am and I love the fact that I can make a man feel like dust under my feet and that he's happy of that fact."[9] Come to her with respect. Get on your knees before she asks you to. Feel lucky she's chosen to grace you with her passionate, painful, unrestrained presence: Ezili red, red, redder.

Sit as obediently as you can, readers, while you move through these pages in service to another, blood-red avatar of black queer femininity come to demand worship. Her kink, too, embodies black feminist theorizing—deviant theorizing that breaks missionary limits on black women's bodily autonomy. In her brilliantly perverse, optimistic study of black women in pornography, Mireille Miller-Young reflects how "BDSM fetishism—particularly the fantasy of black women dominating white men— . . . queers racial and gender hegemonies by exposing their very constructedness. By creating fantasies that explode assumptions about what constitutes proper gendering of, and appropriate pleasure and pain for, the black body . . . [the prodomme's] illicit erotic activism displays the use of what may be generally understood as super-deviant sexualities to empower black women's sexual performances."[10] Noting the perverse power of encouraging "black women spectators to explore their 'darkest desires,'" Miller-Young asks: "Could taking pleasure in the most deviant articulations of black sexual deviance offer a radical tool to negotiate and transform how power acts on our bodies and our communities?"[11] Yes, Ezili Je Wouj answers, screams: yes dirty sluts, yes enemy lovers, yes naughty children, *yes*. Black femmedomme, reddening.

———

Scarlet again, letters bold and rough and scarlet: red block letters shadowed in black spell the novel's title, SALT ROADS, popping boldly from the cover's center. Dominating the scene is a brightly drawn brown woman who stares at the reader with gold-flecked eyes, her full breasts straining the bodice of her strapless red-and-white dress while she lifts flounced petticoats, arms akimbo, her loosely curling hair upswept and lips rouged red. Over her right shoulder stands a white man in a frock coat and top hat who, dwarfed by her dazzling presence, peers from behind a red curtain. And between the two of them a chamber pot with gold swirls rising from its center leaves stars and bubbles floating magically in the air, promising strangeness and intrigue.

Welcome to *The Salt Roads*, the third novel by Toronto-based, Jamaican-born, Guyanese-descended speculative fiction writer Nalo Hopkinson. In the late 1990s Hopkinson erupted on the science fiction (sf) scene as one of the genre's most promising writers, winning the Warner Aspect First Novel and Locus First Novel Awards for postapocalyptic *Brown Girl in the Ring* and garnering critical acclaim for interplanetary romp *Midnight Robber*. But *The Salt Roads*—an experiment in historical magical realism rather than Afrofuturism—jolted readers out of what they'd come to expect. With its mélange of intrigue and exoticism, *Publishers Weekly* searched for words to describe the new novel:

> Whirling with witchcraft and sensuality, this latest novel by Hopkinson . . . is a globe-spanning, time-traveling spiritual odyssey. When three Caribbean slave women, led by dignified doctress Mer, assemble to bury a stillborn baby on the island of Saint Domingue . . . Ezili, the Afro-Caribbean goddess of love and sex, is called up by their prayers and lamentations. Drawing from the deceased infant's "unused vitality," Ezili inhabits the bodies of a number of women who, despite their remoteness from each other in time and space, are bound to each other by salt—be it the salt of tears or the salt that baptized slaves into an alien religion.[12]

The Ezili born from the stillborn child's "unused vitality" is Ezili Je Wouj. "Ezili Red-Eye" she names herself in the novel, "the termagant enraged, with the power of millennia of Ginen hopes, lives, loves."[13] And Je Wouj's primary horse is the red-painted woman on the cover—Jeanne Duval, a historical figure most famous for her tenure as the lover of French poet Charles Baudelaire, lyricized in his "Sed Non Satiata" as a "bizarre deity . . . child-witch of night, with flanks of ebony."[14] But in Hopkinson's reimagination Jeanne is a woman with a (seedy) past and (happy) future beyond her time with her famous paramour, and many more lovers to boot—lovers black, white, male, and female whom she likes to dominate, spank, dress up, and love expansively.

Hopkinson notes that "*The Salt Roads* has received a more mixed reception than my other books," in part because of her explicit depiction of black women's nonnormative, kinky sex.[15] "Some people find it disgusting. Some people find it liberating. My mother's just alarmed," she remarks in an interview.[16] She goes on to explain her commitment to portraying black people "doing kinky sex": "There are all kinds of reasons why it feels particularly taboo to do the latter. For one thing, we (. . . meaning 'black people') are too often the victims of having white sexual fears projected onto our bodies, often in dangerous ways. So we can be cautious about making any room for that to happen. But I think there's a cost when black communities keep too opaque a veil over the fact that black people's desire and sexual inclinations are as varied and human as anyone else's."[17] Hopkinson's choice of sf as the genre through which to explore black kink is not coincidental. Not only are sexual scenes in sf texts often suggestive of BDSM dynamics, as Sylvie Bérard notes.[18] Hopkinson views the work of sf writers and kinksters as parallel projects, creative processes that similarly contest the limits of normative realities. She muses: "It sometimes seems to me—and perhaps whimsically so—that the people who are courageously non-normative in their sexualities are doing in the real world some of the work that science fiction can do in the world of the imagination, that is, exploring a wider range of possibilities for living."[19]

But this wide range of sexualities isn't the only thing that turned readers off, Hopkinson acknowledges. The novel's mixed reception sprang from "all kinds of reasons, not just the sexualities. The novel is also non-linear with multiple viewpoints, and there are differences of opinion as to how successful that was."[20] Hopkinson mentions readers' discomfort with her representations of sexuality and temporality as if these were separate issues, but they may also intersect. The creative temporalities of speculative fiction and kink parallel one another in ways that may be unsettling for those unfamiliar with them. BDSM, Elizabeth Freeman argues, offers a set of sexual practices that self-consciously manipulates time. In a BDSM séance, the top works to pleasurably destabilize the bottom's expectations of time: she gets you worked up, then draws out your orgasm as long as she pleases; leaves you blindfolded and powerless to know what comes next, when the next kiss of the flogger or dildo will grace you; stands back as you impatiently anticipate the sting or relief of her touch, then delivers it in your most unguarded moment. The phallocentric teleology of arousal, climax, resolution explodes in the BDSM scene as past, present, and future loop in and out of each other in dizzying ways. Freeman believes this creative remix of time provides a useful model for understanding historicity outside imperial as well as heteropatriarchal teleologies. "S/M may bring out the historicity of bodily response itself," she writes. "By 'historicity' I mean not only the conditioning of sexual response over time . . . but the uses of physical sensation to break apart the present into fragments of times that may not be one's 'own,' or to feel one's present world as both conditioned and contingent."[21] Here again, the work kinksters do—in this instance, with time—parallels the work that Hopkinson undertakes as an sf writer. Both break time into fragments that propel readers and bottoms into pasts, futures, and alternate presents without being sure where we're going, leaving us with an embodied experience of how contingent and malleable historical realities can be.

Yes, you can get this experience from both sf and BDSM time; but you can also get it from what African diaspora spiritual practitioners call *spirit time*. It's a commonplace among practitioners that you never know how long a ceremony will last because once you start you're no longer on human time. When from one moment to the next an ancestor can return you to the past—or a lwa can pull you to a more expansive present—or an unborn spirit can give you glimpses of the future—you have to surrender any illusion of operating in unidirectional, forward-marching time. Jacqui Alexander puts it beautifully: "Spirit work does not conform to the dictates of human time. . . . Time becomes a moment, an instant, experienced in the now, but also a space crammed with moments of wisdom about an event or series of events already having inhabited different moments, or with the intention of inhabiting them, while all occurring simultaneously in this instant, in this space, as well as in other instants and spaces of which we are not immediately aware."[22] When you understand spirit time, then, it's not far to go to make yourself comfortable in speculative fiction time, BDSM time, or a combination of these. If you write about the genesis and manifestations of Ezili Je Wouj, to a certain extent you *have* to write sf—have to take your reader time-traveling between "fragments of times that may not be one's 'own.'" And if you tell Ezili Je Wouj's stories, you may *have* to thrust your reader into BDSM time—to destabilize her expectations of what comes next and leave her breathlessly, pleasurably confused about where she's going. So when you peel back the image of Jeanne Duval's red skirt and open *The Salt Roads*, know: Ezili Je Wouj will be there to ride you, will take you up and down, back and forth in ways you weren't expecting. Since you can't stop her, try to enjoy the ride.

∞

Wearing a vermillion dress against a vermillion background—oranges layered on red, brilliantly—the cinnamon-brown figure in the portrait stares at the viewer with striking, luminous eyes, a string of red-tinted pearls cinched around her neck and a rust-colored baton brandished in her long-fingered right hand. In 2003, New Mexico–based artist Erin Currier produced a series of portraits titled *Women Warriors*. Currier, who creates art using discarded paper trash, acrylic paint, and glaze, paints "portraits that celebrate figures who resist or defy authority": repurposing the elitist portraiture tradition, she explains, "my use of trash is . . . a poetic incantation—a call for a counter power rooted in the imagination."[23] The defiant figure conjured in the portrait described above is Mary Ellen Pleasant, a nineteenth-century, Northern California–based black entrepreneur who used her fortune to support the abolitionist movement and became known as the Mother of Civil Rights in California. "Pleasant was once the most talked-about woman in San Francisco. When other African Americans were rarely mentioned, she claimed full-page articles in the press," biographer Susheel Bibbs notes. However, "by the end of the century, via the popular press, Pleasant had been labeled 'Mammy Pleasant,' angel and arch fiend, and madam and murderess—her story indiscriminately plunged into myth, misinformation, gossip, and half truths."[24] How fitting, then, that Currier literally dug into trash to extract a portrait of the imposing Mrs. Pleasant, and transform her image from stark shades of black and white into brilliant red.

Traveling west from New Orleans on the steamer *Oregon*, Mary Ellen Pleasant arrived in San Francisco April 7, 1852. Taking advantage of women's scarcity in the city as well as the capital she'd inherited from her first husband, she quickly established herself as the owner of several laundries and boardinghouses that catered to San Francisco's banking and political elite. Pleasant took advantage of these magnates' trust—as well as the financial and personal secrets she collected while serving them her famed dinners—to maneuver for jobs and rights for black San Franciscans. "It is said that for this they nicknamed her 'The Black

City Hall,'" Bibbs writes. "In the 'colored' community . . . she used her money to help ex-slaves fight unfair laws and to get lawyers or businesses in California. She became an expert capitalist, owning every kind of business imaginable, and she prospered."[25] Helen Holdredge, whose sensationalized, fictionalized 1956 biography of Pleasant remains the most accessible text about this figure, evoked her consolidated power in terms that evoke the role, paraphernalia, and "excessive" desires of the dominatrix: "She had become the whipmaster of the city, she could control finances and politics, she was immune from the law; but she wanted more."[26]

Pleasant's more recent (and archivally diligent) biographer Lynn Hudson notes that the woman who bore the simultaneous nicknames Mammy Pleasant and the Black City Hall was adept at playing on gendered, racialized fantasies of black women to advance her social and political power. "Pleasant wasted no time capitalizing on her domestic skills and on the assumptions that as a black woman she excelled at these [domestic] tasks," she writes of Pleasant's success as an owner of laundries and boardinghouses. "Her entrepreneurial success in the West—from its beginning—relied in part on the manipulation and exploitation of stereotypes of black women."[27] Representations like Hold-redge's, which fixate on Pleasant's "unnatural" predilection for dominance in ways that take on an erotic charge, play with another gendered, racialized, and sexualized fantasy: the black dominatrix, the too-powerful, dominating black mother-figure who looms at once fearful and titillating in the sub's eye. Mistress A., a black prodomme, describes the fantasy of the black domina as another facet of the myth of the strong black woman. Her "Confessions of a Black Dominatrix" relates how clients write "in search of a towering, powerful Ebony domme. . . . They want this caricature of a woman. . . . It's part of their kink."[28] The black dominatrix, she finds, has "to play up the notion that all black women are of superior strength, non-emotional and definitely not possessing the same femininity of our white counterparts."[29] It seems evident that Pleasant was quite savvy in playing up the mammy version of the strong black woman fantasy; but is it possible she manipulated the domina version of this fantasy, too? If she was willing to trade on clients' trust in the black mammy, why not on their simultaneous fascination with and fear of black female dominance? "While my job is to deal and trade in fantasy, I don't take the entire burden," Mistress A. clarifies. "Dominatrixes are a bit like espionages, well the good ones at least."[30] Shielded behind the overlapping images of the mammy and domina, what secrets of white male power could Mary Ellen Pleasant—well known as an abolitionist spy—elicit and exploit? How did she take patriarchs' trash and reshape it to become one of those women warrior "figures who resist or defy authority"?

❦

Yellow, yellow welcomed like it's golden. On a page detailing her "Favorite Play," Domina Erzulie explains her predilection for indulging submissives with "golden showers": "What I love about this champagne is the strange empowerment it gives me. It's primal, animalistic, dirty, exciting. I might grab your hair, while pouring my champagne all over your face, your body, your cock. And if you've been a very, very good boy, I might even let you have a taste."[31] Mollena Williams, self-styled "Perverted Negress" and BDSM educator, muses on why this champagne becomes such a coveted reward: "for those who fetishize urine, such scenes can be arousing in different ways. It may be the perceived prurience of the act or the perceived 'dirtiness.' It might be the idea that the top or dominant is so exalted that even their waste material is sacred and precious, and such ritual ingestion is an honor."[32] When the goddess pisses on you, she's showering you with her power—a power that you can bathe in, that you can make your own.

And if there's a lwa for whom a golden shower is a fitting tribute, it's Ezili Je Wouj. Colin Dayan explains Je Wouj's relationship to Freda as one of conversion, in which Je Wouj takes the ethereal, oneiric, luxurious trappings of Freda's power and brings out their fleshy, earthly, elemental undersides. She writes: "It is as if the extremes of love and restraint, enacted for the community by the generosity, tears, and surrender of Ezili Freda, lead to a more savage transformation: the flowers, perfume and basil of Ezili Freda turn into (or merge to form) the blood, flesh, and dirt of Ezili-je-wouj."[33] And the French champagne that Freda adores turns into the champagne of Domina Erzulie's golden showers. Don't forget, the Ezili are water lwa; so how could there not be an Ezili who pushes us to tap into the cosmic power of our own bodily fluids, the water that comes daily from between our thighs?

And yes, the contemporary Montreal where Domina Erzulie's submissives live may be excited by seeing and feeling her urine because they find it "animalistic, dirty." But this represents only one possible relationship to that bodily fluid. Historically, urine has been touted for its cleansing properties. In her 1677 treatise *The Compleat Servant-Maid*, Hannah Woolley's recommendations for laundering stained clothes included: "Before that you suffer it to be washed, lay it all night in urine, the next day rub all the spots in the urine as if you were washing in water; then lay it in more urine another night and then rub it again, and so do till you find they be quite out."[34] Using urine as bleach or as a detergent called "chamber lye"—a combination of fermented urine and ashes—was a common means of washing clothes in Europe and North America into the nineteenth century. During the same time period, lant (aged urine) served as a household cleaner whose effectiveness came from its high ammonia content. Not only a cleanser, though, urine also became a beauty secret. In Enlightenment England and France, women urinated in their hands and rubbed their skin to give it a fresh glow; laboratories now replicate this effect by adding synthetic urea to lotions. The medical uses of urine are also extensive and ongoing. Pharmaceuticual companies extract proteins and hormones to use as ingredients in medications including Pergonal, Premarin, and Urokinase. But urine's medicinal properties need not be chemically mediated. In *The Water of Life: A Treatise on Urine Therapy*, John Armstrong details the effectiveness of urine therapy—that is, drinking one's own urine—on diseases including gangrene, cancer, diabetes, tuberculosis, heart disease, malaria, wounds, burns, and asthma.[35] Nearly ten million people currently practice this therapy in western Europe alone.

Vodoun, too, recognizes urine as a strong cleanser and medicine. One of the most powerful ways to spiritually cleanse a house is to use a floor wash made with first morning's urine (and other ingredients). And if you get hold of someone else's urine, you can use it for them or against them: yes, you can mix it with herbs to make healing medicine, and yes, too, you can store it in a bottle and pray over it to wish them harm. So one way to understand the deep thrill of a golden shower is to imagine the vulnerability and power of pushing past contemporary Western taboos on bodily fluids in order to experience that "champagne" as a healing, one that submissives can feel on their flesh and take into their orifices. *And* one with an edge—because urine cleans with a little burn to it, doesn't it, its power a mutable one that can run for or against you; but in that moment of the golden shower, you have no choice but (because you have made the choice) to submit to it. Lay down, submit, and let the flesh in all its messiness—its leaking, its uncontrollable gushes, its bringing what's inside out and what's outside, in—overpower you. You see, the piss, "blood, flesh, and dirt" of Ezili Je Wouj don't manifest with the intention to be offensive or shocking to her servitors. They're meant to return us—brusquely, violently if need be—to the basic elements of our bodies, those parts we eschew as waste rather than welcoming as power. Yes, we should all love the Freda in ourselves but we should love the Je Wouj too, and just as hard. Domina Erzulie proclaims herself "a divine creature to be adored and worshipped" because she is "earthy, tactile, playful, energetic, intense, sensual, erotic," and Je Wouj's blood, piss, and other effluvia are powerful because they are all these things.[36] So hold out your hands, let her grab your hair, open your chest and mouth, and know— golden showers cost extra, but Domina Erzulie makes it worth it.

Two scarlet women, tangled together in sheets moist with sweat and sex and perfume; two women, their bodies literally marked scarlet. Hopkinson introduces *The Salt Roads'* readers to Jeanne Duval in Paris, 1842, as she lounges in bed with white French lover Lise. Sequestered in her room with doors locked, windows drawn, and surfaces littered with half-eaten food, the cabaret dancers are enjoying a two-day furlough in bed—having sex, sleeping, playing games, drinking wine, smoking hashish. Their eyes are red from the hashish—je wouj—and between their legs is red, too: Lise's from "the thick red bush of her jigger," Jeanne's from the menstrual blood that drips onto her legs. As Jeanne reclines on Lise's thigh she feels her lover's hand tugging her tightly curled hair, stroking it and enjoying its texture (much as Baudelaire would in his famous poem "La Chevelure").[37] But Jeanne literally flips this situation. She quickly turns to plant her face between Lise's legs, licking her, holding her down and pulling her closer as she "pitched and galloped like runaway horses" and called out, "cursing me sweet."[38] So Baudelaire's most famous paramour first appears in the novel not only as a lover of women but as a lesbian top—one who holds white French womanhood down in dirty sheets and refuses to let her up until her cursing ends in a spectacular orgasm.

Then, begging some rest before they "do it again and once more again before the night even falls," Lise suggests another game they can play: scrying for their "true loves."[39] This so-called white magic was a common amusement among nineteenth-century European women, usually considered an innocent diversion. But Lise and Jeanne put an edge to this familiar women's magic. Without enough water or wine to gaze into, Lise suggests they use the mixture of urine and menstrual blood in the chamber pot.

The combination of piss and blood becomes at once erotic and esoteric, a lovers' game and a medium for divination. If this sounds dirty to you, that's part of the point. Nineteenth-century Paris was at once a very sophisticated and very polluted place, as Hopkinson remarks in a discussion of this scene—one where horse manure mixed with human waste on the streets as chamber pots were routinely emptied out windows.[40] Surrounded by filth, European metropolitans became very concerned about separating what was dirty from what was not; the ability to shield oneself from dirt became a mark of class and racial privilege. The rising European bourgeoisie was equally concerned with *who* was dirty—which individuals, yes, but more importantly which genders, sexualities, classes, and races were sexually impure. "As the nineteenth century drew on, the iconography of dirt became a poetics of surveillance, deployed increasingly to police the boundaries between 'normal' sexuality and 'dirty' sexuality," Ann McClintock notes, glossing the latter as "masturbation, prostitution, lesbian and gay sexuality, s/m, the host of Victorian 'perversions.' "[41] But Jeanne and Lise, both physically and sexually dirty, choose to regard their dirtiness—their stinking, unemptied chamber pot, filled with effluvia from between their legs—as something at once erotic and magic; something they can enjoy together, something they gaze into like a mirror, something they try to see a future in.

But the romance and magic of dirt don't work the same for everyone, Jeanne quickly discovers. Inhaling hashish and gazing into the pot, the lovers see a vision: a man "dark as coal, as mud," wearing a stained apron and reaching for the hand of a woman in a pink gown. Lise begins to weep: "He was so foul . . . black as the devil! . . . I am to be wedded to a black, and toil all my days . . . and have nigger babies."[42] Jeanne replies: "Well then, my beauty . . . they will look like me."[43] As in other kinky scenes, Jeanne and Lise make a game out of manipulating time here. Their scrying plays with the tense Lynda Hart identifies as the performative time most characteristic of BDSM, "the future anterior—that past that will have been": that is, readers witness Jeanne and Lise looking into a future that, for us, is the past.[44] Citing Catherine Clement, Hart muses that "the future anterior is a locution in which one finds the future retroactively, 'a memory curious about its own future. . . . The future anterior alters history: it is the miraculous tense, the tense of healing.' "[45] But for this black woman top, the future anterior of kink proves neither miraculous nor healing. The future Jeanne predicts—one readers know as their past, present, and maybe future—is one where her black girlhood repeats itself: where the birth of black womanhood ("nigger babies" that look like Jeanne) is greeted *once again* as a failure and a source of sorrow. Lise's exclamation leaves readers to wonder if her desire to bottom for Jeanne is tinged with racism, if she thrills in being overcome by the *extra* dirtiness of Jeanne's blackness. It also positions us to see that—far from kinky sex or dirt fetishism proving "an anarchic force for good"[46]—lovers' racial (and other) power differentials must be addressed if kink is going to prove empowering for black women, even black tops. Black femme sexual dominance may be "a radical tool to negotiate and transform how power acts on our bodies and our communities," but can't be black women's *only* tool.[47]

So Hopkinson commands another force to destabilize the power relationships Jeanne remains enmeshed in, even between dirty sheets. Directly after this scene ends, Hopkinson takes readers back to Haiti to witness the birth of Ezili Je Wouj at the burial of a stillborn black baby. And wandering through the ether, searching for an anchor, this new spirit descends into Jeanne's body. "I am here. In someone's soul case. And though I beat and hammer on its ribs, I am caught . . ." the lwa tells us as she settles inside Jeanne. "Blind, linear, I quiet inside the ginger woman's body."[48]

"Some people have reported that I was born in slavery, but as a matter of fact, I was born in Philadelphia," Mary Ellen Pleasant quipped in her 1902 autobiography. "My father was a native Kanaka and my mother a full-blooded Louisiana negress."[49] Most biographers beg to differ. Bibbs and Holdredge place Mary's birth sometime between 1814 and 1817 on a plantation near Augusta, Georgia, where she entered the world as the daughter of a planter and an enslaved Voodoo priestess. Separated from her parents at an early age, she bounced around the country as a child—perhaps a slave, perhaps an indentured worker—until she settled in Massachusetts. There she married James Smith, a wealthy mulatto and active abolitionist. The two worked together in abolitionist causes, serving on the Underground Railroad and working with New Bedford's Anti-Slavery Society until he died suddenly in the mid-1840s. In 1851 she moved to New Orleans with second husband John James Pleasant. This deep Southern relocation, Bibbs stipulates, was motivated not only by "slavers hot on her trail" but by desire to pursue her maternal heritage by studying Voodoo: "LaVeaux had invented a way to use Voodoo to aid the disenfranchised, and Mary, who should have inherited a voodoo priestancy from her mother, wanted to learn it. Said the only eyewitness of this study, LaVeaux's granddaughter, 'She (LaVeaux) was teachin' Mrs. Pleasants Voodoo so she could use it some way.' So, from Mam' zelle LaVeaux Mary learned to mentor her people and to use the secrets of the rich to gain aid for the poor—a 'model' that would serve her well in San Francisco."[50] In San Francisco, legend has it, Pleasant became the city's first Voodoo queen.

Holdredge's biography elaborates several accounts of Voodoo ceremonies Pleasant presided over in San Francisco. She cites neither written nor oral sources for these accounts, which repeat, almost word for word, Robert Tallant's questionable descriptions of reverence for Li Grand Zombi in *Voodoo in New Orleans*.[51] Holdredge introduces readers to her version of Voodoo with a tale of how Pleasant acceded to her queendom in a St. John's Eve ceremony. Following Tallant to the letter, Holdredge clothes this ceremony in scarlet: gathering by the light of a huge bonfire, participants, she writes, wore red handkerchiefs knotted around their waist, while Pleasant made her entrance in a crimson gown. The ceremony's focal point became a barred box containing a snake that celebrants humbly petitioned as the Great Serpent. With a convulsive shudder, Pleasant strode atop the box and spoke as the serpent's oracle, uttering "words which fell strange and alien on those unacquainted with the ceremony."[52] Holdredge imagines that the ceremony then broke into a bacchanal of song and dance: "The dancers, without stopping, drank rum from the vessels which they passed hand to hand. As weariness engulfed the dancers after three hours they let themselves be mastered by passion and tearing the bandannas from their sweating bodies they rushed away in pairs, each man holding a woman, and disappeared into the encompassing darkness."[53] After sensationalizing a sexual finale for this event, Holdredge goes on to imagine Pleasant staged abridged Voodoo ceremonies for her elite boardinghouse patrons—ceremonies that dispensed with bonfire and snake worship and got straight to the sex. "Such primitive rites were not for white men," Holdredge opines. "Instead, there was a minimum of food, a great deal of champagne, and ten beautiful quadroon girls to dance with the white men."[54] And sleep with them, of course.

The details Holdredge doesn't borrow from Tallant, the ones she concocts herself, go to fictionalizing the dirtiness of Pleasant's ceremonial work. Her accounts are replete with pungent effluvia: free-flowing alcohol and its attendant piss, sweat streaming from writhing bodies, the implied wetness of culminating sexual acts. And then, of course, there's the prurience of these gatherings, where Pleasant appears something like a femdomme presiding over a play party whose participants enjoy erotic dance and taboo (Voodoo) play. Holdredge's dirt fixation isn't entirely misplaced. Indeed, as Karen McCarthy Brown writes, one of urban Vodoun's most important functions is to keep its followers in touch with dirt, with the earth.[55] So, in ceremony, people who no longer till earth get dirty, people who no longer do manual labor get sweaty, people who no longer live in agrarian community touch skin—not necessarily sexually, but perhaps. In short, participants are challenged to be in touch with their elemental, physical selves. This, of course, would register as dirty to the elite white San Franciscans who patronized Pleasant's boardinghouses as well as those who read Holdredge's book. Pleasant capitalized on such squeamishness, first charging her boardinghouse clients to get dirty at mock Voodoo ceremonies then having them pay her to clean them up again. Literally, she laundered their clothing; figuratively, she kept their dirty secrets in exchange for favors. Holdredge imagines that after her crowning ceremony, Pleasant traded severe black dresses for low-cut, bright-colored gowns she wore while strolling down the street with a new haughtiness. "To her followers she was a woman of power, the Voodoo Queen of their cult," Holdredge envisages. "To others her changed appearance betokened an uprise of prosperity; more than ever prominent men flocked to her."[56] Yes, why wouldn't they?

Red: no crimson, already crimson, pushing through to redder. On her blog, Domina Erzulie gives a detailed account of a public punishment she inflicted on a submissive whose (undetailed) actions embarrassed her. Leading him into a BDSM dungeon on a short leash, she tied him prone with his bare ass exposed. "I love humiliating a man that way, it gives me a warm feeling," she explains.[57] Then, drawing from the bag of whips and paddles she'd had him fetch, she began spanking him—slapping him with her bare hands until he begged for mercy, then continuing with a paddle and flogger. She reminisces: "I took my time with the blows, every stroke I gave him, I gave for his own good. Every stroke I gave, as I was watching the color of his buttocks getting redder by the minute, gave me great satisfaction . . . It made me feel warm inside. Why? . . . because I do it freely for my own satisfaction and show him not to embarass me ever again!"[58] Domina Erzulie lovingly recounts several such corporal punishment stories on her blog. "I love drums. Do you want to be my drum?" she asks submissives interested in corporal punishment scenes. "From light to extreme. I delight in seeing you squirm and scream."[59] One source of delight in such scenes seems to be her ability to color bodies red: again and again she describes with satisfaction a submissive's backside as it becomes *red, redder, crimson* under her hand or ruler, bearing "red splotches" and "red marks across his white flesh." Ezili Je Wouj, come again.

Another source of delight seems to be the spirit in which she acts these scenes out: the fiery red spirit of openly embraced revenge. Domina Erzulie always links intense corporal punishment to a perceived slight on the part of the dominant—he arrived late, or expressed doubt that a female dominant could spank him *really* hard. But the punishments she metes out—five hundred blows with the flogger, a back full of welts raised by an eighteen-inch ruler—seem pleasurably, indulgently out of proportion to submissives' offenses. Domina Erzulie's erotically charged, generously administered vengeance links her to one of Ezili Je Wouj's most known and feared characteristics: this spirit is most often called on by people with a taste for revenge, and especially for exacting swift and memorable retribution on behalf of wronged lovers. The fury behind the vengeance she enacts, however, derives not from individual misdeeds but from the cosmic injustice she rages against—the loss, accident, deprivation, and disease that impinge on (especially women's, especially black) lives without fairness or reason. Maya Deren describes the rage of Ezili Je Wouj as "the cosmic tantrum—the tantrum not of the spoiled child, but of some cosmic innocence that cannot understand—and will not understand—why accident would ever befall what is cherished, or why death should ever come to the beloved."[60] This tantrum is cosmic, yes, but it is also historical: a product of the dramatically increased vulnerability to premature death that her mostly black, often female servitors negotiate. Pat Califia, reflecting on the problems facing (white) women channeling powerful spirits like Je Wouj as part of BDSM-as-ritual work, opines: "The biggest problems, for me, are related to the real-life oppression of women. It is very hard to channel loving dominant female energy in such a poisonous context. It feels to me as if the goddess is pissed off, and it is sometimes hard to know what to do with all that cosmic rage."[61] How pissed off will the goddess be, then, when she's a woman *and* black? You should be ready to accept five hundred of her lashes and be grateful.

And make no mistake about it, skewed racial and gendered power dynamics lend a charge to the corporal punishment scenes this black prodomme enacts. Noting with satisfaction how much she "love[s] humiliating a *man*," Domina Erzulie delights in "leaving light red marks across his *white* flesh" and reddening "his *white* bottom with the ruler." The red-on-white punishments she devises for these men are colored with revenge for their maleness and whiteness—for the privilege they exercise in the world outside her dungeon, that she temporarily "corrects" with her red marks. Though she doesn't tag them as such, these scenes veer into "race play": that is, play (according to Mollena Williams) that "embraces and explores the . . . racial identities of the players within a BDSM scene."[62] Williams engages in race play as a mode of spiritual work, one she compares to the Ordeal Path of shamanic journeys. "Whether you are finding power in surviving a bitter defeat, or finding power in victory, the power exchange inherent in race-based play is dynamic and demanding," she reflects. "By overcoming, whether obliquely (*via survival*) or obtusely (*by turning the tables on the 'oppressor'*), we can find profound truths and power within these scenes."[63] The most optimistic hope for race play, when the domme is a woman of color, is the same hope entertained for the appearance of Ezili Je Wouj in ceremony. Namely: that bearing the brunt of a Je Wouj–esque "cosmic tantrum" changes something in the world sense of submissives and servitors—that it gives them an embodied sense of what race, gender, and power feel like when the black woman's pain, pleasure, and strength *matter*. When Domina Erzulie rains the last blow on the "already crimson bottom" of the man who didn't believe a (black) woman could spank him hard, she proclaims triumphantly: "He would never forget this, for sure." Any more than you'd forget the appearance of a raging, vengeance-red Je Wouj.

But sisters, let's be honest. Part of the bravery of this kind of play—part of why it requires goddess-like strength to allow yourself, as a woman of color, to embody the cosmic tantrum—is the overwhelming likelihood that once the ceremony and/or BDSM scene is done, participants will walk outside without much having changed. Responding to male masochist fantasies that femdomme BDSM creates a "feminist utopia" in which women are finally "fully liberated and universally recognized as the Superior Sex," Ann McClintock aptly retorts: "the 'feminist utopia' exalted by these men is a paradise arranged and organized for male pleasure. In the private security of fantasy, men can indulge secretly and guiltily their knowledge of women's power, while enclosing female power in a fantasy land that lies far beyond the cities and towns of genuine feminist change."[64] And when the fantasy hour the submissive has paid for ends, white cisgender male privilege still cushions him—and endangers Domina Erzulie—in the twenty-first-century Montreal streets they return to.

This power shift at the end of a BDSM séance parallels the sudden descent into impotence that accompanies the end of a possession by Ezili Je Wouj. When the "raging tears of Erzulie Ge Rouge" cease, Deren writes, she arrives at "that moment that has been called her paralysis."[65] Realizing she'll find neither solution nor respite to the cosmic injustice she rails against, her (horse's) body collapses, goes limp, and must be carried from the ceremony. Deren concludes her discussion of Ezili's visitation with the observation: "The wound of Erzulie is perpetual: she is the dream impaled eternally on the cross-roads where the world of men and the world of divinity meet."[66] Similarly, despite the mantle of divinity she creates for herself in scenes, Domina Erzulie still routinely finds herself thrust from the "dream" of the dungeon into a "world of men" where part of her work is dealing with the pernicious racism that haunts the BDSM community—which is, Williams reminds us, a microcosm of, rather than a respite from the racism of a larger society. Her website also becomes a space where she rails against the insultingly racist responses she gets from potential clients, one of the most egregious reading: *"Hi i am dom Man love to have anal with color girls if you like I make you this offer you are mine for 2 hour (I can do what ever i want to you Sure in no much Pain level but anal fisting gag."*[67] Domina Erzulie's response: a few choice words and a picture of a brown-skinned domme (herself?) in pink-red stiletto heels, crushing shut the mouth of a white man lying flat on his back on the floor. Because make no mistake, Ezili Je Wouj *never* gives up; she may leave in a moment of paralysis but she always, always returns, redder than ever. Her revenge has no end.

———

Blood red, the marks Jeanne's open palm makes as it lands across the "pale . . . moons" of his bare ass and blood red, the marks her teeth leave there, too.[68] You may not, but Hopkinson considers the opening bedroom scene between Jeanne and Lise "pretty daily sex."[69] More provocative, she hopes, is a scene that imagines "a famous white poet in bondage, bottoming to his black female lover"—a scene that nearly got *The Salt Roads* banned from a U.S. public library.[70] This erotic interlude takes place in Paris, 1844, at a time when Charles Baudelaire had established Jeanne Duval as his mistress and paid for her clothing, food, and lodging. Their afternoon of rough sex begins with Charles bent at the waist and bound to his writing desk with Jeanne's shawl, his frock coat thrown over his head and his underwear pulled down to his ankles. Spanking and biting him to punctuate her words, Jeanne declares: "Today . . . I think I'll show you what it feels like to be a woman."[71] She inserts her index finger into his anus as he strains and begs her to stop, and in return she asks: "Do you feel how you are? . . . How dry? . . . How tight? How unwilling? . . . Has a woman ever felt this way when you've entered her?"[72] Hers is an act of revenge: revenge for Baudelaire's ineptness as her lover, revenge for his inability to recognize women as sexual *partners* rather than objects to facilitate his pleasure. At his affirmative response Jeanne pushes her finger further while he moans in pain, relenting only when he promises to learn how "to prepare a woman—nay, even a man, should you come to that—so that they are eager and ready for your embrace."[73]

Readers may recognize this scene as a pleasantly perverse iteration of contemporary BDSM gender play, one of a set of practices that Margot Weiss groups as *cultural trauma play*: scenes that "replay hierarchies based on gender, class, race, or age," using "social or historical structures of exploitation as fodder for SM eroticization."[74] Gender play that creates "roles in which real power and scene power are discordant"—in which rich men pay to get down on their knees and clean a domina's house, or dommes dress male subs in lingerie and humiliate them for acting like sluts—counts as the form of power exchange that receives the most interest from cultural critics, Weiss notes.[75] In the analysis of scholars like McClintock and Foucault, SM "is understood to disrupt the heterosexual logic that animates sex-gender-sexuality binaries because roles are chosen, rather than naturalized" and "are decoupled from a sexed (or otherwise imposed) body and instead performed or enacted."[76] In Jeanne's play, learning *what it feels like to be a woman* isn't about breasts or vaginas but about experiencing powerlessness, restriction, and disregard for bodily needs. Even while building sexual energy, this power exchange also expresses Jeanne's commentary—and deep-seated anger—about her quotidian, intimate experiences of gender oppression; and, for the time/space of the scene, orchestrates a *pause* to this oppression. Borrowing from Walter Benjamin, Freeman discusses the pause as the time manipulation characteristic of cultural trauma play. "Not an interval between one thing and another" but "itself a thing, analytically and experientially available," the pause allows Jeanne to momentarily press *stop* and step outside the racial, gendered, and class disadvantages that, both before and after the scene, she experiences relative to Charles.[77] And she thoroughly enjoys the respite, too.

After their kinky sex ends with Charles howling "fuck me" until he's spent, Hopkinson creates a pause of a different kind: a line break that signals a temporal shift.[78] On the other side of the break, Charles, dressing to receive guests that evening, returns to being the partner who issues commands, calling Jeanne to ready the wine. Also dressed for company, Jeanne returns to being the one struggling against physical restraints, her corset making it difficult for her to move to do his bidding. Looking out the window at the rainy evening, she broods: "For all the sweet warmth in the apartment, I had the small, constant feeling that I wanted to get out, out . . . I wanted to be out, to go. I wanted to go down to the docks and stare at the greasy sea. Or not down; up. I wanted to rise into the air and fly free."[79] As the pause closes Jeanne finds herself feeling more hemmed in than before, more desperate to escape. For whom has Jeanne and Charles's gender play been liberatory, then? Weiss urges nuanced considerations of the politics of cultural trauma play that refuse to conflate bedroom power with social power. She argues for "considering the material conditions of SM performance, alongside the material—although often discursive—effects of SM play," pointing out that in the case of race play some scenes "enable the further disavowal of white privilege and racism, while others enable more ambivalent, open-ended readings of social power; some make visible, and thus available for reimagining, the normally invisible construction of racialized belonging, while others make spectacle, and thus detach the audience from such productions."[80] The material conditions of this scene—which takes place in an apartment that Charles rents, plays with clothing that Charles bought, and ends to accommodate a party where Charles shows off his latest acquisitions—never favor Jeanne. Charles can easily enjoy the theatrical reversal of gender roles in their rough afternoon games then, once clothes are donned and night falls, happily let this spectacle dissolve.

Just as the pause closes and the world plays itself forward again, the voice of Ezili Je Wouj surfaces in the text. Filtering in her blood-red perceptions of the lovers' power dynamics, Je Wouj's appearance disrupts the action of the scene; but rather than introducing the disjunctive time of the pause, her observations insinuate the conjunctive time of the palimpsest. Hopkinson layers Je Wouj's bold-printed narratives between Jeanne's normalfonted thoughts, and those narratives serve the function that Weiss suggests politically efficacious BDSM scenes should. They "make visible, and thus available for reimagining, the normally invisible construction of racialized," gendered power between the lovers. As Jeanne prepares for Charles's party, Je Wouj observes: "Charles has just bought Jeanne a new gown, with slippers and jewels to match . . . He's asked her to dress in them all, will invite her to sit under the new lithographs. He will . . . make sure to place her under the picture of Hamlet berating his mother Gertrude for her second marriage: 'In the rank sweat of an enseamed bed, stewed in corruption . . .' Charles fancies corruption, and women in it. Tonight, he wants to show off all his possessions . . ."[81] Viewed through Je Wouj's eyes, Jeanne joins Charles's collection of art and jewels as a prize that crowns him as the edgiest, most avant-garde of gentlemen poets. The author of Les Fleurs du Mal enjoys her kinky sexual creativity but also (literally) labels her corrupt for it while he sneers, unstigmatized; if Jeanne punishes Charles for his misogyny in the afternoon by evening Charles is punishing Jeanne for her sexual power. Ezili Je Wouj, witnessing this inequity, takes her revenge as she can. While Charles displays Jeanne to his friends as rank, Je Wouj exposes Charles to readers as petty, narcissistic, cowardly—and an indifferent lover to boot.

At the close of the chapter, Je Wouj muses on differences between Jeanne's feelings for Lise, whom she loves with "**deep, helpless adoration,**" and her more transactional love for Charles. "**Her love is bought, and Charles must pay,**" Je Wouj notes. "**Her love buys silks, watered as though they've been retrieved from locked chests in sunken ships; gold, that streams and flows around her neck and wrists in chains of liquid light; jewels that trickle and tripple from her ears. She's covered in the stuff, she soaks in it and it buoys her up when Charles is cruel.**"[82] The imagery here is at once opulent and eerie, the stuff of sunken ships and expensive wrist manacles repeating elements from a story that Jeanne heard as a child and that Ezili recalled pages before. This is a sailor's tale of a slaver that began to ship water and drowned the enslaved chained below, their bodies found sea-swollen and bearing the imprints of feet trying to climb their way to air above deck. Clothed in sunken silks and gold restraints, Jeanne at once becomes the enslaved who drown in their chains and those who strain for air in pure desperation; she founders in her relationship with Charles even as she's buoyed up by it. Charles pays for clothing, her lodging, her jewels, her wine that night, he pays and pays for her love. And in moments, pauses like this afternoon she makes him pay in other ways, too. But no matter what, Charles is still in charge of the ship; and he doesn't let Jeanne forget it for long.

∽

She was, you may know, a friend of John Brown. Mary Ellen Pleasant's tenure as "whipmaster" of San Francisco scandalized Holdredge in part because Pleasant was motivated not just by profit but by payback—by a desire for social justice that included vengeance against the white patriarchs who underestimated her. "She looked at her guests and dreamed of another goal—social equality—and she knew that the name of her god was Equality," Holdredge writes.[83] In 1858 Pleasant, now a prosperous proponent of radical abolitionism, advanced a large sum of money to John Brown for his attack on Harpers Ferry. Though Brown and his raiders were captured and executed, bitterly disappointing their backer, Pleasant continued with other means for raiding the elite's power base. Chief among these was the art of blackmail—an art she also learned from Marie Laveau, Bibbs and Holdredge speculate. Pleasant routinely set boarding-house guests up with sexual companionship then blackmailed them to keep their secrets. When these encounters resulted in pregnancies she asked both parties to pay to "take care of" (adopt out) illegitimate babies, thus expanding the network of blackmailable parties to include birth parents, adoptive parents, and potentially the children themselves.

Pleasant's penchant for blackmail eventually led her into a much-publicized legal battle. In the early 1880s she developed a close relationship with Sarah Althea Hill, a beautiful strawberry blonde from Missouri. While her primary business relationships were with men, Pleasant was known to take young black and white women on as protégées. The nature of Pleasant's relationships with these young women remains uncertain; some historians suspect she was their madam, others intimate she was their lover. Contemporary writers, Hudson notes, "also implied that she made 'sapphic' gestures toward young white women. One author . . . suggested that at precisely the time Pleasant 'felt rich and powerful,' her memoirs reveal 'errant words and phrases that suggest something outré in her relationships with young ladies.' "[84] One observer of Pleasant's relationship with Hill inveighed: "Mrs. Pleasance [sic] has a very peculiar relationship to [Sarah Althea Hill], one inexplicable upon ordinary principal [sic] or upon any reasonable ground. Her intimacy with Miss Hill . . . was one that ought not to have existed."[85] Veiled descriptions like these make "rich and powerful" Pleasant's "peculiar relationship" with Hill sound not only like a sexual partnership, but like one built on power exchange—that is, a domme/sub relationship in which Pleasant played the dominant role. Whatever their arrangement, Pleasant acted as Hill's benefactress—supporting her financially and emotionally—when Sarah Althea filed for divorce from U.S. senator William Sharon.

In 1883, Sarah Althea sued Sharon for divorce, charging him with desertion and adultery. Hill claimed that Sharon secretly married her in 1880 and supported her in a suite at the Grand Hotel; Sharon countered that he rented her room and paid her $500 a month for sexual companionship. Contemporary observers suggested that Pleasant engineered her protégée's relationship with Sharon as well as its subsequent dissolution. She may have been motivated to best Sharon in court as revenge for financial losses suffered when Sharon edged Pleasant's business partner Thomas Bell out of the Bank of California in 1872, as well as when Sharon refused to pay Hill's expenses (including Pleasant's hush money). Even Hudson, Pleasant's most careful biographer, acknowledges that "the theory that Pleasant was out for 'triple revenge,' as one author calls it, may have some merit."[86]

Although Hill (and Pleasant) won the divorce case, the affair marked a turning point in Pleasant's power in San Francisco. Whereas she previously appeared in newspapers as an influential figure in the city's life and politics, during the trial political cartoons satirized her as a wizened, conniving black nanny. Sketched as a short, thin, dark-skinned, and desexualized figure, she was no longer represented as the "towering, powerful, Ebony domme" whose dominance San Franciscans might find titillating as well as imposing.[87] The public judgment weighed against her, Hudson sums up, amounted to fear that "she had too much money and too much control over white people. . . . What could be worse than a mammy, a docile, obedient slave who turned out to be working for the other side?" The power to bring down a U.S. senator, the power to dominate young white womanhood, the power to "make men—in this case Sharon—pay for sexual favors," the power to fund this whole enterprise: this was just simply *too much* to be undermined or contained by caricaturing Pleasant either as the long-suffering mammy or the Jezebel domina. And so, Hudson notes, "the public scrutiny of the 1880s—the racialized and scandalous cartoons and headlines included—contributed to her financial decline and tainted her reputation."[88] Nonetheless, Pleasant stood by Hill for years after.

When the verdict was overturned in federal court and Hill lost her right to alimony, leaving her destitute, Pleasant took Hill into her home and cared for her until Sarah Althea's declining mental health led to her institutionalization. A good top knows how to care for her bottom, always.

❧

Golden, golden, golden again—stretching bigger, rounder, pop! A link takes you from Domina Erzulie's website to Voodoo Fetish Productions!, which features video clips for sale. Scroll down and you'll find "Popping Golden Balloons in Public Park," a three-minute clip available for $3.99.[89] Here Domina Erzulie, dressed in tight jeans, sunglasses, and button-up top, greets viewers in a springtime-green park holding two very full golden balloons. Reaching for a third, she puts the golden latex between her lips and starts to blow, blow, blow, until—the shimmering balloon bursts spectacularly in her upturned face. Then, placing the second balloon on a concrete platform, she faces away from the camera as she sits harder and harder, moving her hips forcefully and finally popping it "with my nice round butt in my tight jeans." The last balloon receives special treatment: she lounges on her side and massages it with her bare feet, squeezes it between her thighs, and captures it when it "blows away only to come flying back to me so I can finish it off, surprised, with my fingers." Lucky, happy golden balloon!

The target audience of these and other Voodoo Fetish Productions! balloon clips are looners (balloon fetishists) who take sexual pleasure in blowing up, popping, and/or sitting and lying on balloons. Like many fetishists, looners often locate the root of their sexual practices in childhood. They recall either extreme fascination with balloons—the skin-like feel of their latex, their bright colors, their ability to grow from small to big—or intense fear of the balloon's popping, which they later overcome by sexualizing the pop. "Balloons activate all facets of our senses," sex therapist Kimberly Resnick Anderson muses when interviewed about balloon fetishists on TLC's *Strange Sex*. "So, they're pretty to look at, they're colorful, they're cheerful, they have interesting shapes and sizes, they resemble breasts and penises."[90] More recognizably than with many other fetishes, maybe, looning offers pleasurable ways to remember, nurture, and indulge the child in the adult kinkster. Though Susan Donaldson James puts it crudely, she has a point when she remarks on ABC News: "For children, balloons can make the heart soar, but when an adult tucks his balloons into bed at night, he could be considered a 'looner.'"[91] We could put this another way, though, and say the looner is an adult caring for the child-self whose heart soared at the sight of balloons. This aspect of sexual self-care can be considered a link between—rather than a mark of difference from—this paraphilia and rougher BDSM practices like flagellation, race play, or golden showers. Speaking back to academic and clinical texts that insist that BDSM either endlessly repeats childhood sexual trauma or has nothing to do with it, Hart suggests that many kinky sex practices *do* find points of origin in childhood trauma. However, she posits, they replay that trauma metonymically rather than mimetically.[92] That is, BDSM practitioners take one part of a traumatic childhood experience—the nun's ruler, the balloon's pop—and weave that into another scenario, one where the child-self can finally find release, comfort, and pleasure. So when Mollena Williams engages in race play she's getting off, yes, but also giving herself a chance to take care of the girl-self once fascinated, ashamed, and terrified by her childhood reaction to *Roots*.[93]

And many people forget this, but Ezili Je Wouj is a caretaker of children, too. You can always call on her to help children in physical as well as spiritual danger, and she often surfaces in children's hospitals, especially surgical wards. She also comes to help children unwanted by their parents, ushering them back to the spirit world before they're born or acting as their guardian once they are. In short, Ezili Je Wouj ferociously protects the kind of children people are most afraid or ashamed of having. And why wouldn't she? Ezili Je Wouj is, after all, the cosmic child. Deren sees in her both the "child's innocence of reason" and "the hurt of a child [that] mounts and transcends both its own cause and solution."[94] This Ezili is the one who'll never learn that blood, flesh, and urine are dirty, the one who can never accept life's unfairness to the black women she loves, the one who'll never change, calm down, or listen to reason. Just as the dominatrix is misrepresented as a child abuser even while she's caring for the child in her clients, Ezili Je Wouj is often feared as the cosmic angry black woman when she could more aptly be welcomed as a woman outraged and protective on behalf of the injured child in us all. As one practitioner puts it: "Most people only contact her for her angry side or when they want revenge. . . . She's tired of only being invited to the negative revenge situations and not the fun stuff."[95] Why not the fun stuff? Why not recognize the cosmic black woman's rage as a force that can be generative, inspiring, even sexy as hell?

But maybe you do. Maybe you come to Domina Erzulie's website because you like the idea of getting your ass beat even though that terrified you as a child. Or maybe, after being humiliated for years for wetting the bed, you want someone to delight in peeing on you. Or maybe you're there because after you snuck all the balloons from your little brother's birthday party into your room you felt ashamed and confused and don't want to be anymore. Then maybe you've come in search of Ezili Je Wouj: the lwa who exists to take care of all of those parts of you because they're all parts of her, all aspects of her cosmic force, all reclamations of the edges of our bodies and psyches we've been taught to be ashamed of but that fuel her red fire. Well, if that's what you want then go on and get it, girl! Go on and get what you need from the red power femme and know you deserve it, all of it.

—————

Rosewater, rose wine, rose red: red can also be softer, yes, red can also be rose. Readers familiar with Baudelaire's biography already know this affair ends badly for Jeanne. After seventeen years of tumultuous partnership— when Jeanne is in the advanced stages of syphilis she contracted from Charles—the poet leaves Jeanne for a younger, white French love, Apollonie Sabatier. Refusing to end Jeanne's story with this break, Hopkinson instead imagines an *after* to their relationship: one that leaves Jeanne "**dancing in the groove I've laid for you, dancing a new story to your life**," as Ezili Je Wouj puts it.[96] Jeanne discovers the future love she glimpsed in the chamber pot was hers, not Lise's. Her final lover in Hopkinson's novel is Achille, a black chef who arrives in her quarters wearing an apron stained with red wine spilled while cooking beef Bourguignon. He invites her to live with him in Paris, where he opens a chic restaurant the lovers run together. Disabled from a stroke caused by now-terminal syphilis, Jeanne finds her last years with Achille her happiest. "Achille kisses my balding scalp. Tells me he loves me," she recounts. "I hold my aching head high when I walk in the streets. Sometimes I have flour on my chin instead of powdered chalk. Sometimes I have ink on my hands instead of gloves, but I am a woman of property, and I am loved."[97]

If *The Salt Roads'* first sex scene is the dirty one between Jeanne and Lise, its last is a playful one between Jeanne and Achille. It begins as Jeanne, taking in the rosewater lingering on Achille from pastry-making, quips: "You smell like a girl, all cheap perfume."[98] She haughtily tosses him a gown and orders him to put it on. As he eagerly wriggles into the dress, excited to please the "happy old rouee" issuing him commands, his lover relates: "No one seeing the bulge he made in my frock would think him a girl. But we had a solution for that, he and I. Sometimes we would bind that poking flesh up against his belly, then put my pantaloons on him . . . Sometimes he loved it better so, to pull up the dress he was wearing, to see the frilly underclothes beneath it."[99] Achille's delight in frilly underclothes looks like *petticoating*: erotic fetish play where female dominants dress masculine submissives in girls' clothes—usually complete with petticoats—and teach "bad boys [to] become good girls."[100] While petticoat discipline originated in the Victorian era as a form of humiliation for nonconforming boys, contemporary practitioners explore ways to delight in the femininity both of the petticoated "girl" and the petticoating mother figure. One contributor to *Petticoat Discipline Quarterly* extolls the feminine virtues of play with "a cute pinafore, silk clothing, dainty shoes, and the comfort of panties": "I believe petticoat discipline to be effective, fun, and helpful to society and family . . . Restraining or scolding is of course necessary; but the lesson I want to teach is how wonderful the nurturing, loving, sensitivity of femininity is! I would rather have my man, boy, or rowdy girl melt into the joys of silks and lace . . ."[101] And so, soaked in rosewater, Achille melts and melts while Jeanne smiles at her newly created little girl.

Playing with fetish, the girly costume that Jeanne creates for Achille also plays with time. While her scene with Lise looked forward to the future (anterior) and her scene with Charles paused (the present), her play with Achille creates a contrary-to-fact *past* conditional: that is, an alternative past in which Achille giggled his way through girlhood, and Jeanne found her own version of the joys of motherhood. "The conditional temporality of 'what could have been,'" Saidiya Hartman speculates, is a critical one for writers to explore when imagining black lives.[102] Playing with "a narrative of what might have been or could have been" allows writers to *perform abolition on the page*, she posits.[103] That is, if contemporary black unfreedom originates in past violence, imagining alternative pasts is necessary to begin creating possibilities other than the living deaths that were supposed to be our lives. Jeanne's petticoating scene composes a meta-past conditional, as character and author simultaneously engage in eroticizing the *what if*. That is, in order to imagine a sex scene that's expansively empowering for her black dominatrix protagonist, Hopkinson chooses to veer outside the archive and script conditions that speculate *what it would have look liked if* Jeanne ended her life in a space of financial and emotional security—a space where, as Jeanne tells us, "I am a woman of property, and I am loved." Only when the material conditions in which the BDSM scene is embedded provide a measure of safety, only when scene power isn't entirely discordant with real-life power, can erotic power exchange work for this black woman in ways that don't come crashing down after the last orgasm.

To make this possible, Hopkinson imagines a kinky, feminist version of an ideal relationship for Jeanne, even though—or precisely because—she knows such a thing almost certainly never came to pass for the historical Jeanne Duval. In Hopkinson's fantasy Jeanne and Achille, secure in their success as business partners, enjoy becoming bedroom partners in multiple ways. While readers have seen Jeanne, the consummate top, take care of all her lovers during sex scenes, Achille also takes care of Jeanne in bed in another way. When she's sick he stays by her side and, she says, "cares for me well, whispers me stories in the evening."[104] Throughout the novel Jeanne expresses horror at the idea of bearing children, relating how a stillborn baby girl nearly killed her mother and so equating maternity with death. But in her scenes with Achille she can experiment with a past conditional mothering where she's not only safe playing with her little girl but, in moments of vulnerability, is safe being taken care of like a little girl. Now, what if that *really had been* black women's past? **"A few months later, she dies a happy woman, Jeanne does,"** Ezili Je Wouj tells readers shortly after this scene. **"At first when I got trapped in her body, I set her on the path of joy out of curiosity, but now I find that I am glad that I could be of service."**[105] And it's only after Jeanne's happy death that Je Wouj finds herself liberated from her horse's body and **"free! . . . soaring, soaring . . . like dancing, like singing, this flight."**[106] Where will she land next, the reader is left to wonder? If Ezili Je Wouj comes for you, will you be ready to open up to her red-loving, heart-twisting, thigh-spreading service *and enjoy it*, like Jeanne did?

In 1878, Pleasant—who, as Hudson notes, "at a time when many African Americans across the nation experienced a retreat from civil rights and the promises of citizenship . . . reached her financial zenith"—took up residence in a dwelling ominously dubbed the "House of Mystery."[107] Pleasant commissioned and oversaw the construction of this thirty-room, gilt-and-cupid-adorned mansion at 1661 Octavia Street. She never lived there alone, though: her business partner Thomas Bell and his wife Teresa—another of Pleasant's protégées— moved into the Octavia Street mansion with her. Though Pleasant claimed to live as the Bells' mammy (a ridiculous claim, given her wealth), the nature of their relationship garnered much speculation. Was Pleasant the lover of Thomas, Theresa, or both? Was theirs a relationship of equals or did Pleasant somehow have Thomas and Theresa in her control? San Francisco observer Charles Dobie wrote of the Octavia Street mansion, "People were purported to live beneath its frowning mansard roof but the only person I ever saw emerge was the black witch who held them all enthralled."[108] As late as 1987, Hudson reports, "the *San Francisco Chronicle* claimed that Pleasant kept Bell as her prisoner in the mansion and fed him dog food."[109]

Pleasant's contemporary detractors suggested she kept the Bells in her control by supplying them with babies. During the Sharon trial, defense witnesses testified that Pleasant sold illegitimate babies to women looking to trap wealthy men into marriage by faking pregnancy, and that Theresa Bell was among those who employed her baby-selling services. Sarah Althea's astrologist, Mrs. Wanger, testified that Mrs. Pleasant "got the babies for Mrs. Bell, and Mrs. Bell pulled the wool over Tom Bell's eyes."[110] A Mrs. Weill testified that Pleasant had sold Theresa Bell the baby of an unmarried girl named Bertha Bonsell, and the baby was then passed off as one of the Bell twins. Pleasant rebutted that she found a home for Bertha's unwanted baby with a woman on Bush Street and that "our babies were born ten or fifteen days before Bertha's." When the attorney asked, "Whose babies do you mean when you say 'our babies'?" she replied, "I mean Mr. Bell's babies."[111] This testimony ascertains not only that Pleasant was in the business of finding homes for unwanted newborns, but that she had no compunction about reporting this activity. Perhaps one of the homes where she placed newborns was, in fact, her own. Perhaps, by her doing, Thomas and/or Theresa Bell were unknowingly raising children that weren't biologically theirs. Or perhaps Pleasant and the Bells had purposely crafted a kind of queer family in which all three shared child rearing—in which the Bell's twins were, as Pleasant testifies, "our babies."

Whatever the case, after Thomas Bell died in 1892, the household at Octavia Street went awry. The Bells' oldest son, Fred—purported to be the baby rung in on Thomas—took his mother to court, claiming she was unfit to oversee his father's estate and that Pleasant was in fact (mis)managing the Bell fortune. "Mammy seemed to exercise an unaccountable power over [Fred's] mother's mind," Fred's attorney claimed.[112] Fred himself lamented: "In the 'house of mystery,' in the home of my people peace would ever reign, if that negress— 'Mammy Pleasant'—was in some foreign clime. She is the cause of all our trouble and trouble will reign until she departs. Just how she maintains the weird influence over Mrs. Bell I am unable to say."[113] The Bell children won their case and Pleasant was evicted from the Octavia Street mansion. Her fortune nearly exhausted by these decade-long legal battles, she died in 1904 living in a cottage on Geneva Street.

Make no mistake about it, though, Mary Ellen Pleasant never left San Francisco. In 1925 the House of Mystery was torn down and replaced by Green's Eye Hospital, now known as the Healing Arts Building. Next door stands the city's smallest public park, Mary Ellen Pleasant Memorial Park. Ghost tours lead visitors by this site nightly, where they're instructed that they may sense Pleasant's presence via a crow alighting or a sudden downpour of rain. If they make a respectful request of the Voodoo Queen at 1661 Octavia Street, they're told, it's sure to come true. But spiritualist John Thompson tells a slightly different story. "Unlike other famous San Francisco ghosts, Pleasant does not haunt one location," he claims. "Instead, her essence is claimed to be felt in dozens of local addresses."[114] Her appearance has changed since her death, he notes, so that she has come to resemble Erin Currier's portrait of her: her skin is darker, her expression steelier. "She is well spoken and proud, showing kindness to minorities and street people," Thomas reports. "She has a short temper when dealing with whites, especially journalists and the wealthy, and she takes some delight in frightening such folk."[115] He adds an important warning: "She should be approached with respect and good manners, and by no means should one ever call her 'Mammy.' "[116] Mistress, Queen, Madame, yes, but *never* Mammy: because you see how she enjoys raining down just punishment on the disrespectful, still. Mother of Civil Rights in California, Mary Ellen Pleasant demands all children approach her with the reverence she's due.

⚜

Once upon a time in the land of fever, there lived a scarlet pussy.[117] As I revised this homage to Ezili Je Wouj, Minneapolis-based musical artist Prince joined the ancestors on April 21, 2016. "During his 57 years of life, Prince consistently showed us Black femme extravagance," Ekundayo Afolayan eulogized. "From his purple suits to press n' curls and high pitched moans, Prince showed us how to authentically and fully live out our truths."[118] Prince's femme embodiment included alter ego Camille, initially slated to put out a self-titled album and credited with performing several songs including "Scarlet Pussy." Prince sings about Camille in "Shockadelica" as a dominatrix who holds lovers in a trance: "She got you tied with a golden rope . . . And when you've cried enough / Maybe she'll let you up / For a nasty ride in her shockadeli-car / She'll make you beg, girl."[119] In the outpouring after his death, many Prince devotees remembered the artist's revolutionary work in lyricizing black life in kink. Many more queer, black, femme, bigender, disabled, racially ambiguous, auto-erogenous, slutty, and non-metronormative writers honored Prince with childhood stories of how his music and persona became nurturing, possibility-opening presences in their lives as misfits, weirdos, crips, and freaks. "This was someone different, wild, real and awesome—a kindred spirit candle in the window," K. T. Billey wrote of the artist she called "our dirty patron saint of pop."[120] Prince, you took care of Ezili Je-Wouj's scarlet pussy children for so many years, in so many ways. Rest for eons in her care, purple majesty.

PHOTO BY CINDY ELIZABETH

PHOTO BY CINDY ELIZABETH

bridge

FOR THE
PARTY GIRLS

As a young femme in the Bay, I lived for women of color tea parties with dripping names: Butta third Sundays at the Oasis, Mango fourth Saturdays at El Rio. Those weekend afternoons I'd happily slip into a sea of black & brown women, admiring the polished dyke party girls I wished I could be. Club dykes leaning under fake & real palm trees sporting Minnie Mouse buns & chokers, Tims & overalls, ordering golden Red Bull & vodkas & laughing with certainty they were in the very place in the world meant for their flying high & grinding low.

One Saturday a few months after I'd broken up with a girlfriend, Mango was moving to a close & I was in the bathroom line, resigned that once again no fine-ass party queens were nodding my way. In front of me a woman with a loose, generously greased curl started up a conversation. She was drunk, so drunk her eyes didn't focus when she told me she lived just up the street & asked did I want to come to her place to watch movies? She moved close enough to smell stale alcohol & her skin next to mine seemed yellowed & overlotioned & lonely, somehow. Looking back, I see a late-stage alcoholic trying to make a connection with someone next to her. She repeated her question twice. Looking in her brown eyes as I made an excuse I saw a reflection of what it looks like to want to be one of these party queens, just like I did—but to fall into somewhere so deep you can't quite find yourself for yourself.

Party queens are like sirens: sometimes they feel so good, & sometimes they take you under. Like Mango or Butta, partying, addiction, & healing are recurring scenes in black queer women's lives—ones we don't talk about to everyone, maybe, but you know once you're part of the life. Most days no one but us cares about our joyful partying or drowning sobriety. No studies measure black queer women's substance use, even though researchers find high rates of addiction among white lesbians & black straight women. So we find our own language to make sense of the possibilities & dangers of partying. It's the language of mermaids: sounds of plunging headlong into altered consciousness & splashing back to the surface, too. Language always on the edge of becoming a love or blues song, that I hear as the soundtrack to scenes in this next chapter: Sharon Bridgforth's performance processional Dat Black Mermaid Man Lady, Azealia Banks's Mermaid Balls, & the life of late swimmer Whitney Houston. This song is dedicated to all of those of us who lived black & queer by the Bay, whose reflection is always looking for the Pacific; & especially that deepsea drinker at Mango, who I've never seen again & never forgotten.

FOUR

IT'S A PARTY

Dontcha wanna dance, say you wanna dance—with somebody who loves me . . . Chandeliers glanced glittering lights off sequined gowns and décolleté, Kardashians and former child stars smiled brightly for cameras as *the* premiere music industry party of the year went on as scheduled on February 11, 2011. Despite speculation the event would be cancelled, Clive Davis's thirty-seventh annual pre-Grammys party kicked off that night as planned at the Beverly Hilton. An image of Whitney Houston—standing center stage with arms outspread, face lifted ecstatically to the sky—projected onto screens behind the music mogul as he ascended to the podium to address guests. "By now you have all learned of the unspeakably tragic news of our beloved Whitney's passing," he began, tapping himself on the chest to indicate the heaviness of his heart. "Whitney was a beautiful person and a talent beyond compare," he eulogized. "She graced this stage with her regal presence and gave so many memorable performances here over the years. Simply put, Whitney would have wanted the music to go on, and her family asked that we carry on."[1] Davis asked partygoers to observe a moment of silence honoring the singer and the room fell into a deep hush. Then, announcing the night's festivities would be dedicated to Whitney, Davis pronounced: "And now, on with the music." Performers offering tributes included a beautiful, reverent Alicia Keys, who invited guests to sing with her: "Whitney, ooh oh oh oh oh—tell you—no one can get in the way of what we feel for *you*."[2]

Four floors up, in suite 434, Whitney's body remained in the room where she'd been found that afternoon. At 3:50 her assistant, Mary Jones, discovered her employer unconscious in the bathtub, face down as if her head slid on the back of the tub. Submerged in a foot of hot water, the singer was surrounded by a menagerie of pill bottles; on the counter, a small spoon with white powder and a mirror with white residue lingered. Six weeks later, an autopsy found that Whitney used cocaine "just probably immediately prior" to drowning and determined her death an accidental drowning with contributing factors of atherosclerotic heart disease and cocaine use.[3] When consulted about the coroner's report, UCLA's Dr. Michael Fishbein speculated what Ms. Houston's final moments might have entailed. "The immediate effect of cocaine is that it interferes with the electrical system of the heart," Fishbein explained. "An analogy might be a swimming pool pump. You can have a perfectly good pump, but if you cut the electrical cord, the pump stops working. If the heart stops pumping blood, all the organs are deprived of oxygen. The tissue dies and the person dies."[4]

During the pre-Grammys week that Whitney spent at the Beverly Hilton, the singer surrounded herself with water. She turned heads wandering through the hotel perpetually wet as a mermaid, hair dripping onto mismatched clothes. She was a fixture at the pool, where mornings found her swimming, lounging, and ordering drinks. With surprise, guests noticed the forty-eight-year-old doing poolside handstands, enjoying her newly returned stamina. "I started back swimming," she told former musical director Rickey Minor. "Look at the tone. And I'm getting my wind back."[5] Two days before her death, when she crashed E! News' interview with Clive Davis, Brandy, and Monica, Whitney flitted on screen with sopping hair and greeted interviewees with cheery hugs and kisses. Monica asked playfully why the diva was once again wet, and Houston replied sunnily in her lilting, now-husky voice: "I went swimming. I do two hours a day. Two hours a day, I have to."[6] When guests watched her swimming in the ten-foot-deep, Olympic-sized Aqua Star pool on the morning of February 11, who would have guessed she would drown in a shallow bathtub that afternoon?

The last decade of Whitney's life found the Prom Queen of Soul tangled in exploitatively public struggles with drug and alcohol addiction. "Now I'll grant you, I partied," Whitney admitted in her infamous 2002 interview with Diane Sawyer—meaning (she explained) she liked to get high on cocaine, marijuana, pills, and alcohol.[7] After interventions staged by mentor Davis and mother

Cissy, the singer entered elite rehab facilities and worked with a sober coach. But her sobriety ebbed as consistently as tides. Meditating on spirituality and addiction, Richard Rohr likens recovery to learning to breathe underwater. No individual can stop the "drowning waters" of addiction from engulfing her, he writes, but "we must at least see our reality for what it is, seek to properly detach from it, and build a coral castle and learn to live under water."[8] Working the twelve steps builds the castle, he continues the metaphor, while trusting in spirit guides the drowning to return to breath. "Only those who have tried to breathe under water really know how important breathing really is," Rohr reflects.[9] But try as she might, Whitney never learned to breathe underwater. Try as she might, Whitney drowned.

Why did such an unfathomably wealthy, talented artist—a woman gifted with the voice and beauty of a siren—need to escape so completely, deeply into *partying*? Pressures of the music industry? An unhealthy marriage to recording artist Bobby Brown? Some speculated that Whitney's disintegration had less to do with the relationships that fame brought her than those it cost her. A week after her death, LGBT activist Peter Tatchell published an article leadingly titled: "Whitney's REAL Tragedy Was Giving Up Her Greatest Love of All—Her Female Partner Robyn Crawford." Tatchell met Whitney and Robyn—often referred to in the press as the singer's "roommate" or "assistant"—at an HIV vigil in 1991. Remembering the pair as "madly in love . . . a gorgeous couple and so happy together," he muses: "Whitney was happiest and at the peak of her career when she was with Robyn. Sadly . . . she was fearful of the effects that lesbian rumours might have on her family, reputation and career. Eventually she succumbed. The result? A surprise marriage to Bobby Brown."[10] He invites readers to sympathize with Whitney's loss and self-medication: "Giving up Robyn—they'd been inseparable for years—must have been emotionally traumatic. Whitney's life started going downhill soon afterwards. . . . She went on drink-and-drug binges—evidence of a troubled personal life and much unhappiness. It seems likely that the split with Robyn contributed to her substance abuse and decline."[11]

. . . *With somebody who loves me.* Black women who love women grapple with addiction at rates up to three times those of their straight sisters, studies suggest; and unlike those of white lesbian counterparts, their rates of drug and alcohol dependence don't decrease with age. In *Amazon Spirit: Daily Meditations for Lesbians in Recovery*, Eleanor Nealy remarks that growing up lesbian—especially "Black, Latina, poor, or differently-abled" and lesbian—means standing outside "the circle of this society's definition of acceptable women," as Audre Lorde puts it. "Our addiction helped us learn to survive," Nealy continues. "It enabled us to tolerate living on the margins. It helped us push aside the feelings of exclusion, rejection, and abnormality. Whether we used drugs, alcohol, food, or sex, we found it easier to survive."[12] After the singer's death, Robyn Crawford penned a eulogy to her beloved Whitney that suggests the pop princess partied to survive, too. "She was working hard to keep herself together, and I think she felt that if she admitted any feeling of sadness or weakness she would crumble," Robyn remembers. "One time, back when we were young, we were out, we were partying, and I said, 'Listen, I have to go. I'm tired. I can't make it.' And she looked at me with her eyes wide and said, 'I've *got* to make it.'"[13] Robyn's tribute concludes: "She *was* the action, for such a long time. She's out of the action now. I hope she can finally rest."[14] Yes, after all the hours of swimming, singing, partying at her final pre-Grammys celebration, Whitney rested in her bathtub. And in the ballroom downstairs, the music went on.

Whitney, Prom Queen of Soul, both survived and died performing a black queer gender we don't often stop to think about carefully enough: the siren-like figure of the party queen. We all know her, high as a kite and bright until dawn, turning the club into a sacred blaze of light that crests and falls like full moon into morning. But who loves the party queen in the meshes of the afternoon; who watches her as she takes care of herself? Yes, partying, addiction, and healing are daily, underdiscussed facets of queer black women's lives—lives undertaken in the absence of any societal investment in our sobriety or healthy substance use. Where do we go to explore and refigure the possibilities and dangers of "partying" for black lesbian, bisexual, and transwomen? Since there's nowhere on land that's safe for the party queen, she might as well dive underwater in search of mermaids. Might as well seek out the deep-plunging, ever-resurfacing Lasirenn and, finally, dance with somebody who loves us.

I need all my mermaids on stage. But only Ariels; we don't need no Ursulas![15] Welcome to the vogue ball under the sea: Azealia Banks's sold-out Mermaid Ball at Manhattan's Bowery Ballroom, June 3, 2012. The room is swirling with sequins, fins, and gold bustiers, fluorescent octopus sculptures and crab-shaped balloons, blue cotton candy and seapunk trap beats. *Yaaass*, aquababes! Just after midnight MC Jack Mizrahi calls the night's mermaids to the stage for the $1,000 costume/voguing contest—mermaid realness—and surrounded by snaps, dips, and iridescent fins the bubble-blowing merqueen Bubblina is crowned winner with tiara and roses. Finally, at 1:00 AM the party's star takes the stage. "Banks entered her ball as any semi-aquatic celebutante would," commented *Rolling Stone*'s Matthew Trammel, "flanked on either side by her girls, and wearing nothing but seashells, jewels, some well-placed pasties and her milky, mischievous smile."[16] Rocking long green hair, a bare left breast, and navy and salmon translucent spandex, she greets her hometown crowd with love and the questions of the summer: "Who's already drunk? Who's already high? Who's fucking tonight?"[17]

If you ask Azealia she'll tell you that partying—alcohol, drugs, and sex—can be an art, one of the arts that brings her to the stage tonight. Drugs and orgasms massage her creativity, she tells *Billboard*; she does her best writing in the middle of the night fueled by wine, weed, and masturbation.[18] And like any other art, they open space for emotional and spiritual growth. Azealia started partying after breaking up with a controlling boyfriend she met when she was seventeen and he was forty-three. "Once we broke up, I went into this deep, deep depression. I was doing a lot of drugs," she tells *NME* magazine. "And I went to a lot of places with myself. I saw a lot of things in other realms. My circuitry started to switch. In a good way. Those things, they knock the crust off your third eye. Just like, wooooo—you can see ghosts and shit."[19] Ghosts and shit: haints, spirits, and brown-skinned, green-haired mermaids?

Glittering hard like a hallucination, the Mermaid Ball at the Bowery is the beginning of Azealia's year of *Fantasea*: the new mixtape whose release she's promoting that night as she performs its lead single, "Jumanji." The following week she releases a second single, "Aquababe"—"livin' lavish, aqua-fancy, she get it, splash it," she sings—then on July 9, her mixtape's cover art surfaces on Twitter.[20] Above the pink, curvy title, it features a richly colored version of the mermaid who took the stage in June: a chocolate-skinned siren with long, green hair mixing into the darker waves of the water she rides, her pink tail curving upward and her face and bare-chested, seastar-pastied torso spotlit by a deep brown (third?) eye shining in the purple night sky. For spiritualists like Azaelia—"always outside picking up rocks and sticks and doing weird witch-craft stuff," divination and candle spells[21]—this *Fantasea* mermaid might look a lot like Lasirenn: "Ezili of the waters," the Haitian mermaid who lives and sings in rivers, lakes, and oceans. Brown-skinned and pink-tailed, this marine, riverine lwa is known for her long shiny hair, which she spends hours combing as she gazes in her mirror and floats alongside sister water spirits Labalenn and Lurucan. She lives at the bottom of the water in a palace decked with shipwrecked gold—*livin' lavish*—and makes her own music, sending songs to the surface to draw women to her side—*she get it, splash it, then dip it back in.*

And if you want to get drunk, high, or freaky on a Sunday night, Lasirenn is the lwa who can ride along with you. Lwa of the watery unconscious, she's also the lwa of altered consciousness. She's the spirit who swims with you as you move beyond the limits of your rational self to "consciousness of the intuitive world," as you do what you need to, to "let go of the mundane world around you and plumb your own inner seas of unconsciousness and talents"[22]— spending the night drinking, smoking, masturbating, and writing, maybe. This Vodoun Ariel can take you to physical and psychic places you've never been before—but she can also pull you back. She's the lwa of the "lighter blue domain" of surface waters, not the "deep, deep depths" of rock bottom.[23] Like the twin fish of the Pisces symbol, Lasirenn will take you down—underwater, under possession, under the influence—but she'll bring you back up: back to the shore, back to yourself, back to sobriety. She'll open the night sky like a bright moon-eye and help you sway in that place where you're neither stuck on ground nor drowning in undertow, in that liminal, semiaquatic space where you can breathe underwater and let your consciousness expand. So all my mermaids, all my Ariels and Ursulas, all my aquababes: who's drinking tonight, who's partying, who's fucking?

———

"At the bottom of the Ocean and sometimes at the Juke Joint and in the Sky and swamp."[24] This is the setting that Sharon Bridgforth gives her performance processional *Dat Black Mermaid Man Lady*, a jazz/blues/spoken lyric celebration first workshopped in 2013 with support from the New Dramatists Creativity Fund. *Black Mermaid*'s characters are two gender-fluid singers who perform as conarrators, moving with layered sound, movement, and lyrics to "sing, move, tell stories, call the audience to process, chant, holler back, build altars—celebrate life."[25] They sing/tell the stories of HoneyPot, Miss Kitty, and dat Black Mermaid man lady: rural Louisiana jazz women, gender queers, and healers who navigate lives of woman-izing, piano playing, knife carrying, gambling, drinking, chicken frying, and conjuring as they train a next-generation healer. "By the end of the piece," Bridgforth explains, "we discover that the narrator is the next gen-eration healer and that himshe has been conjuring herhe existence into being through the telling of Dat Black Mermaid Man Lady."[26] Daniel Alexander Jones and Kelly Erin Sloane riffed the script into song in the inaugural New Dramatists readings September 16–20, 2013, and October 6–10, 2014, which Bridgforth tagged "Mermaids in NYC."[27]

At the bottom of the Ocean, moving through with music and breath: girl, Sha-ron's taking you home. Under seawater and swampwater are ancestral space for Bridgforth, whose father's people are from watery Algiers, a New Orleans community on the Mississippi's west bank. This below-sea-level neigh-borhood, submerged under waist-high flood waters (as it often is) the fall Dat Black Mermaid Man Lady was first workshopped, is revered and feared as New Orleans's cradle/crucible of spirit and music—of Voodoo, Hoodoo, and jazz. Underwater is Bridgforth's spiritual homeplace, too. A creative spiritualist/healer who calls herself a "Transdenominational practitioner of Jazz," Bridgforth was initiated in 2015 as a priest of Yemoja, Yoruba mermaid spirit of the ocean and West African antecedent of Lasirenn.[28] For many years she also practiced Buddhism, a tradition that imagines human beings afloat in an "ocean of existence" where all things are connected; where the Udana likens those who have attained understanding to "great sea monsters who roam the endless depths, who sport and play in an ocean without any shore."[29] Like floodwaters from the Gulf, like Yemoja Asesu, like any mermaid worth hisher salt, Bridgforth takes everyone assembled for Mermaid some-where in the ocean without shore.

And sometimes at the Juke Joint, drinking and hip-swaying and carrying on: girl, Sharon taking you out. In the partying, fighting, fucking, elevating uni-verse of Bridgforth's performances, the juke joint is home and spiritual space too. Homespace for bulldaggers and sissies, an everynight space where, as Omi Jones writes of Bridgforth's work, black "queer is the norm";[30] where long-nail girls, trouser womy'n, himshes, and any, every black gender and sexuality can both party and be at rest. Ritual space for conjuring new pos-sibilities for black folk and black love, a music- and dance-driven space that Matt Richardson likens to Vodoun ritual.[31] What lubricates everyone here so that homecoming and spirit-raising can happen is partying—using alcohol, drugs, and sex to temporarily reconfigure the senses of the long-nail girls and trouser womy'n who come in search of joy. As Alison Reed writes of Bridgforth's *love conjure/blues*, "getting drunk or high" is part of "calling forth the ritual space of the bar, or the juke joint, as a potential 'site for transformation. . . . Our senses combust so that we release.' . . . The bar ritual free[s] the senses and loosen[s] gender conventions."[32] But as Reed also notes, "what is toxic can be tonic" and vice versa, and gin and tonic can become toxic in Bridgforth's work.[33] Addiction weaves through her juke joints, with *love conjure/blues'* Lushy Boudreaux losing her lover because of her alcoholism, HoneyPot and them earning the title of "professional drinkers," and gambling addict Miss Kitty betting on cards long after hisher luck runs out.

Underwater and above land, sky and swamp, drunk and sober, addicted and recovering, man and lady: Bridgforth's juke joint offers us conceptual space open enough to hold all these in relation rather than in tension, an oceanically broad, oceanically fluid space where contradictions dissolve so new possibilities can emerge. A recovering alcoholic, Bridgforth neither denies the pleasure and possibility that drinking offers black queer partiers nor romanticizes addiction in her work. Instead, she conjures the Black Mermaid man lady as an apparition who offers addicts ways to reintegrate those parts of themselves they've split off from. Hisher ways are routed in the *fact* that tail-chasing, cross-dressing, watermelon-eating black queers are an image of the divine; and that if we recognize our divinity, maybe we don't always need a drink or a bet to elevate our spirits. In their study "Toward a Grounded Theory of Lesbians' Recovery from Addiction," Connie Matthews, Peggy Lorah, and Jaime Fenton underscore "the importance of self-acceptance, both as a lesbian and as a recovering alcoholic and/or addict" as "fundamental to . . . ongoing recovery."[34] Self-acceptance, they elaborate, is developed and maintained by three processes: *learning to recover*, acquiring the tools for sobriety offered by Alcoholics Anonymous (AA), therapy, and self-care; *relationships with other people*, including with friendship networks and family of origin; and *relationship with something bigger than self*, with a higher power.[35] *Dat Black Mermaid Man Lady* offers images of what all these facets of self-acceptance look like for Voodoo-, spirit-, and jazz-soaked black Louisiana queers, fleshing them out not through psychological realism but through metaphor and myth. And what self-acceptance looks like is a Black Mermaid man lady, the truest myth of the black Atlantic.

Ohh oh oh, I'm your baby tonight. On the sweaty, waning-moonlit Saturday night of August 9, 2003, hundreds of attendees pressed eagerly into Atlanta's Taboo Bistro & Bar to celebrate Whitney Houston's fortieth birthday. Forty candles and more blazed at this white linen party open to the singer's fans, who enjoyed gazing at birthday cakes decorated to represent musical themes from throughout her twenty-year-career. White linen and lace cascaded throughout the club, set off by ribbons and flowers in Whitney's favorite colors, fuschia and purple, and at 1:00 AM—an hour after her birthday ended—the guest of honor arrived in a white-and-purple outfit to match. The joyfully awaited diva entered looking hot, unsteady, and disoriented. "She was stressed out," fan Rakaia Jackson noted. "She was attempting to get her jacket off, and she could barely do that."[36] The party broke up two hours after the guest of honor's confused arrival, and the next day party publicist Donald Fields remarked cryptically to the *Atlanta Journal and Constitution*, "It's safe to say we're all exhausted today."[37]

Six months later Whitney entered rehab for the first time. She checked out of the undisclosed facility after five days, announcing she was "continuing the prescribed treatment program" at home.[38] As she did, mother Cissy organized a massively attended vigil against substance abuse—which became a Prayer Vigil for Whitney Houston—at Harlem's Abyssinian Baptist Church. Less than a year later a court order sent the singer back to rehab, this time at the Crossroads Centre in St. John's, Antigua. Promotional photos of the elite treatment center picture its facilities cradled by blue skies and bluer waters, residents welcome to enjoy two calm, palm-shaded swimming pools and a panorama of magnificent marine views. "Far away from the distractions and demands of everyday life," one seaside image promises, "the facility overlooks the tranquil blue waters of Willoughby Bay, the largest bay on the island."[39] Whitney knew these blue waters well. She first visited Antigua in the late 1980s, when she "just wanted to relax and go somewhere she could meditate and be inspired."[40] Coco Beach, Mamora Bay, Galleon Bay, Pigeon Point Beach, Rendezvous Bay: TiTi Thwaites, the driver who ferried her from one beach to another to swim, sail, and lounge, remembers her "love of the water and sense of adventure," her feeling of freedom on the island.[41] "Very homey, very earthy, very untouched," she described Antigua to *Ebony* magazine in 1994, soon after purchasing a house overlooking the water on the south coast's Shirley Heights.[42] When Whitney told Oprah that she once contemplated "going to an island and having a fruit stand . . . me and my daughter, living on a little beach on a little island," was Antigua the island she imagined?[43] Was this where she fantasized she and daughter Bobbi Kristina—herself an avid swimmer—could live the peaceful life of mermaids? *My fantasy, I'm your baby tonight . . .*

Whitney left Crossroads after completing the standard twenty-nine-day treatment. She entered outpatient programs twice more over the next five years "to support her longstanding recovery process."[44] After her death, many blamed Whitney's extraordinary life and career for her "failure" to remain sober. "Why did Whitney fail rehab? Too much talent," the title of an article by *New York Times* writer Charles Duhigg asked and answered. His think piece outlined the common view that Whitney's relapses were fueled by her inability to participate in the group recovery processes integral to programs like Alcoholics Anonymous. "What Ms. Houston couldn't do—because her life catered to the belief that she was peerless, the star of the show, an incomparable diva—was find a group of peers whom she could compare herself to, and believe that *if they can struggle and persevere, so can I*," he opined.[45] But in fact, Whitney's need for multiple rehab stints was in no way extraordinary but painfully ordinary. Only 40 percent of clients who entered Crossroads during the time of Whitney's stay were still abstinent a year later, and sobriety rates for less exclusive centers were lower. "Addiction is a chronic disease," Hazelden Foundation rehabilitation facility director Dr. Omar Manejwala explained to CBS when consulted about Whitney shortly after her death. "Relapse is very common. Evidence suggests that the majority of the people need repeated treatment. If the initial treatment is only partially effective, we don't call that a failure."[46] Relapse rates are higher for women who love women, too. "The negative effects of internalized homonegativity/heterosexism can be complex and when not dealt with can lead to a cycle of relapse," Minnesota's Pride Institute documents, and the Recovery Connection explains: "Without specific gay-friendly treatment components, an LGBT person is at increased risk of leaving treatment without addressing the underlying issues relating to substance abuse and addiction."[47] Ever-regal, Whitney may have gone in and out of rehab like any diva, why not? But she also went in and out of rehab like any black queer, unable to find a recovery program—seaside, poolside, or outside—that could teach her how to breathe in the particular, black Atlantic waters that were her home.

⟡

And *this* is what happens when an aqua-fancy mermaid leaves home and crosses the black Atlantic. On October 13, 2012, Azealia Banks brought her Mermaid Ball to a sold-out venue in London where the wine was free, the merfolk wore pearls and starfish, and the sharks were real. Because this Ball was hosted at the Sea Life London Aquarium, and—"packed in like sardines in a tin ('this fish is brined, brined!') and with the temperature not-so-steadily increasing"[48]—the crowd swayed madly between fish tanks to Azealia's performance of *Fantasea*. Situated on the South Bank of the Thames, the Sea Life Centre houses one of Europe's largest collections of aquatic life with the mission to educate visitors about "the world of marine creatures they meet" and "to raise awareness of marine conservation issues and threats to our sea creatures."[49] So watch and learn, public pool mermaids: this is an educational under-the-sea Ball. What do you learn about jellyfish when you watch them after a few glasses of Azealia's wine and a few verses of "Aquababe"?

Azealia's always there to school haters, yes, but she's all about education, too. She's vocal about what kind of formal education youth need. "Young black kids should have their own special curriculum that doesn't start from the boat ride over from Africa," she tells *Playboy*. "All you know as a black kid is we came over here on a boat, we didn't have anything and we still don't have anything. But what was happening in Africa? What culture were we pulled away from? That information is vital to the survival of a young black soul."[50] And she's just as public about the kind of occult training that black folk need. Her Twitter asserts: "black people are naturally born SEERS, DIVINERS, WITCHES AND WIZARDS. we have REAL supernatural powers, and the sooner we ALL learn to cultivate them and access the them, the sooner we can REALLY fix shit."[51] Learning to work *this* kind of science can (she says) come from books, nature walks, and yes, partying. Not only does she learn about "ghosts and shit" from taking drugs, but she made sure she learned *how* to take drugs to open her third eye. "She started reading '60s acid guru Dr. Timothy Leary's psychedelic manifestos, and grazing the internet for the psychedelic experiments of Alexander Shulgin— the legendary psychonaut who first publicised MDMA as a recreational drug,"

Gavin Haynes reports in his interview with her. And after that self-study, "Psychedelics opened her up. She went deep . . ."[52]

Now Azealia's trying to educate her fans, too. She offers them "feminist proverbs": "Mermaids only swim underwater, because under the water, the fish don't stink."[53] And she encourages self-examination: "Do you wanna be a public pool bitch or do you wanna be a mermaid? #askyourself."[54] Unlike European sirens, black mermaids are teachers—teachers who may call you out and snatch you up to teach you something you weren't planning on learning in the first place. Lasirenn does this every day. Any woman walking by the water—especially if she's navigating difficult times—can be pulled underwater by this Ezili, where she'll spend three restorative days and nights with her and receive (literally and figuratively) in-depth instruction in healing arts. "Legend says that if you see Lasirèn, you're about to receive a profound and sudden insight, one that might change your life," Skye Alexander writes in her study of mermaids. "Like other mermaids, Lasirèn likes to grab humans and take them to her underwater home—a luxurious palace decked out with treasure from sunken ships. But unlike most mermaids, she prefers to capture women. Some drown, but those who return have learned from Lasirèn how to heal and see into the future."[55] Lasirenn will ask her own version of Azealia's question—*do you wanna be a public pool bitch or do you wanna be a mermaid?*—and if she makes the right choice, the water-dweller returns to land after three days. She comes back with the knowledge she needs to be a priestess of Lasirenn, a graduate of initiation anba dlo (underwater): meaning, her time with Lasirenn entitles her to work as a manbo without the time- and money-consuming rites usually required to enter the priesthood. Watch and learn, public pool mermaids.

What are those three days underwater like? Anba dlo initiates can never tell you. But maybe they're something like a *trip*: like a vacation, yes, but also a like a psychedelic experience. In their classic treatise *The Psychedelic Experience*, Timothy Leary and Ralph Metzner define that titular phrase as "a journey to new realms of consciousness" that can "occur in a variety of ways: sensory deprivation, yoga exercises, disciplined meditation, religious or aesthetic ecstasies, or . . . through the ingestion of psychedelic drugs."[56] The psychedelic experience, they explain, has three phases. In the first, you float unmoored from external reality—"beyond words, beyond space-time, beyond self"[57]—like the first moments of initiation anba dlo, when you drift down through waters suspended in the oceanic, unaware of time passing on land. Then you move into the longest phase, where you bathe in "sharp exquisite clarity" of new, otherworldly visions . . . subaquatic visions of Lasirenn's castle, gold, and esoteric revelations, reflecting back to you lavish, expanded possibilities for who you can become.[58] The final stage is the return to everyday reality and self, to land and who you now are. *Livin' lavish, she get it, splash it, then dip it back in.* That final stage is the hardest part of Lasirenn's educational journey. Because when you're in Lasirenn's castle no one needs to teach you how to swim without stopping or breathe air underwater; magically, these things happen on their own. But when your mermaid days are over and the high of ocean depths dissolves, you need to return to terrestrial life armed with tools for surviving the everyday—tools that make life liveable enough so that you don't jump back underwater to stay. Lasirenn is the aquatic teacher who grounds you with those skills. This is why you come back to land with a miraculous knowledge of healing arts, so you can heal the pain of being present to life on land; and with the ability to see the future, so you know you can make it okay. So, like Azealia, you can believe you're "never gonna end up a broke bitch."[59]

<hr/>

Now, this is how dat Black Mermaid man lady comes to visit partyers in their dreams. In *Dat Black Mermaid Man Lady*'s opening sequence, traveling jazz singer and fearsome femme HoneyPot is causing the ruination of folks' nerves and "busting up our good gotdangit time" by sending her right-hand bulldagger Duck to shoot up the juke joint every time someone crosses her.[60] She busts in one evening targeting Mo Pretty, a singer who's taken to impersonating her on the road. Before Duck unleashes her full fury, David, a "teeninchy" man with "a heart like Goliath" who's had too much to drink—and has Mo Pretty hidden in his bed—steps up and "decide to open a ministry up on honeypot in de joint."[61] With everyone hanging on his words, he describes the Black Mermaid man lady he sees in his dreams: "black black like a most beautiful night sky. eyes shining like stars. skirt deep blue/dark like skin. hair gots a thousand fishes and pearls hanging all the way down past behind. this man lady . . . take my hand pull me down down down to the bottom of the ocean. at the very bottom. i see things. like. down there is all them people you donn killeded."[62] Maybe, he continues, the mermaid man lady shows him their faces to let him know that none of them deserved to be taken down—and he's sure Mo Pretty doesn't, either. "Gotdangit honeypot," he finally shouts, "just keep yo black ass up on the band stand. Slay peoples with yo music. That the treasure. It yo treasure to give. It ours to receive. And therebythroughinandwhatnot what you give circle back to you. It your treasure posed to circulate you know. not your rage."[63] HoneyPot breaks down, cries, and embraces Mo Pretty, whom she invites to join her traveling act. "And now. us," the narrators sing, "we all swear when we rest. that black mermaid man lady with blue back dress and fishes and fishes and pearls come by our dreams. leave trails of sand and sea weed. wet in the night."[64]

HoneyPot and her crew are "professional drinkers" who "keep a level of it in the system at all times. sippy cup always full and available."[65] In Bridgforth's *delta danti*, she also collects a swarm of men and women lovers who enjoy her honey like bees. But her drinking and sexing aren't what call for an intervention in *Dat Black Mermaid*; it's the violence that accompanies them. The gun-spraying, knife-throwing violence that HoneyPot wields acts as a jarring metaphor for the violence of addiction—a disease defined not (just) by someone's excesses of drink, drugs, or sex but by the uncontrollable destructiveness that accompanies those excesses. Someone you love blowing through your shared space, sometimes when you expect it but most times when you don't, tearing up everything around them and not thinking about consequences: isn't that what it's like to live with an addict in your life? And could all addicts become killers, potentially? In his reflections on iboga, the sacred rootbark used for curing addictions in Gabon, Cameroon, and Congo, Vincent Ravalec posits that the karma he incurred as an addict is more problematic than that of a one-time murderer. "I was killing someone bit by bit during thirteen years and that someone was me," he admits.[66] Recovery, then, is nothing less than preventing murder—nothing less than resisting the reign of violence that's "busting up our good gotdangit time . . . causing the ruination of our nerves."

Teeninchy, drunk, sex-struck, and sanctified, David comes to set off HoneyPot's process of *learning to recover*. Her education is not only a group practice but a community ritual, a backwaters Louisiana echo of an AA meeting, *and* an iboga initiation ceremony. The juke joint ritual proceeds through call and response—"everbody" in the joint answers David's proclamations with shouts of YEAH!—and Honeypot's healing can only take place through communal support: "something break. / we feel it / we hold it open for she. / honeypot get in it / sing."[67] As HoneyPot sings, "david pour he spirits on ground / . . . david pour he spirits on honeypot head / . . . david spit he spirits round de joint . . . david say / it donn."[68] This healing through community Africanizes one of the central teachings of AA: that while "isolation and alienation" are symptoms of addiction, "recovery is dependent on our ability to recognize our need for connectedness with others."[69] At the same time, it Americanizes the three-day iboga ritual practiced by Central African Bwiti, a ceremony undertaken to break addictions and other chronic diseases. In this community healing, practitioners envelop initiates in song, dance, and cleansing as they ingest the psychoactive iboga, known to reset the brain to its preaddicted state; initiates symbolically die as addicts—"break"—and are reborn to new possibilities—"get in it / sing."[70] In all of these ceremonies, participants seal their work by joining in a circle that represents the unbrokenness of community: to intone the Serenity Prayer in AA, dance counterclockwise around initiates in the Bwiti initiation, or sing *circulate, lawd circulate* while HoneyPot cries in the juke joint.

What "resets" HoneyPot in the juke joint are neither twelve steps nor a sacred root, though, but music. *Rest, i guess i'll let it rest . . . yes, i'll let it rest . . . yes lawd, let it rest,* she sings into the space the community holds open for her.[71] HoneyPot's songs serve as "tools for conjuring," bridges between the material and the spiritual world that perform the ongoing work of rewiring the senses.[72] The songs that circulate around and through HoneyPot engage her body and spirit in the same time and place, moving to heal them not as a duality but as a unity. Similarly, music is sung and played continuously throughout the three-day iboga ceremony not for aesthetics but for efficacy, as an integral part of the "reset" that the ritual seeks to effect. Music's work "is in large part vibratory. The mogongo and the harp are not only playing music, they are transmitting information, and often it's active information, even interactive."[73] Writing on musicality and the jazz aesthetic, Omi Jones links awareness of "pulse and vibration in language" to a similar metaphysics of song in Yorubaland.[74] "This attention to sound as vibration and animating force is the principle behind àfǫṣẹ, the ability of the word to manifest reality," she writes. "Words—when sounded—are a very particular making, are their own distinctive kinesis as the words transform the physical plane and are action."[75] The time/space where this action occurs is what jazz calls *the break*: a transitional passage when the song's prevailing texture is interrupted and makes way for solo improvisation, "the necessary rupture for something new to spring forth."

And the song HoneyPot shares with folks after her break *does* change the physical plane in this performance processional, ushering the materiality and spirituality of water into the joint and bringing everyone there to the bottom of the ocean. "yes lawd / rest lawd / yes lawd / rest lawd / rest in the night / come what might / jus / rest," the narrators sing as the story of Honey-Pot and David comes to a close.[76] Sibilant s returns syllable after syllable like the rush of waves, resonant liquids r and l string together in the watery sounds of *rest lawd*, intoning a sonic imprint of the arrival of dat Black Mermaid man lady in everyone's dreams. They go to sleep and wake with sand, saltwater, and seaweed in their beds, while HoneyPot, Duck, Mo Pretty, and David all travel "on da road / slaying the peoples / with they songs. together."[77]

I'm every woman, oh OH oh! If you're winding your way up North Gate Road through five acres of woods in Mendham Township, dressed in "summer vogue" and following skyward-bound purple balloons to Whitney Houston's twenty-sixth birthday barbecue, then you know you're *somebody*. Right? Then you're one of 450 people who received a glossy, poster-sized invitation with the pop princess's glowing image on its front, announcing: "You are cordially invited to attend an outdoor barbecue in honor of Whitney Houston's twenty-sixth birthday, Saturday, August 12th from 4 P.M. Dinner served at 8:30 . . . Tennis and swimming available."[78] If you bring your designer swimsuit and take up the hostess's offer of swimming, you'll have the pleasure of lounging the late afternoon away in what reporter Roger Friedman calls "an oasis in Whitney Houston's backyard: a swimming pool the size of a small manmade lake."[79] When working with designers to customize her estate in 1987, she explained, "They said, Whitney do you want a nice oval pool? I said, Listen, I want to swim. I don't want to play. I want an Olympic size swimming pool with my initials on the bottom of it."[80] After floating over the curving, entwined *WH* lightening the blue pool floor, happily sunkissed, you'll drift toward three white tents draped with fuschia curtains and brimming with purple and cream balloons, just in time to watch Whitney and new friend Bobby Brown start the party dancing to the remix of "I Wanna Dance with Somebody." And you can't miss the camera-catching moment when, in a blaze of sparklers, servers wheel in two cakes—carrot, to symbolize the carats of her so-many gold records—topped with frosting replicas of her album covers and the assembled *who's who* of black music sings a joyous happy birthday. "I loved this party! I mean, I had a ball. Everybody that came had a good time, I hope," she tells reporters. Asked why she threw such a bash for her twenty-sixth birthday, she smiles radiantly. "Because I made it past 25," she proclaims, clapping gold-bangled hands above her head in celebration.[81]

"Just peace and love, for everybody. That's all I want," she laughed when *The Insider* asked for birthday wishes.[82] When Whitney moved into the Mendham estate, family and friends imagined this five-bedroom mansion—redesigned to melt into circular living spaces, airy ceilings, generous windows, and soft pastels—would become space to cultivate just that. "I was thrilled with [Whitney's] new house and hoped it would be a place where she could one day settle down and start a family," mother Cissy remembers.[83] At eighteen, Whitney moved into a small apartment with Robyn in nearby Woodbridge. Enjoying money coming in from Whitney's modeling and Robyn's basketball scholarship, the pair crossed to Manhattan to spend time in the few dyke bars where black women drank and talked trash—the Duchess, the Cubby Hole. "Whitney Houston always looked like a 'femme': coiffed and sleek, a Jersey girl who could be tough," writer and bar-goer Hilton Als remembers, "but she had an even butcher personal assistant"—Robyn—"who could deal, if it came to that."[84] The twosome met as camp counselors in East Orange and, like sister-lovers Lasirenn and Labalenn, quickly "got to the point where you couldn't tell where one ended and the other began," a camp-goer remembers. "When they were together, they'd act as if no one else was even in the room. They had their own world."[85]

Whitney's publicist Ken Reynolds was one of many music insiders to reflect that "Robyn was very much a protector, Whitney's guardian."[86] During his slow dance with Whitney at her twenty-sixth birthday festivities, producer Narada Michael Walden—noticing shades of stress and depression clinging to her even as she partied in her shiny white suit—mentioned an eighty-two-acre beachside resort in Hawai'i where she could go to recoup and reset. Robyn immediately made all arrangements for their ten-day trip to the Kona resort, where she fetched meals and did Whitney's bidding so the diva could "relax and look at the ocean."[87] "She was the *true* bodyguard," Walden muses.[88] And while she remained circumspect about their relationship, Whitney was open about the sweetness, love, and emotional security that living with Robyn brought her. "Robyn and I have been friends since we were kids. For so many years," she told Friedman as they sat by her pool. "I'd rather have a friend, somebody that likes and loves me for me. I'd rather have the companionship, someone I can trust. A lot of people like me 'cause I'm Whitney Houston, 'cause I have a big house. But intimacy is different . . ."[89]

Not everyone in Whitney's life was ready to celebrate her version of intimacy, though. "Thrilled" as she was about her daughter's move from Woodbridge to Mendham, Cissy "was less thrilled . . . when she invited Robyn to move into the Mendham estate with her."[90] The oil painting portrait of herself that she gave Whitney for her twenty-sixth birthday must have seemed to glower disapprovingly from the fireplace where it sat. The Houston matriarch was outspoken about her dislike of Robyn from the time "Nippy" (Whitney's family nickname) met her until after her daughter's death. "I had a bad feeling about that child from the first time I saw her," she declares in her memoir. "There was something about the way she carried herself, a kind of arrogance, that I didn't like. . . . She also seemed abrasive and unapologetic about that. While Nippy would usually bend over backward to get along with people—sometimes to a fault—Robyn had a strong, assertive personality and said exactly what she thought."[91] The butch protectiveness and swagger that impressed Als and Walden sat uncomfortably with Mrs. Houston. "As I would later learn," Cissy continues, "she was also gay, although that had nothing to do with why I didn't like her."[92] But when Oprah questioned the singer's mother about the above excerpt—"Would it have bothered you if your daughter, Whitney, was gay?"— she replied unequivocally: "Absolutely," she wouldn't have liked or condoned it "at all."[93] Whitney's bodyguard Kevin Ammons remembers Cissy and Robyn erupting into frequent, loud arguments over Robyn's attachment to Whitney, "who hated being in the middle, but . . . wasn't giving Robyn up for anything."[94] With so much family pressure piled onto so much public scrutiny, Whitney's ability to hold onto her alliance with Robyn "as long as she did is a testament to her strength in her difference," Als appreciates.[95]

I'm every woman, ha ha ha, my GIRL! For the first thirty-five years of her life, Cissy and Robyn were the most powerful women in Whitney's wide open, tightly closed world. They were her childhood and her young womanhood, her models for black wife-and-motherness and black dykeness, her first femme and her first butch. And if they could never, ever accept each other—then they couldn't really accept all parts of Whitney, either. So how could she? Cissy does remember one moment of alliance between herself and her daughter's companion. Not long before Whitney's twenty-sixth birthday bash, Robyn paid Cissy an unexpected visit. "She told me that Nippy was using drugs, which was news to me."[96] Robyn admitted that both she and Whitney had been using recreationally but that "Nippy likes it too much," that she was unable to stop and would stay high as long as there was a stash in the house.[97] "Now, I might not have liked certain things about Robyn, but I will say this: She cared a great deal for Nippy, and she wanted to protect her," Cissy acknowledges. "Nobody had the courage to come tell me that Nippy was getting into something that was bad for her— nobody except Robyn. She didn't have any kind of relationship with me, but she still came to me in person to try to help Nippy. I always respected Robyn for that."[98] Robyn knew a drowning swimmer when she saw one—and had a loud enough voice to shout when she saw Whitney couldn't keep breathing in the monogrammed, Olympic-sized waters she created for herself.

❧

I just want to thank everyone who came out, dressed up, and joined my little "fantasea."[99] On July 14, 2012, Azealia Banks's Mermaid Ball splashed down on Pacific shores, arriving at Hollywood's Fonda Theater in Los Angeles. And, yes, this Ball leaves much for partyers to fantasize about. "First sights upon walking into Azealia Banks' Mermaid Ball: Gigantic seahorse balloons, choreographed dancers 'reading' and 'voguing' and gyrating go-go girls wearing nothing but flesh-colored spandex and shimmering pasties," Brittany Graham remembers her pleasurable sensory overload in a *Vibe* review.[100] With seminude mermaids dancing provocatively in side boxes throughout the all-female lineup, Azealia's golden coast ball becomes the best kind of pussy fest. "Predominantly female, the event's roster of radically inventive and relatively new artists allowed the Mermaid Ball to function as both a celebration of second-wave 'girl power' as well as a showcase of the impressive talents of young women in hip hop and electronica," Kat Bee gushes in her writeup.[101] Whether it's literally high femme Brooke Candy bouncing across stage in platform tennis shoes or hoop-earringed hood girl Rye Rye rapping with blindfolded dancers behind her, maybe you're spinning fantasies about what you'd do if you got into bed with one of those sexy-ass performers. And Azealia, who loves to mix business with pleasure, just might be spinning some kind of fantasies herself.

Proud *Playboy* model Azealia is open and unabashed about the sexual creativity that's part of her partying. Months before her first Mermaid Ball she offhandedly came out as bisexual in an interview with the *New York Times*. The story reports: "Ms. Banks considers herself bisexual, but, she said, 'I'm not trying to be, like, the bisexual, the lesbian rapper. I don't live on other people's terms.'"[102] Azealia states more straightforwardly for *Billboard*: "I like sex."[103] She especially enjoys sleeping with her male security guards ("I am going to call my next record *Business and Pleasure*, because I'm always mixing the two") and her close female friends ("it's a proximity thing").[104] But while male lovers are easier for her to come by, she says, her sexuality remains female-centered. "Pussy is way more sacred than penis," her *Playboy* interview concludes pointedly.[105] Or, as she puts it in "Idle Delilah," "puss is deeper than the deep blue sea."[106]

Azealia closes her now-bicoastal Ball with its unaltering ritual: confetti and balloons rain from the ceiling to celebrate her performance of breakout club anthem "212," a song that spits verse on verse about her sexual deliciousness. "She wanna lick my plum in the evening . . . guess that cunt's getting eaten," the first verse brags, while the last verse tests "dude . . . you do eat poom, hun?"[107] Mermaids just come with that *good good*, with that extra sweetness in the black Atlantic—that fluid, wet sexuality that easily slips outside straight/lesbian binaries. You have to recognize "puss . . . deeper than the deep blue sea" to find Lasirenn, too; you have to sing for her male and female lovers when you're trying to call this mermaid. "I don't see Mistress Lasirenn, I ask Agwe Tawoyo for her. Lasirenn, we are here, we are watching for you," you begin, and end: "Oh Balenn! Oh call Sirenn! Oh there is no friend like Sirenn! I say: oh there is no friend like Balenn!" Another fishy femme who likes to mix business with pleasure, Lasirenn swims at the center of a divine maritime threesome. This water Ezili is "married" both to Agwe, male admiral of ocean currents, and Labalenn, "the dark, intuitive sister who swims below LaSiren's cool blue domain."[108] Part of the divine healing that Lasirenn brings black women is the ability to embrace whatever and whoever makes us wet, to accept all the complex, unexpected ways our desires work. Meditating on a prayer flag by Rudy Azor that depicts a luxuriously outspread, sparklingly orange-tailed, levelly three-headed mermaid, Ursula Szeles sees: "Azor's three-headed portrayal communicates visually the triple consciousness of black women-loving women. In other words, Azor's rendition of Lasirenn serves black women-loving-women's self-understanding as gay, black, and female. Triple consciousness is managed with guidance from this Afro-diasporic water spirit."[109]

The easy love of fish can confuse those who walk without this triple consciousness, and Azealia faces her share of biphobia and slut-shaming. Some listeners question her queer credentials: "Do you believe Angel Haze and Azealia Banks are queer women? . . . I don't think I've ever heard either address their like for women because from what I understand both are bisexual?" one tweet asks.[110] And not only the Twitterverse, but even Azealia's ex-lover has questioned the healthiness of her luxurious interest in sex: "He convinced me I was a sex addict because I wanted him to come to town," she recounts in an interview.[111] But Azealia remains clear that sex, too, opens her up to self-discovery; and that pussy-centered as she is, sex with men is an important part of that. "Not to get all deep and shit, but my dad died when I was 2," she tells Arye Dworken. "And there's always been this part of me that's super curious about men. Even when I was little, I was always getting in trouble for like, kissing boys. I've always been a very sexual person. When I started having sex, there was this piece of me there that I needed to unlock."[112] What if black women just need oceans of loving—from parents, friends, coworkers, selves, women, men—in order to unlock all of who we are, and some of that loving comes to us through sex? With her siren's song and her school of lovers human and divine, Lasirenn models the divinity of this deep blue openness to love and feeling. Oh there is no friend like Lasirenn, girl, no friend like one who opens herself to all of your loves and joins your fantasea.

———

And this is how dat Black Mermaid man lady brought home a sisterfriend, a riverine beauty who carries everyone to her ocean. One day HoneyPot's grandmother's older brother Ole Caney Sharp "sent for suga who sent for sweetie jr who sent for delroy's" until "let's just say word got passed to honeypot to come on home."[113] When she bursts into his living room and stares into her great-uncle's eyes, HoneyPot knows what he's called her to do: find his great-grandson Merrit, who "had done got lost up in da north. / parently / the boy heart got crushed / when he come to find that reports of that there promised land / was riddled with inflations. merrit got to chasing bad womens and the numbers steada he dreams. / then bad mens with guns got to chasing him."[114] HoneyPot travels to him and then, as her crew spreads false rumors that he's been killed in the streets, takes him back South disguised as a singer in her band. "Honeypot and dem / throwed merrit up in a dress and heels and wig and pearls and lipstick and such. / then they stood he ass center stage. to hide in plan site."[115] But HoneyPot and dem were in for a surprise: "what no body could have knowd to expect were / merrit / got the voice of a angel stored in he ass. / so when honeypot had donn told merrit to just stand there hush. / feeling so pretty and all backed up with broken dreams and trouble / merrit say he couldn't help it. he just had to open he mouth / let all he heart and soul release."[116] He held his notes so long, hard, and high that glasses burst in folks' hand, and "it were lengendary. / the peoples jus lost they mind. got to falling out and jumping up and reaching for / the hem of he she garment. merrit open that crowd so wide and so fast / till they started calling him / miss kitty."[117] The club's bouncer, Slice, leaves her post to throw herself at the new singer's feet and declare her love, and HoneyPot lets Slice join her crew as muscle—"not that bunch need it / all them knives and guns packed up in all dem tittes and draws."[118] Miss Kitty returns to Ole Caney Sharp's house with hisher new name and new love, and "merrit donn disappeared into he love of dresses and sounds and things / so we now calls he miss kitty. / slice live to make miss kitty happy / and miss kitty love he some slice."[119]

Merrit is delivered from a gambling addiction that's threatening hisher life through *relationships with other people*; and the first of those "others" is the self he's been hiding. Merrit has been living with something invisible inside him, "the voice of a angel stored in he ass." His *ass*? In his canonical essay "Is the Rectum a Grave?," Leo Bersani suggests that a man having something up his ass is "self-shattering"—that it disrupts the ego coherence of men enculturated to believe that manhood means impenetrability.[120] "If the rectum is a grave in which the masculine ideal . . . of proud subjectivity is buried, then it should be celebrated for its very potential for death," he proclaims. And it's no penis or dildo, but maybe having that voice stored in he ass *is* self-shattering for Merrit.[121] That voice of an angel is a high-pitched, feminine voice he shoves inside him in hopes of approximating the "masculine ideal," but its storage up his ass blocks his potential to develop a livable self: a self defined by creativity with respect to gender and sexuality as well as vocal virtuosity. After having been stuck in the black masculine stereotype of the gambler and womanizer, pulling that voice out of his ass leaves room for self-re-creation. Merrit's been psychically constipated, "all backed up with broken dreams and trouble," then as he croons *baybayyy* "all he heart and soul release"—and the crowd introduces himshe to the person heshe's become, Miss Kitty.

Having opened up to Miss Kitty, heshe then opens up to relationship with Slice. Theirs is the romantic storyline of *Dat Black Mermaid Man Lady*: when Slice "laid down at merrit feet / pledge to never leave / something bout that touch merrit soul."[122] Slice—a trouser womyn who works traditional male jobs of bouncer and bodyguard—and Miss Kitty—the Merrit who "disappeared into he love of dresses and sounds and things" but still uses masculine pronouns—embody the creative genders that Bridgforth calls "the boths and the neithers," both/neither woman/man.[123] Their gender queerness is not the story of their relationship, though; the narrators never dwell on it, and it's neither the source of their attraction nor a barrier to their union in anyone's eyes. The everydayness of this black trans love emerges as part of its healing quality. "There are lots of trans folks who are not receiving any love from their families and it's hard for them to create partnerships," black trans activist Tiq Milan states in a video interview titled "Love Is Revolutionary When You're Black and Transgender." "So when that does happen . . . it's countering this dominant narrative that there's a pathology with transgender people, that's showing that we are happy and healthy and we are deserving of love, absolutely."[124]

And finally, Miss Kitty circles back to hisher relationship with hisher family of origin, represented here by grandfather Caney. "Ventually. / honeypot and dem bring miss kitty and he slice by ole caney sharp / so the ole man can see / everthing is / all / right na," the narrators conclude.[125] Refusing to engage stereotypes of the black homophobic and transphobic family, Bridgforth stages a reunion in which Merrit's disappearance into Miss Kitty is greeted as a sign that "everthing is / all / right na." The role of family in Miss Kitty's recovery—the joint efforts of Cousin HoneyPot and Grandpa Caney—echo E. Patrick Johnson's reflections on the ways returning *home* may be integral to the wellness of black queer folks, for whom family of origin is where we first learn to recognize and resist oppression. Caney Sharp's house offers an ideal version of what Johnson calls *homeplace*: "that site that first gave us the 'equipment for living' in a racist society, particularly since we, in all our diversity, have always been a part of this homeplace: housekeepers, lawyers, seamstresses, hairdressers, activists, choir directors, professors, doctors, preachers, mill workers, mayors, nurses, truck drivers, delivery people, nosey neighbors, and (an embarrassed?) 'etc.' SNAP!"[126] And as Miss Kitty becomes part of the "etc.," the diverse *everbody* that populates the juke joint and the bottom of the ocean in *Dat Black Mermaid*

Man Lady, the voice that heshe's pulled out of he ass will bring other characters into the reach of the Black Mermaid man lady come to heal them.

∞

Your love is my love, and my love is your love . . . Imagine you're peachy-skinned,
pigtailed, and six going on seven, sunning in the hottest part of the summer
when day stretches so long it might break, and every afternoon there's a pool
party and barbecue going on in your very own backyard—yes, *every* single
summer day. In 1970, Whitney's family moved from "the bricks" of Newark to
their first house in East Orange, New Jersey. Purchased with an advance from
Cissy's debut solo album, the four-bedroom, white clapboard house at 362
Dodd Street came with a surprise for her three children: an in-ground swimming pool in the backyard. "Because we had that backyard pool, our house
became a gathering place," Cissy remembers. "That first summer, I think Nippy
spent almost all of her time in the pool. Between that, the pool table in the
basement, and John [Whitney's father] grilling burgers and hot dogs in the
back yard, we always had a bunch of kids hanging around."[127] Toni Gregory—
Whitney's first best friend—remembers the Houston house as a second home
to Dodd Street kids, their pool (along with the McDonalds' down the street)
the big neighborhood attraction in summer. Whitney taught Toni to swim there
by laughingly pushing her into the pool then waiting for her to splash her way
out.[128] Sometimes the fun at 362 Dodd Street went on so long Cissy would
wake to find children had slept over in her basement without her knowing it,
and Whitney was sending them home with new clothes Cissy had bought for
her daughter. "They welcomed everybody," Cissy remembers of her children
with a mixture of appreciation and exasperation, "and anything they had,
they'd share it with their friends."[129]

In the years she went to the red brick elementary school up the street—then
Franklin Elementary, later rededicated Whitney E. Houston Academy of Creative
and Performing Arts—Whitney's world revolved around her backyard pool,
the basement where Cissy gave her singing lessons, and New Hope Baptist
Church in Newark. "She was always in the house, shy, or going to church with
her mother," Toni's brother Raymond remembers.[130] At first Whitney pushed
back against choir director Cissy's insistence on dragging her along to New
Hope. Eventually, though, Whitney—who was always a little different, always
teased by other girls—came to find comfort in the church. "It was at New Hope

that Nippy got saved . . . cried and accepted the Savior into her life and heart," Cissy recounts. "And she never let go of that faith, even through all the turmoil and hard times to come."[131] It was also at New Hope that Whitney made her singing debut, soloing in the choir at age eleven. "She would get up and sing like she was in front of a thousand people, and there'd be 60 or 70 people at the church," her friend Helena Hollinshed remembers. "She would sing her heart out."[132] Young Whitney could also quote scripture like the church elder she would never become. One of her favorite passages was Matthew 3:16, Jesus' baptism in the River Jordan: "And when Jesus was baptized, immediately he went up from the water, and behold, the heavens were opened to him, and he saw the Spirit of God descending like a dove and coming to rest on him."[133]

Now imagine you're sixteen going on seventeen—still peachy-skinned, long-legged, and Afro-crowned—and you meet a handsome older girl, a college-bound girl with almond-shaped eyes, basketball muscles, and a smile like lightning. You walk arm in arm with her, you plan imaginary trips to see the world together, and maybe you want her to kiss you in just the way she does. So what's it like to go to the church you love on Sunday morning, now, after spending the rest of the week with the girl you love? *Your love is my love, my love* . . . Maybe sometimes you feel like a fish in the ocean, swimming among your own kind. Because the pews in Newark's black churches are lined with gay men and lesbians, sissies and unmarried aunts. "A random sampling of black ministers in the Newark area found many are aware of lesbians, gays, bisexuals and transgendered men and women in their congregations, singing in the choir or working in a church office," journalist Linda Ocasio notes. "And they are willing to welcome them with open arms."[134] But maybe other times you feel like a mermaid on land, somewhere no one recognizes the fullness of who you are. Because even if they lead the choir and sew its robes, teach Sunday school and usher weekly, queer folks' centrality to black church life goes unacknowledged. Rev. Reginald T. Jackson, pastor of St. Matthew AME in Orange and executive director of New Jersey's Black Ministers Council, recognizes, "You have gay people in leadership positions already," but qualifies—"*not openly.*"[135] Rev. Joe Carter, the New Hope pastor who presided over Whitney's funeral but refused to make a statement about the 2003 murder of fifteen-year-old black lesbian Sakia Gunn in Newark, proclaims "that most black churches understand themselves as a 'biblical people,' and while the Bible refers to 'Adam and Eve' (and not 'Adam and Steve'), we welcome gay people in our congregations as long as they don't 'come out.'"[136]

A biblical people, like Naomi and Ruth. Of course, Whitney knew their story: When Ruth's husband died, her widowed mother-in-law Naomi told her to return to her family but Ruth refused. "Do not ask me to leave you, for I never will," Ruth pleaded. "Where you go, I will go; where you live, I will live; your people shall be my people; and your God shall be my God. Where you die, I will die, and be buried. Nothing but death itself shall part you and I."[137] And so Naomi and Ruth traveled together, walked around the Dead Sea and crossed the River Jordan to reach Naomi's hometown of Bethlehem. In some ways, Whitney and Robyn lived the story of Naomi and Ruth, too. "Not long after I met her, she said 'Stick with me, and I'll take you around the world,' " Robyn remembers of Whitney. "And we went around the world." Across the Atlantic and the Pacific, the Mediterranean and the Caribbean, "all around the world first class." Through all those years Whitney studied scripture, prayed alone in her room, and through all those travels she and Robyn remained as discreet about their relationship as Rev. Carter could desire. "I have never spoken about her until now. And she knew I wouldn't," Robyn proclaims in Whitney's obituary. "She was a loyal friend, and she knew I was never going to be disloyal to her."[138] . . . *And my love, is your love.*

The Fantasea Mixtape was a COMPLETE tribute to Yemaya.[139] Yes, Azealia Banks can be slippery when she wants to. When *Fantasea* dropped days before the Los Angeles Mermaid Ball, *Spin* asked: "What does all this undersea enchantment *mean*?" Her deadpan answer: "It doesn't mean anything."[140] But after her Mermaid Ball tour ended, Banks's Twitter revealed that her earlier answer was a lure—that in fact both her mixtape and mermaids paid homage to Yemaya, Cuba's mermaid orisha and counterpart to Lasirenn. Of course, Miss Banks knows Lasirenn too. She urges black followers to learn about Cuban Regla de Ocha, Haitian Vodoun, and North American rootwork, and affirms working closely with African diaspora spirituality without indicating which tradition she follows. When asked her religion, she replied: "I don't want to say, but I'll tell you about one form of the religion. It's called 21 Divisions." She went on to explain her family connections to the practice: "When they brought the slaves over to the Caribbean, they syncretized all their African gods with Catholic saints. So in 21 Divisions there are black gods and goddesses, and my mother practiced that when I was little. Whenever problems happened, we turned to 21

Divisions to fix it. . . . You can cleanse people with root work or do bad things to them. But 21 Divisions is celestial."[141] With this mother-centered answer, she makes clear that her love of black goddesses mirrors one of Lasirenn's deepest principles: "Lasirenn ties past and future generations."[142] This black mermaid's far-reaching hair isn't vanity but memory, strands of DNA twisting back across generations to connect with her mother and mother's mother and her mother before her; her long, long, black and shining locks imprint genetic traces of "black gods and goddesses" who are our ancestors and family line.

These lines of ancestral connection are neither romantic nor pacific. For Azealia and other black mermaids, transgenerational connection ties us to oceans of pain. In the Banks family, this means intimacy with addiction: Azealia's father was a "cokehead," alcoholic, and sex addict who died of pancreatic cancer brought on "from red meat, coffee, cocaine and Courvoisier," she told London's *Sunday Times*.[143] It also means a heritage of mental illness: shortly after her father's death Azealia's mother suffered a breakdown. "It got bad . . . Real bad. Like *Mommie Dearest* bad," she narrates. "My mom was stressed. She was a single mom with three black daughters in New York City. My mom was a hard worker so we had a good upbringing and were never poor, but my mother was just crazy."[144] Black transgenerational trauma spreads deeper than this individual family suffering, though, as Azealia vigorously vocalizes. "Y'all motherfuckers still owe me reparations!" she laughs to *Playboy*. "Really, the generational effects of Jim Crow and poverty linger on."[145] Lasirenn's historical connections reach back to touch this collective trauma that shadows all black family dysfunction. Her beautifully fishy form—only half-human in an anthropomorphic pantheon—embodies the history of enslavement. Because mermaids weren't part of precolonial West African imaginaries, Karen McCarthy Brown speculates that Lasirenn's mermaid incarnation transculturates the sirens that Africans saw carved on slave ships' masts. So "the Vodou *lwa* Lasyrenn," she writes simply and incisively, "may have roots that connect, like nerves, to the deepest and most painful parts of the loss of homeland and the trauma of slavery."[146] Transgenerational connection means living with those most painful parts twisted into every hair on our skin, so ever-present that diving into addiction—downing another bottle, sliding another line of coke down your mermaid's mirror—sometimes smiles like generous relief.

Never pacific, ties across generations are also never static; *transgeneration* also entails *transformation*. Azealia's father died a cokehead but her mother did not: after his death Azealia remembers no more drugs or alcohol in the house. Mrs. Banks's mental illness prompted Azealia to leave home at fourteen but her recovery brought her daughter back. Azealia's favorite person to spend time with now is her mother, and a smiling Instagram picture of the two bears the joyful caption: "You can see where I get my craziness from!"[147] Witnessing her mother's painful *and* healthful transformations provides Azealia with a model to tap into family craziness and turn it around, to use that energy—much like sex and drugs—as a tool for creativity and self-discovery. And Azealia's Big Mama Lasirenn directs children back to memories of Africa not to retraumatize, but to recover tools for collective healing: to move us toward "a glimpse into the collective wisdom found in the underwater world of the ancestors" because, as Azealia puts it, "we have REAL supernatural powers, and the sooner we ALL learn to cultivate them and access the them, the sooner we can REALLY fix shit."[148] If hair is memory—the transgenerational inheritance that constantly grows with us—then, well, being a black mermaid is all about rocking a weave. You start with what your parents gave you, your natural hair: "I don't process my real hair at all. I'm natural underneath my weave," Azealia insists to *Allure*, touting this as her secret to keeping her hair healthy. But from there, you sew in the colors, lengths, and textures that *you* invent, that tell the world who you're choosing to be. And that, Azealia says, is how she became a mermaid. When she arrived at fashion designer Karl Lagerfeld's party with a long blue and green weave, "I looked like a fish, it was real pretty, greens and blues and purples and shit. Then somebody made a Twitter page called Azealia's Mermaid Hair, and people just picked up on it, boom boom boom. I was just like, all right, I'm gonna take it."[149] And *that's* how you find a black goddess in you who can help you breathe underwater and on land too, help you blend in with mermaids and fashionistas: you take what your mama gave you and add on, and on, and on.

Stumbling on her land legs like any Ariel, Miss Bank$ has stepped in a lot of mess since floating away from her mermaid balls. In one summer she spattered her name across the media promoting skin bleaching cream, promising to vote for Donald Trump, filing a police report against Russell Crowe, and calling singer Zayn Malik a "sand nigger" and "dick rider." When Twitter suspended her account for that tirade, many of us watching sighed with exasperation and concern. One Twitter user worried, "Azealia Banks must be on drugs you know, this ain't even funny she actually needs help" and in an interview conducted in a cemetery Banks admitted to Richard Godwin, "My mother has never reprimanded me but she reprimanded me after the thing with Zayn [Malik] happened."[150] Banks apologized and reflected, "I realised you're not keeping it real by being a crazy girl. You don't lose anything by keeping your mouth shut. So maybe it's time to stop being a crazy girl."[151] Maybe it is, and maybe she *does* need help—but only she can tell us. The mermaids are here for you, Azealia girl, just tell us what you need.

—·—

And last but not least, this is how *Dat Black Mermaid Man Lady*'s narrator swore off empty sweetness so s/he could fill up enough to become the community's next healer. The narrator's drug of choice is that white powder we call sugar. "suga / donn made my ass plum crazy," the narrator laments. "i have always knowd the fact of this / but i had to bow down to it that day long time ago / that day i ate that very large piece of devil ass white cake."[152] That day, s/he followed a pretty lady into a sugar shack where HoneyPot and dem were playing, "a place i knowd i had no business at / cause i knowd wasn't gonn be nuthn but pure ass suga up in there . . . womens / cake / and liquor."[153] When the narrator finally gets up courage to ask the pretty lady to dance she obligingly answers, "why sho." Reciprocating hisher attentions, "next thing i knowd the ver pretty lady say / would you lik some cake / i say why sho. next thing i knowd the very pretty lady say / would you lik a drank / i say why sho."[154] As the narrator finishes this sugar-on-sugar Miss Kitty ascends to the stage, and the combination of hisher spiking bloodsugar and Miss Kitty's angelsweet voice knocks himher into another dimension: "all i recall is her thick juicy red lips opened / and BAM / next thing i knowd / i find myself face up on the floor / laughing and singing and talking to dead peoples."[155] And there, s/he meets that Black Mermaid man lady face to face. "*the dead people turned to water and the water turned to mountains and the mountains rose to the sky and the sky turned into the big full moon and the big full moon turned into itself and it grew and it grew and it grew,*" s/he sings, "*until it burst back down into the water and the water rose up tall tall tall and black with seven deep blue skirts rolling around it with fishes and fishes and pearls flowing all the way down past behind.*"[156] Hisher communion with the man lady is abruptly broken by a thwack from HoneyPot's shoe, snatched off and thrown into the narrator's forehead "to hush me / and all my singing and talking and dancing with dead people and the moon."[157]

Now, sugar is a key ingredient in many addictive substances—alcohol and food, to start—and a metaphor for even more: sex, cocaine, heroin. But it has particular resonance in New Orleans environs, where this labor-intensive cash crop drove chattel slavery. Hugely profitable in the nineteenth century, cane cultivation faced different pressures in Louisiana than in the tropical Caribbean. Winter frosts denied the year-round growing season that made Caribbean cane so rich, so late in November enslaved laborers were pushed to harvest with inordinate speed. By mid-century, market demands for ever-whiter sugar drove growers to invest in costly steam vacuums, which in turn prompted schemes to extract more labor from the enslaved to recoup their capital. As former bondswoman Ceceil George recalled of Louisiana cane fields, "Everybody worked, young, and ole', if yo' could carry two or three sugar cane yo' worked. Sunday, Monday, it all de same . . . it like a heathen part of the country."[158] To encourage the enslaved to continue this toil without the revolts that disrupted Caribbean plantations, owners offered workers incentives during the murderous harvest. In grinding season, planter Frederick Law Olmsted reported, the enslaved were given "better and more varied food and stimulants than usual," including alcohol and tobacco; these addictive substances were also offered as rewards for producing to the master's desire.[159] Not only did these "stimulants" give "them the strength for, and pleasure in, their labor," Olmsted fantasizes, they offered the enslaved "a degree of freedom and social pleasure."[160] But what if you start to lean into tobacco's break to your fatigue, to relax into the way alcohol massages your muscles and your spirit—what if you grow dependent on the drugs shoveled into you during harvest? If addiction was grown as frantically as sugar on these plantations—well, then to be a black addict in postmanumission Louisiana was to be back in the position of the enslaved, looking for a "degree of freedom" but finding only "devil ass white . . . suga."

In hisher diabetic, clairvoyant trance, the narrator is pulled down so s/he can talk to all those dead cane workers, those ancestors who guzzled whisky and dipped snuff to keep going. Then those ancestors transform: the dead become water, and the water becomes that Black Mermaid man lady. Lying flat on hisher back in the sugar shack, the narrator comes to pick himherself up by grasping at the "tall tall tall" mermaid man lady's hand—by literally reaching out for *relationship with something bigger than self.* "Tall tall tall and black . . . with black black shining eyes," this hyperblack higher power swims in a longtime Louisiana tradition of Africanizing North American religion.[161] Cane field workers developed a kind of worship that Richard Follett calls "Afro-Christian devotion": Catholicism adapted so that the enslaved could "shout and pray lak ya wanted ta do" and sacraments were performed by blacks themselves, including a preacher named Mingo who diverted water from the pond "whar dey drew water for the sugar house" to baptize his fellow enslaved.[162] Not only is this mermaid black like the processional's characters, though, heshe is also *both and neither* like them—yes, the man lady is also genderqueer. When the narrator—played simultaneously by a man and a woman, remember—looks up into the shining eyes of the Black Mermaid man lady, s/he stumbles on a kind of affirmation that most black queers in recovery struggle to find: an oceanic reflection of the divinity of being black *and* quare. Like the *"big full moon"* that *"turned into itself and it grew and it grew and it grew,"* the entranced narrator receives divine permission to become himherself in all the ways that look and move like the Black Mermaid man lady.

Dat Black Mermaid Man Lady concludes with this divine becoming: with the now sugarfree narrator slipping into her place as the community's new healer by connecting deeply, more deeply with the Black Mermaid man lady. One day, the narrator returns from a trip to the swamp with a young girl to find the community's elders—"miss mama david ole caney sharp the gurl mama / mama biggranny"—waiting for himher.[163] "Oh oh," s/he moans as these elders form a circle and start turning her around with their canes, "speaking in silence / till i feel like i feel when i eats me some suga but i ain't had no suga . . . / till i can hear they thoughts / which feel like my thoughts / and next thing i knowd / i find myself face up on the ground / not from suga / not laughing / not singing / talking to dead peoples."[164] And there the narrator is again but not again, staring at the full moon that rises from the center of the elder's circle as it bursts to become water and rises to become the black mermaid man lady. "And the black mermaid man lady become all above and around," the narrator sings, "and reach down down / down for me / and take me / wrap so tight around me / herhe become me."[165] This is an initiation anba dlo where the ocean comes to land, takes the narrator under without himher moving from her stance on Louisiana earth and makes himher a priest of ocean power with no other ritual than their deep connection. Could the narrator have continued to reach out for the Black Mermaid man lady by eating, drinking, and following sugar? Why sure. But while sugar visions isolate himher from the juke joint community (until HoneyPot intervenes with a shoe to the head), these visions arise from and build community as all the elders "moving so fast / they clapping so loud /

they singing so sweet / they grab me spin me right / they turn me left / they stomp / they shout / say / Love."[166] Say Love, say Love, say Love, the Black Mermaid man lady sings, until you're soaked in a gentler sweetness that lifts you and takes you down and "i stomp / i shout / i say / I."[167]

So this, finally this is how you learn to breathe underwater when you're black and queer. (Sing.) You let yourself fall under the sea, tonbe dan lanme; and there you look at the Black Mermaid man lady with fishes and fishes and pearls and flowing down behind and realize that you *are* himher, you are that safe coral castle at the bottom of the ocean floor where you can take in what you need. You reach for the ancestors around you and ask how to make a workable present out of a painful past, how you divert that water from the sugar mill to baptize yourself and weave your hair like waves flowing down behind. You go down and you come up, you go down and you come up again, you go down and you come up from the underwater juke joint swampland public pool Black Atlantic Bristol Bay Aqua Star to a place where you can live. Lasirenn, Labalenn, chapom' tonbe nan lanme; M'ap fe bebel ak—Lasirenn, Labalenn, chapom' tonbe nan lanme.

PHOTO BY CINDY ELIZABETH

bridge

BAÍA AND
MARIGO

You read this book like a song, so you can't forget the dedication. Every letter, every keystroke fell to conjure a world for my very beloved daughter, Baía. When I conceived her in a doctor's office overlooking a frozen lake in 2008 or named her after the San Francisco Bay in 2009, I couldn't imagine all it would mean to mother such a beautiful black girl queerly. Teaching her it's okay to kiss girls, introducing her to uncles' husbands—these are the easy parts. Teaching her she's perfect & powerful just because she is, opening space for her to be Queen B of all she imagines, mirroring back how she matters when the news pronounces her future dead: this is the hardest, queerest part of black mothering. "Queer," as I wrote not long before she was born, "in the sense of marking disruption to the violence of normative order and powerfully so: connecting in ways that commodified flesh was never supposed to, loving your own kind when your kind was supposed to cease to exist."[1] Raising Ezili Freda as a black girl in Texas is the queerest, most wonderful thing I've ever done.

During three of the four years it took to write this book, I was trying to carry another child. Parts of the second chapter were written in bed during my first miscarriage, a child my mother dreamt a little boy. Three months later I was pregnant again, with a placid, calm spirit I was sure was a girl. I always thought my second child would be a son but now it seemed powerful juju baby Baía, obsessed with Disney's Frozen, had conjured a sister to play Anna to her Elsa. I named her Marigo: Kreyòl for "bayou" & also for Marigot, the capital of St. Martin where Matt's family is from. She would have been my baby girl, my youngest, my daughter of promise, my Anaisa.

Miscarriage is a common experience of black mothering, too. "Rates of every kind of pregnancy loss—miscarriage, stillbirth, preterm birth and infant death—are significantly higher for black women than for any other racial group," I wrote shortly after that pregnancy ended. "No genetic factors have been isolated to explain this discrepancy, and rates of loss do not vary significantly by socio-economic status. . . . This leads pregnancy loss expert Elizabeth Czukas to speculate, 'the continuous, low-grade stress of racism may be the factor that unifies all African-Americans, and may contribute to the increased risk of pregnancy loss.' "[2] My baby girl, my youngest, my daughter of promise, my Anaisa was an unbearable child—a child who refused to be born. This baby, too, I'm continually seeking to mother queerly. Mothering Marigo means saying her name, being angry with her for leaving her sister & compassionate about her decision not to live this life, insisting on the possibility of conjuring a world where she could move from imagination into flesh.

This book is for your sister, Marigo. Yours still waits to be written, on that day when the black girls from the future arrive.

ARTIES'S SONG

Erzulie, O! If my mother dies, I'll cry. If my father dies, I'll cry. If my wife leaves, I'll find another. Ana-Maurine Lara's debut novel Erzulie's Skirt opens with a conversation between siren Erzulie and her (sometimes) husband, ocean lwa Agwe, as they greet the morning and tell stories about humans whose lives twist through their existence. Erzulie laments that she receives less elaborate offerings than the boats, flowers, and fruit devotees offer Agwe, but he retorts: "You have so many husbands and wives I don't know how you manage." Erzulie laughs and acknowledges: "My arms reach far and wide—far and wide!"[1] Many people, she smiles, "love me, marry me, give me fruits, flowers, cigarettes and beer, perfume and all those good things."[2] So many husbands and wives, lwa and men and women who themselves have other husbands and wives, lovers and children. Definitely *not* the Virgin Mary she's often syncretized with, Ezili reaches her divine love "far and wide—far and wide," practicing cosmic polyamory. Noting that the word comes from Latin *poly* meaning *many* and *amor* meaning *love*, the Polyamory Society imagines polyamory as "the nonpossessive, honest, responsible and ethical philosophy and practice of loving multiple people simultaneously. . . . Polyamory embraces sexual equality and all sexual orientations towards an expanded circle of spousal intimacy and love."[3] To love Ezili—and I do, I love every Ezili in every page of this text—is to embrace her polyamory: to welcome her loving presence without ever imagining it could or should be exclusive, heteronormative, forsaking all others, until death do us part.

Over the course of this book my meditations on Ezili have gone in many directions—so many I've sometimes said to myself the same thing Agwe says to Erzulie, "I don't know how you manage." Often I haven't managed to draw all thought lines together; and that unresolved plurality, too, became part of following the fractal mode of theorizing that is Ezili. Laboring with love through the diverging, converging subjects that visit these chapters, I've found that engaging Ezili as a mode of theorizing means embracing theoretical polyamory. Like most scholars, I was raised to be academically monogamous: to be "married to" a single, coherent subject, "faithful to" a line of theorizing. But because Ezili asked and I couldn't say no, I tried to open my conceptual relationships here. A philosophy as well as a practice, theoretical polyamory encourages movement between different modes of theorizing: music videos, popular songs, dance, film, erotica, speculative fiction, and fashion all "married" into one theorizing enterprise—all accorded as much explanatory power as academic prose to make sense of black queer lives. It also brings into the same sheets a variety of intellectual producers whose ideas might not easily fit together. Would Azealia Banks's ideas of black women's sexuality mesh with Edwidge Danticat's? Would Domina Erzulie's political affiliations line up with Laurence Magloire's? I was challenged to find the angles at which the answers to these questions become yes: to find the space where disparate ideas, aesthetics, and politics come together under Ezili's skirt.

Lara frames Erzulie's Skirt as a leisurely morning story Erzulie spins for Agwe and, by extension, the novel's readers. Her tale introduces us to many kinds of polyamory: love of more than one person, more than one lwa, more than one community, more than one kind of family. And more than one kind of Vodoun, too. Because while Erzulie and Agwe belong to the Haitian Vodoun pantheon, the divine characters that move through Lara's novel largely come from Dominican Vudu. "Some will say that Dominican Vodou is Haitian Vodou, just practiced in the Dominican Republic," Hector Salva explains. "This is not true, Dominican Vodou (La 21 Divisiones) is a separate practice and lineage and although there are many of the same Lwa, the practice and manner in which they are served is different."[4] Vodoun, too, isn't one but many: its lwa and rituals vary from Port-au-Prince to northern Haiti, and even more widely in the Dominican Republic, Puerto Rico, New Orleans, and Montreal. Luxuriating in the multiplication of Ezili, this book has backgrounded the multiplicity of Vodoun itself. Still, I couldn't end without offering a glimpse of Vodoun's many iterations. That glimpse focuses on Anaisa, the most beloved of Dominican female luases and the youngest daughter of Ezili Freda, who serves as tutelary luas for many of the characters in Erzulie's story. "You like that," Agwe says when she identifies one of the characters as Anaisa's daughter, and she replies: "Of course! Anyone that comes from water is alright with me."[5] Anything that comes from water, anyone that Erzulie loves, belongs under her skirt.

❦

On the spring-heady evening of May 4, 2015, Bajan pop star and fashion icon Rihanna glided onto the red carpet of the Metropolitan Museum of Art Gala draped in an imperial yellow, fur-trimmed cape decorated with miles of embroidered gold flora, so luxuriously long that three handlers trailed behind to carry its train. The show-stopping garment—designed by Chinese couturier Guo Pei and handmade by one Chinese woman over the course of two years—was chosen by this first black Dior Girl in honor of the Gala's 2015 theme "China: Through the Looking Glass." With a gold headpiece crowning her locks, a tiny pink dress peeking out from underneath the cape, and lean, stiletto-clad legs emerging from its fur-trimmed opening, Rihanna stole the show. Hers was a royal statement. "In imperial China, only the emperor was allowed to wear yellow. Yellow was the most precious color, the most noble color," Yahoo beauty editor Noel Duan wrote of her ensemble. "Rihanna and Guo Pei are making a statement about Rihanna, about what a queen she is. It is kind of crazy that she's wearing something only a male emperor would be allowed to wear. Only Rihanna could pull it off."[6]

Rihanna is the queen of ever-changing looks, her hair moving from red to blue in the blink of an eye, her outfits eclectic and playfully gritty one day and ethereally haute couture the next day. But besides flawless fashion sense, what unites her looks is their sense of playful, carefree black femininity. "If 2014 saw the meteoric rise of the Carefree Black Girl trope," Hannah Giorgis writes, "then Rihanna was the island wind beneath its weave."[7] In the eighteen months leading up to Rihanna's Met Gala brilliance, the Carefree Black Girl movement championed the need for media representations of black women and girls that challenge stereotypes of Jezebels, Mammys, and Sapphires. Jamala Johns praises this movement for depicting "the freedom and exuberance of simple moments and pleasures: clutching flowers, enjoying the company of your equally stylish friends, reveling in creative endeavors, and even finding the ethereal beauty in not-so-carefree moments. . . . For women of color, such basic depictions continue to go underrepresented."[8] Except on RiRi's Instagram page, where they're the only moments that matter. "RiRi crafts notably rebellious black female self-determination in this spirit [of the carefree black girl], eschewing propriety in favor of a carefree, self-indulgent womanhood not contingent on respectability," Giorgis reflects. "Rihanna's defiant ascent to superstardom offers glimpses into a world where all black women can revel in (or rebuff) the limelight on our own terms and laugh while we're doing it, where our creativity, beauty, and worth are not graded against the impossible sliding-scale rubric of white femininity."[9] Rihanna's carefree black girlhood takes us to the other side of the looking glass, into a wonderland where black women and girls "transform themselves . . . change and circulate as they wish."[10] Yes, on the steps of the Met Rihanna comes dressed for "Through the Looking Glass" in more ways than one.

Looking like the queen of carefree black girls that night, Rihanna also looks like a goddess. After all, who else lives on the other side of the mirror? She steps out in yellow channeling Anaisa Pye, the divine carefree black girl of Dominican Vudu. Derived from indigenous Taino, her name—meaning little child of the golden river flower—tells you what and how she loves. Anaisa dresses in imperial yellow, too, and loves accessories as lavish as Rihanna's headdress and heels: expensive yellow flowers, rings on every finger, mirrors, makeup, Spanish fans. Laughing like a river and bright as a sunflower she arrives cheerful and full of laughter, always the life of the party. Freda's spoiled youngest daughter—a child who gets what she wants in multiples—young Anaisa is the spirit of multiplicity as much as of female youth. "Anaisa Pye is known as the Queen of the Seven Roads, she who spins seven times, and each turn is an avatar of the previous one. She is the Lady of the seven altar [sic] egos and Lady of the seven split personalities, Lady of Seven Manifestations, Queen of the Seven Crossroads," Sancista Luis reflects. "Anaisa Pye is the first to say she only has seven, but this of course is known by her servitors as 'a little white lie,' and is a way for her to protect her identity."[11] Seven multiplied by seven and seven again: because in a world that refuses black girls love and safety, we need as many Anaisas as we need carefree black girls, to remind us that we deserve adoration in multitudes. "There is no surviving, yet alone thriving, as a Black girl without being carefree," Ashleigh Shackleford writes. "There are 50 million ways to be a Black girl and 50 million ways to be carefree"—and

70 million ways to be Anaisa and 70 million ways to be divine, too.[12] Carefree as she looks, bringing Anaisa into the world is a herculean task. Every Anaisa born requires the 500,000 hours of labor that went into Rihanna's cape and something else, too: the audacity to believe that somewhere in a universe not too far away, a black girl can be the empress of everything and enjoy it, too. So gaze on and appreciate, appreciate everywhere you see Anaisa in all her lush, flowing, gold-embellished yellow royalty: the most beloved black daughter has arrived, the only girl in the world.

My great-grandmother Arties Phillips was born November 13, 1894, in Goodwater, Alabama. From the moment she entered the world under Scorpio sun and autumn moon, she was never ever alone, never ever *the only*. Ten sisters came before her—Alice, Emma, Ellen, Annie, Mittis, Laura, Satthee, Lillie, Mattie, and Mavis—and she had four brothers, Henry, John, Talmadge, and Harry. She was a long-limbed, skinny child with Cherokee cheekbones and high, burning attitude. The Alabama Phillips were plain country Negroes, multiracial and multilingual: their people migrated to Goodwater and Sylacauga from Georgia, where they were Cherokee and Geechee. Arties learned to speak Geechee with her sisters but never taught it to her children. She kept it as a language to speak only with other black women, my grandfather told me, making sure she could talk big women's business without little ears knowing. Christened Eulabelle and nicknamed Doskie, my great-grandmother didn't like either of those names; sounded too much like cows, she told my grandfather. So when she was old enough she started calling herself Arties until everyone in the family called her that, too. Great-grandma Arties, the brownskin of many names.

Life in Goodwater just didn't suit young Arties, not at all. Of all the Phillips sisters she was the one who loved a good time, the one who sought out a party, the one her siblings never imagined keeping a man or raising children. But what else was there for a black girl becoming woman to do in Goodwater? Named because of its location near a spring, Goodwater—a small farming town with less than six hundred souls at the time of her birth—really wasn't near much else. One by one her sisters married, three of them to Thomas boys and four of them more than once. But Arties made up her mind: she was *not* going to be a farmer's wife, not going to bear child after child while she spent days in the field and nights sweeping field dust out of her house. So she bought a ticket on the Georgia railroad train that came from Columbus, Georgia, and took her to Birmingham, Alabama, where she spent the rest of her life.

She lived near the train tracks in North Birmingham, listening to the coming and going of cars in the Magic City, all the goods and smells and bodies that passed her en route from somewhere to somewhere bringing little pieces of the world closer and closer. Arties was one of many young black folks—mostly men—migrating to the rapidly industrializing Birmingham from rural Alabama at the beginning of the twentieth century, eager black bodies vying for manufacturing jobs where they were paid a fraction of white workers' wages and crowding into housing in the country's most segregated city. Young, beautiful, laughing, and defiant, Arties lived by train tracks where she breathed air thick with smoke and wind and grass and metal too mixed up to sort out. At a crossroads where everything was full with this energy, *this*, that circled hotly everywhere, collecting in walls and grass and sidewalks and every surface, the heat of eyes and hands that used to be somewhere and got forced out to make room for steel and cities—hanging on things like the smell of Cahaba lilies, wanting to speak and see and warn and comfort and learn from all these new passages of bodies. Yes, everything everywhere was too full to not be seen and heard and wanted, and Arties wanted what she did.

Erzulie tells Agwe the story of Haitian Miriam and Dominican Micaela, two poor black women who meet in Santo Domingo, become lovers, and undertake a perilous passage across the Mona Strait to the U.S. territory of Puerto Rico. While the couple is making the difficult decision to leave, Miriam has what she hopes is a prophetic dream about life in the United States. "I dreamt of that man again, that beautiful man who had come to take care of us," she tells Micaela. "He is handsome and serious, not like the charlatans from here. You and I were both together with him, but of course, he was mine. I dreamt that he fell in love with me and bought me a house . . . a proper house. A real home of my own."[13] While neither Miriam nor Micaela has other lovers during their many years together, maintaining complementary relationships where each partner brings something she needs—love and sexual companionship from Micaela, financial security from the dream man—remains an unrealized ideal for Miriam. Polyamory is a shining hope for her much like the streets of New York, which, in her imagination, are paved with gold lying ready for black women to pick up and make their own.

Micaela's dream rises out of African diaspora sexual cultures, echoing the "dual sexual system" that Gloria Wekker explores in her brilliant study *The Politics of Passion: Women's Sexual Culture in the African Diaspora*. Wekker documents a working-class Paramaribo sexual culture where black women have simultaneous and/or consecutive relationships with women and men to allow for maximum satisfaction of their needs, with each partner expected to provide something essential: sex, money, food, clothing, housework, child care, emotional support. The unwritten, communally recognized rules of what's "fair" to expect from a partner are called *kamra prikti*—literally, bedroom obligations. "Whether relationships were between a man or a woman or between two women, Surinamese Creole partners were expected to bring equal resources to the association," I wrote of this system in my first monograph. "The more money [a woman] brings in, the less she will have to perform sexually solely to please her partner; the more often a male partner is impotent and cannot please her in return, the less housework she must do. At any time she can choose to take other work or other lovers to fulfill unmet needs, since sexual integrity is understood not as exclusivity but as a woman's assurance that she gives what she can and receives what she needs in any partnership."[14] In no way an offshoot of global northern polyamory movements, this dual sexual system and its kamra prikti are well over a century old. Without "free love" available to them, poor black women developed this complex system to mitigate their ongoing unfreedom in years following emancipation in 1873. Needing love and material security too, they created a framework of sexual honesty that *works for them*: one where doing right by your partner is not about monogamy, but about responsibly sharing sexual and other resources.

Theoretical polyamory initially seemed to me like the man of Miriam's dreams, an immediately attractive, moon-brilliant vehicle to take me beyond the disciplinary boundaries that unsettled me for years. But as anyone who's been poly can tell you, multiplying your alliances multiplies the work you do—multiplies the prikti you're beholden to. Theoretical polyamory is in no way, shape, or form an invitation to shoddy interdisciplinarity any more than ethical nonmonagamy is a license to sleep with anyone behind your partner's back. Trained in literature, I delved into religious studies, dance history and theory, film theory, BDSM studies, and performance studies (among other things!) to write these meditations on Ezili. To get a lot out of working between ways of theorizing, I had to give a lot too. I've had to be respectful of all the disciplines and theorizings I enter, to know their histories, possibilities, and limitations. And to be as self-reflexive and honest as I could, but without taking up too much space in the conversation that is this book, letting my theoretical loves speak with voices stronger than mine. This was *not* easy to write—that book of literary criticism I proposed as a second project in my tenure file would have been so much easier and done long ago! But experimenting with theoretical polyamory opened possibilities for me to say things I couldn't otherwise embody in academic prose, and to be accountable to many different ways of knowing and loving. I've given what I could, and gotten what I needed in ways that were never possible for me when I was writing that first book, meditating on polyamory but not theorizing through it.

—◈◈—

On May 17, 2012, Rihanna and best friend Melissa Forde were photographed laughing and holding hands as they left Malibu restaurant Giorgio Baldi. Rihanna flawlessly sported long hair with wistful bangs, gold bracelets and pendant, taupe stilettos, and a two-piece white crochet ensemble: a semitransparent tube top paired with a peep-through midi skirt, her dark thong visible through its eyelets. Pictures surfaced on celebrity website Celebuzz, which tweeted nastily: "Dear Rihanna, you've gone a little too far with this 'outfit.' May be time to class it up and put some clothes on?" The singer responded with aplomb: "@CELEBUZZ your pussy is way too dry to be riding my dick like this."[15] The twenty-four-year-old was transparently exasperated by a year of record slut-shaming and ready to brandish her unabashed sexuality—her hard, wetness-craving dick—in her defense. In 2012, press criticized Rihanna for reuniting with abusive lover Chris Brown, spread rumors about sneaky sex with singer Drake, and linked her to actor Ashton Kutcher and basketball pro J. R. Smith. Asked whether she'd also hooked up with actor Ryan Phillippe, she quipped: "No no no, I hate to burst your bubble, but no. I am dating girls, I am just kidding!"[16] Of course there was no shortage of rumors about that, either. The month before RiRi and Melissa shared another hand-holding dinner at Giorgio Baldi and Rihanna tweeted: "I'm on my first date in almost 2 years" and "#date-night my lover for the night @mforde11."[17] The following month Rihanna and pop star Katy Perry proclaimed their intentions to have sex with each other, RiRi naming Katy as the woman she'd go lesbian for. Which led one blogger to comment about Rihanna's busy sex life: "So you know when you have a pet and it gets to Spring and they get all horny and start trying to have sex with chair legs and whatnot? Well Rihanna is just like that."[18]

Virulent slut-shaming is an occupational hazard for a black woman celebrity like Rihanna, but one she refuses to take lying down—lying down under a dry pussy, anyway. This, too, is part of what it means for her to move through the media as a carefree black girl. "The way black women are portrayed today in popular media makes it hard for a carefree black woman to openly express herself sexually while trying to avoid such labels," Deja Jones observes. "Just ask the carefree black girl who chooses to embrace love as the movement. She is often forced to find a way to differentiate herself from the jezebel, which depicts black women as sexually promiscuous and driven."[19] Rihanna, who entered the music business and its rumor mill at age sixteen, initially found her sexualized media persona unwieldy and uncomfortable. "I had to fake it till I made it. That's what I had to do," she told Oprah about how she became comfortable in her sexual skin. "I had to pretend that I was as comfortable. I really was not . . . But . . . I'm 24. I can do that now. I can experiment and try things."[20] And by the time Celebuzz made the mistake of taunting her, Rihanna had seized on her controversial sexuality as a personally and professionally gratifying power play. "Rihanna's marketing strategy has seemed rooted almost entirely in the novel idea of not people pleasing, of never kowtowing, and of being totally unedited," Lizzy Goodman noted in her 2014 *Elle* interview.[21] Tellingly, that interview concluded with Rihanna revealing her fondest Christmas wish: "A big, trimmed dick."[22]

Rihanna turns slut-shaming into earning power with the same femme fierceness that Anaisa Pye turns it into divine power. Anaisa is everyone's girl . . . but *only when she wants to be*. Though Belie Belcan is her husband, Houngan Hector concedes "she is known to have relationships with the majority of the male lwa"—except in her path as Colonel Anaisa la Fronte, when she only sleeps with women.[23] "She is often misunderstood . . . as a harlot, prostitute, femme fatale or lady of the night, and although she often manifests her energies and uses her feminine wiles in humans in a way that we may suggest or misunderstand her as such, she is so much more," Sancista Luis writes.[24] The male lwa themselves often try to reign in her sexual generosity, including Belie Belcan's ally Candelo Cedife. "Often Candelo scolds or chastises Anaisa for her flirtatious ways," Luis reports, "but Anaisa knows all the mysteries of charming both men and spirit, and she does the same with Candelo Cedife, who has a soft spot for her."[25] As she manages Candelo's patriarchal disapprobation, Anaisa overlaps the strategies of feminine erotic self-definition that Rebecca Ann Rugg calls "flirtatious femme" and "iron femme." While the former invites and revels in being the object of sexual desire on her own terms, the latter makes clear that this erotic invitation puts the femme in a position of power: that she remains "iron" while the desiring butch or man reveals his "soft spot" for femininity.[26] So the carefreeness of Anaisa's meandering desire reveals its own fem(me)inine strategy, an unapologetic seductiveness that disarms slut-shaming by exposing and stroking masculine powers' soft, desiring underbellies. *Candelo, your pussy too dry to be riding Anaisa's dick like that. Let her juicy it up for you a little, na?*

While finding her life in Birmingham, Arties met a pretty, easygoing, easy-drinking, light-skinned man from Georgia named George Stapler. Luxuriating in each other's brown beauty and warm skin they married, creating three children in three years: William Clarence, John Talmadge, and Hattie Pearl, with Hermann following three years later in 1923. George died shortly after Hermann's birth and his children remembered very little of him. What they *did* remember, though, was the string of men who came through the house after him. My grandfather was mortified by the men who spent evenings with Arties when he was a boy, drinking and enjoying music while he hid under the bed to do homework. Census records tell me Arties never remarried but she didn't waste away without men's company, either. The 1930 census lists "Cartsis Stapler" (their misspelling) as the head of her household at L and N Railroad, recording that she was living with a man named Moses Mahone as well as her four children. So even though she did marry and have children, yes, her sisters—who always talked stories about their wild baby sister—weren't wrong, either: a lifetime of monogamous wife-and-motherhood, lived in deference to a male head of the house, was just not in Arties's stars or plans. *Praise be.*

Because however they felt about their mother's creative erotic life, all Arties's children followed in her footsteps: by unanimously refusing to enter into any kind of partnership that looked like the farmer-and-his-wife model she was so determined to leave behind in Goodwater. Lanky, well-groomed, music-loving

Clarence never married or had children. Instead, my bachelor great-uncle—who lived with his mother until her death, then stayed in her house until his own—seemed to find something special in the company of other men (and the bottles they shared). John, my grandfather, entered into an illegal marriage with a woman he met while stationed in Germany during World War II, giving a false Chicago address on his marriage license to evade Alabama's antimiscegenation laws. Unmarried and opinionated, Hattie Pearl—her mother's daughter, the family's wild child—had three children with three fathers: Edward Earl Merrett, Evelyn McDonald, and John Robert Rawlings, as well as a stillborn baby girl whose birth caused her own death at age thirty-four. And baby Hermann died before having a partner or children, falling to his death on the train tracks near his house one night when he was drunk. Their love lives were messy and unresolved and half-glimpsed and unexpected—just like their mother's, just like mine. Her life helped make all of ours complicated, pointed out to us that there are so many more ways to love than we know when we're born and so many more ways to sugar our tea, forced us to be related to all kinds of loving even, *especially* if they made us uncomfortable. Loving was never bad because it was unmarried, unconventional, temporary, or drunk in the house at L and N Railroad; it was only bad when you didn't get what you needed, from whom you wanted.

—•—

On the hand-drawn map of Ayiti Quisqueya that prefaces Erzulie's Skirt, curving lines trace the trajectories that Miriam and Micaela travel separately and together in Erzulie's tale. Born in El Sur (the southern Dominican Republic), Miriam relocates to the capital after her Haitian-born parents die; Micaela, born in San Cristobal, migrates to Santo Domingo after her mother ejects her from the family home. The lovers cross the shark-infested Mona Strait to the "promised land" of Puerto Rico only to be conscripted into sex work in the U.S. territory, but miraculously escape and return to El Sur to open a colmado. Constructing identities and communities in these "multiple border spaces," as Josune Urbistondo puts it, Miriam and Micaela's loveship finds its un/home through *polylocality*: Yingjin Zhang's term to describe physical, cultural, and economic interconnectedness between "multiple, diverse localities."[27] Wherever they go in the Caribbean or (in dreams) around the black Atlantic, the poto mitan draws polylocales together:

that is, characters' practice of Vudu in Haiti, the Dominican Republic, and Puerto Rico becomes the constant through which Miriam and Micaela make sense of their world. Their commitment to Vudu is also a commitment to blackness, since throughout the region Vudu is cosa de negros, nengre sani, black people someting—a phrase that detractors hurl as an epithet by that practitioners embrace as a source of pride. In "Vudu in the Dominican Republic," Lara documents how Vudu holds space for blackness to become a meaningful identity in a nation that attempts to deny African ancestry by "giving shape to an alternate history where those who reference Africanity are at the centre of cultural meaning production and symbolic resistance to oppression."[28] Everywhere they go, Miriam and Micaela are children of Shango and Anaisa; everywhere they go, Miriam and Micaela are black women who survive violence and oppression by loving other black women.

Polylocality has been one of the practices of my theoretical polyamory, too. Gonaïves, Bwa Kayiman, Port-au-Prince, Paramaribo, New Orleans, New York, Los Angeles, Montreal, Toronto, London, Paris: these are some of the polylocales, the sites and communities that Ezili's Mirrors has moved through. I've loved Ezili in all these spaces, yes; and designed the kamra prikti of my theoretical polyamory so that my primary love and reference point is black feminism, *always and everywhere*. Ezili's theorizing in these polylocales reminds us that black feminism is capacious, that it can include the multiracial, multilingual, multicultural: the mulâtresse Marie Laveau and the métisse Jeanne Duval, the Brooklyn Kreyòlophone MilDred Gerestant and Ballroom language-fluent Angie Xtravaganza, Bajan American Rihanna and Black Cherokee Arties Phillips. But throughout métissage with indigeneity and Europeanness, multiculture and pop culture, black women's experience continues to serve as the poto mitan for the feminism explored in Ezili's Mirrors. As Patricia Hill Collins posits in her classic Black Feminist Thought: "Black feminist thought consists of specialized knowledge created by African-American women which clarifies a standpoint of and for Black women. In other words, Black feminist thought encompasses theoretical interpretations of Black women's reality by those who live it."[29] So wherever I've gone, black women's theoretical interpretations—our words, movement, art, work—serve as points de repère in this book. Throughout these pages, I've moved as a daughter of Ezili Freda and Oshun; throughout these pages, black women's world-making has been the *something* that weaves together the issues of labor, sexuality, aesthetics, migration, transition, addiction, and femme power that cross these meditations.

⊷⊷⊷

"Black iz beautiful," Rihanna captioned a triply dazzling Instagram picture of herself, her cousin Leandra, and Melissa in their jewel-emblazoned turquoise, black, and gold Crop Over regalia on August 3, 2015.[30] The ladies were jumping with celebrated costume band Zulu International, and Rihanna worked the band's *Hunger Games* fantasy theme in Mockingjay-inspired finery by designer Lauren Austin. Her claw-shaped jeweled bra and matching thong sparkled in the sunlight, cyan and peacock feathers bloomed in an elaborate headdress and flight-ready wings, and glinting body chains finished her fashion warrior look. Proudly celebrating her West Indianness on this biggest day of Barbados's annual fete—#Caribbean Gal and #culture, her hashtags proclaimed—she flooded Instagram with pictures of herself partying with the women she grew up with and the women she now world-travels with, with beauties black and brown. "Her love of life and her love of family and friends, the ability to live her life by her life and no one else's . . . make her a Caribbean girl and as captioned in the above pic: a Black girl to be proud of," Ayana Malaika Crichlow appreciates in her op ed "Rihanna Queen of Crop Over."[31]

Crop Over dates back to eighteenth-century Barbados, when it was one of many Caribbean celebrations that marked the end of the cane harvest with food, music, and dance organized by the enslaved. Its cultural origins are as mixed as the harvesters themselves. Crop Over's antecedents reach back to West African harvest festivals including "yam festivals of the peoples of Nigeria and Ghana, the point of origin of the majority of Barbadian descendants" who "believe that such festivals help them forge close bondage with their ancestors and ask for their protection and continued blessings."[32] They also include indigenous Arawak summer harvest festivals, elements of which resurface in Aruba's Dia di San Juan and Trinidad's Carnival fetes as well. Harvest Home, the celebration of the end of grain reaping in the British Isles, was also evoked in slave owners' sponsorship of the festivities. When she comes home every summer for Crop Over, then, Rihanna celebrates the overlapping communities she descends from—African, indigenous, and European. But at the end of Kadooment day, "black iz beautiful": that is, Rihanna understands all of these heritages as part of the ethnic complexity that constitutes blackness in her home communities of Barbados and the United States. "That she identifies as black and does not go out of her way to say she is mixed, or her family has some kind of European heritage in the family tree, that she doesn't play up her eye color or skin shade to identify and signify being a red woman is very powerful and endearing," Crichlow notes. "For her to claim her blackness unabashedly when this world teaches us to be ashamed of our melanin is astounding."[33] Don't forget: whatever her skin tone or eye color, the carefree black girl *always* embraces the beautiful fact of her blackness.

Crop Over coincides with the Feast of Saint Anne, also celebrated as the Feast of Anaisa Pye. "Salve O Gran Anaisa Pye, Gran Cacica, India Mulatta, bella morena de mi devocion," servitors pray as they offer her yellow scarves, champagne, jewelry, and perfume: *Hail Great Anaisa Pye, Great Cacique, Indian Mulatta, beautiful brown-skinned queen of my devotion.*[34] Anaisa Pye luxuriates in her beautiful black girlness, too, presenting herself to devotees as a mulatta whose greatest attraction lies in being morena. India Mulatta, she has polylocal roots in West Africa and precolonial Ayiti alike. "Although many think Anaisa is just . . . an African Spirit, in all her vueltas she is not," Sancista Luis reminds us. "Many vueltas of Anaisa Pye are Native Loa, a Loa de la Raiz; a root Loa who resided in the Caribbean way before the Europeans came to the Americas."[35] Both Anaisa and Cachita—one of her paths, whose name derives from Cacica (female chief)—come from Arawak, and as Cachita she is an avatar of Arawak river spirit Coatrisque as much as Yoruba river spirit Oshun. Catholic practitioners associate her with Saint Anne and Joan of Arc, and her European connections also are evident in her role as daughter of Ezili Freda, lightest-skinned of the lwa. But Anaisa's divine femininity never glamorizes lightening the race, never goes "out of her way to say she is mixed, or her family has some kind of European heritage in the family tree." This India Mulatta remains visibly, glowingly darker than her light-skinned mother, embodying a future for blackness in the mixed-race Americas. Born of many colonial encounters, she insists on claiming her blackness, too, and becomes the lwa other morenos call on when they're looking for love, children, and a loving black future. *Subele que Subele, Subele que eh, Subele la sangre a Anaisa Pye.*

∞

Arties Stapler didn't come to Birmingham to find a life spent between four walls; so while I know home life stories from children and grandchildren, I also know she spent lots of time away from home. She was a longtime member of

Bethel Baptist Church, founded in 1904 and located on the corner of 29th Avenue North and 33rd Street. The church was declared a National Historic Landmark in 2005 because of its significance in the civil rights movement. Activist pastor Fred Shuttlesworth led the congregation between 1953 and 1961, and beginning in these years the church served as a meeting place for civil rights organizing and headquarters for the Alabama Christian Movement for Human Rights (ACMHR). Loving black people as she did, Arties was an ardent supporter of the charismatic Rev. Shuttlesworth and active in the civil rights movement alongside her grandchildren.

While men were the leaders of the church-based civil rights movement in Birmingham, women were its backbone. "Women were indispensable to the ACMHR. As in African American churches, they made up the majority of ACMHR members, 61.7 percent in 1959," Wilson Fallin Jr. documents. He explains: "Although men made the major decisions, women were the chief fund raisers. Women almost exclusively directed candy and bake sales, socials, and dinners. Women organized special occasions like the annual anniversary. They made up most of the choir and ushers."[36] "Run by the men but the women keep the tempo," as Beyoncé sings.[37] I see this black woman's tempo in a motion-filled photograph of a 1963 ACMHR meeting at Bethel Baptist. The church is a sea of black women of every shade of brown (punctuated here and there by black men), all shouting, clapping, and raising open palms to the sky as stained-glass windows crown them and a lone fan blows onto their collective heat. Many women raising hands and voices are elders, and sometimes I see my great-grandmother's face peering glowingly from a middle row with her chin uplifted and eyes and earrings glinting. Not the one and only but one of many many, her presence in a sea of black women is an image of force, possibility, and joy.

My great-grandmother practiced her faith in the wooden pews of Bethel Baptist and in the woodsy outskirts of Birmingham, too. Her black Eastern Cherokee mother, Lucinda Crozier, came from a family of beekeepers and herbalists, and Arties left the bees swarming in Goodwater but took the family knowledge of herbs with her to North Birmingham. When family members were sick, my cousin John Robert remembers, she traveled to the woods to gather herbs to heal what medical doctors couldn't. His stories echo those of ex-slave Martha Patton of Alabama, who recounted in a WPA interview: "Twa'nt no use to send fo' a docta, no'm, 'cause dey didn't have no medicine. My grandmother got out in de woods and got 'erbs. She made sage bam. One thing

I recommember, she would take co'n shucks—de butt end of de shucks—and boil 'em and make tea. 'Twould break de chills and fever. De Lo'd fixed a way. We used roots for medicine too."[38] Sage (as tea and smudge), corn (especially corn pollen and husks), passionflower, Queen Anne's lace, blackberry, sassafras: these are all staples of Cherokee ritual healing and African American rootwork that Arties would have learned from her own mother, that she used to heal her grandbabies too. And she may not have had much use for bees, but she did root out bee balm: a purple-flowering plant that Cherokee women use to bring on their period, calm their headaches, sweat out their flus, settle their stomachs, and make their sleep restful. In her King James Bible, Arties kept the names and phone numbers of church parishioners whom she visited when they were ill: Sis C. Carmichael, Sis L. Clark, C. Newberry, R. Henderson, V. Durant, L. Hutchinson, B. Washington, E. Chapelle. Did she bring herbs with her to these visits, too? When you're trying to heal a community, don't you bring all your tools from all your places?

———

Ezili Ayida Tokan, tout pitit ou yo lan men ou! Ezili Ayida Tokan, all your children are in your hand! Miriam is pregnant with a son, Antonio, when she and her partner Jérémie migrate to Santo Domingo looking for work. The child comes but work does not, and after Jérémie leaves Miriam to raise Antonio alone the young mother meets Micaela, her second partner and Antonio's third parent. Antonio accompanies them on the Puerto Rico crossing but drowns when the raft briefly capsizes. Abandoned by her man, coerced into sex work, and bereft of her child, Miriam's story now echoes one of Ezili's songs: "Ezili marye, li pa genyen chans! Ezili fe jennes, li pa genyen chans! Yon sel pitit li genyen. Li ale an lanme, kannot chavire ave li! Ezili got married, she had no luck! Ezili prostituted herself, she had no luck! She had one sole child. She went into the sea, the canoe flipped over on her!" But while the song ends here, Miriam's story does not. When she and Micaela return to El Sur they take in a girl named Yealidad, raising her as a daughter and healer. "They had shown her how to walk, how to breathe and how to believe. They had shown her the depths of love," Yealidad meditates.[39] So though Miriam is pregnant only once and Micaela never at all, the couple has multiple children, multiple next-generation loves raised by multiple parents. This is a queer family, yes—but also just the way African diaspora women parent. Writing of working-class black Surinamese women, Wekker tells us: "One of the West African features of the Creole kinship system, which has survived to this day, is that children are easily exchanged between households. Especially when a woman is without children of her own, she is 'given' children of her siblings, of other relatives, or of her mati to raise."[40] Her lover Misi Juliette Cummings, she recounts as an example, was brought up by an aunt with no biological children, gave her youngest daughter to her childless eldest to raise from birth, and had a daughter, Wanda, named after a female lover who kept the child after she and Juliette split up.

Treading in this black womanly tradition, I've found my theoretical poly-amory necessitates theoretical multiparenting—the contemporary term given to raising children with more than two parental figures. I started writing keenly aware of my wondrous position as the daughter of many black feminist intellectual mothers and young aunties: Helen Tinsley-Jones, VèVè Clark, Barbara Christian, Gloria Wekker, Nalo Hopkinson, Sharon Bridgforth, Omi Jones. But somewhere along the way, I realized I was writing Ezili's Mirrors—if you'll pardon my cliché—for the children. For my daughter, beloved Baía, who has so many more ways of knowing than can be contained in the kind of book I was trained to write; who excels in science and Spanish, talks with the dead, tells me she's going to be a priestess of the wind, and makes six-year-old black girl's meaning with her body through dance, fashion, hair braiding, and joy. For my graduate students, who imagine futures where black girls can live (super)naturally, flirt with lingerie-clad Rihanna in public talks, slip poems into dissertation chapters, claim Amber Rose and Cardi B as feminist warrior-sisters, and break open language where black trans women can live. The forms of writing, knowing, and becoming I was taught in graduate school—and was supposed to pass on to them—aren't capacious enough to hold all the ways they know. Now this is true of every generation, but theirs is the one I can mentor; so now is my time to make a gesture toward undoing conventions that don't allow for all of what we know to make it to the page. My students will have many black feminist intellectual mothers, too, some of whom will guide them through disciplinary expectations as lovingly as my mother Helen taught me to follow sewing patterns. But I'm writing Ezili's Mirrors to become the queer black mama who cuts those expectations into pieces small enough to be sewn into a wild-colored quilt, putting my patchwork into the academy the way ancestors hung Underground Railroad quilts: as a signal that a safe space has been created here for black folk, that prayers are being offered for our well-being.

When I was beginning *Ezili's Mirrors*, brilliant, lovely José Muñoz made his transition and as I conclude, his introduction to *Cruising Utopia* gleams goldenly in my mind. I try to avoid lengthy quotations, but his is worth every line:

> We are not yet queer. We may never touch queerness, but we can feel it as the warm illumination of a horizon imbued with potentiality. We have never been queer, yet queerness exists for us as an ideality that can be distilled from the past and used to imagine a future. The future is queerness' domain. Queerness is a structuring and educated mode of desiring that allows us to see and feel beyond the quagmire of the present. . . . We must dream and enact new and better pleasures, other ways of being in the world, and ultimately new worlds. Queerness is a longing that propels us onward, beyond romances of the negative. Queerness is that thing that lets us feel this world is not enough.[41]

Muñoz's "forward-dawning futurity" is queer of color time, the warmly illuminated, unreal(ized) future where all our multiparented, unruly, well-loved black and brown children are free to desire creatively.[42] It's also spirit time, the forward-pushing temporality of Ezili. "In her character," Maya Deren writes of the lwa, "is reflected all the élan, all the excessive pitch with which the dreams of men soar, when, momentarily, they can shake loose the flat weight, the dreary, reiterative demands of necessity" and elevate "their capacity to conceive beyond reality, to desire beyond adequacy, to create beyond need."[43] In other words: when they can move beyond the quotidian present to the future, perfect.

I've tried to write *Ezili's Mirrors* somewhere in between the present and the perfect-moving queer future, to push limits, open gaps and fissures for other writers to push through. Like all mothers, I've done this fabulously imperfectly. Luckily, mine isn't the only way to try to touch a black feminist queerness that remains *not-yet*: José did it his way; Gloria, Omi, Sharon, Nalo, and many others continue to do it in theirs. So I hope all the beautiful young black queers and feminists will feel at home in many intellectual mamis' and tanties' houses, will walk through as many family doors as Miriam or Misi Juliette. In order to "dream and enact new and better pleasures, other ways of being in the world, and ultimately new worlds," this generation of black women and queers must be Ezili's children, born of and meant for so many, many loves. *Ezili Ayida Tokan, all your children are in your hand!*

⋙⋘

On February 8, 2015, Rihanna was one of the last guests to arrive on the red carpet for the Fifty-Seventh Annual Grammy Awards in Los Angeles's Staples Center. She entered floating in a lush, two-tiered pink tulle strapless gown by Giambattista Valli, her hair pinned back in a simple bun and her natural-looking makeup harmonizing in shades of browner pink. The gown was so fantastically voluminous it spilled over into three seats, proving visible on the arena's overhead cameras. While there was no shortage of pictures of Rihanna twirling and laughing on the red carpet, some of her most talked-about photos were taken with young black girls. Photographers snapped her smiling and holding Jamie Foxx's daughter Annalise, then bowing down charmingly to put her arms around Blue Ivy Carter. This second, particularly tender picture caught many eyes—not only because of the sweet visual harmony of two black girls in pink hugging, but because of decade-long rumors that Rihanna was sleeping with Blue's father Jay Z and feuding with her mother Beyoncé. Though this was the first meeting between RiRi and Blue, their comfortable hug and easy eye contact suggested a connection between the two carefree black girls. "If you wanted to see what our dreams looked like, you could just look at this single, flawless photo of Rihanna and Blue Ivy hanging out in pretty pink princess dresses backstage at the Grammys," Sally Holmes wrote in *Elle*. "Trading goss, being the ultimate besties. RiRi would pretty much be the coolest babysitter ever."[44] The next day, Rihanna posted their picture on Instagram with the caption: "Blue told me she likes my fluffy dress lol! She was also fully aware that she was in Dior, and not afraid to let ya know ok."[45]

"Auntie OhNaNa," Rihanna calls herself when she takes on the role of "coolest babysitter ever" for young girls in her life.[46] In September 2014 she stood as godmother for her baby cousin Majesty's christening and proudly posts pictures of herself caring for her goddaughter whenever she can. "She may have a carefully curated persona as the bad girl of pop," Shyam Dodge of the *Daily Mail* admits. "But when it comes to her baby cousin Majesty, Rihanna is as soft and tender as they come."[47] Rihanna often expresses child-rearing desires even as she voices doubts about pregnancy, citing childbirth as her greatest fear. She herself was largely mothered by her beloved GranGran Dolly, a woman who didn't birth her but nurtured her to the wild complexity of adulthood. Call it Caribbean tradition ("Island Gals" Rihanna captions a selfie of herself and Majesty),[48] but creative mothering arrangements like Rihanna's and Dolly's are an essential part of carefree black girlhood. Black mamas, grangrans, godmothers, and cool babysitters need flexible, expansive kinship structures both to raise a next generation of carefree black girls, *and* to keep the carefreeness of their own black girlness alive. Sometimes a baby girl needs more than one mama so she can grow up with more than one model of womanhood, and sometimes a black mama needs a comother so she can keep taking care of herself. Describing her own inventive mothering style—including home birthing, teaching journaling classes, and single parenting by choice—"carefree black girl disguised as a mama" Simone Jones argues passionately that unconventional mothering needs to be recast as a strength rather than a deficiency in black families.[49] Instead of calling mothers like Rihanna's irresponsible or mother figures like Rihanna bad role models, she opines, "The mother shaming shit needs a rest. Point blank. If we did that, it'd make it easier for women to become whole and ultimately be even better mothers. . . . Maybe 'mom sabbaticals' would exist without the guilt or fear of being called a bad mother. Little girls would have examples of full, grown, developed feminine energies that respect and revere their complete selves."[50]

Comothering that models "full, grown, developed feminine energies" not only produces healthy girls; it produces images of divine black girlness. Like RiRi and (we hope) Majesty, Anaisa ascends into self-realization under the tutelage of inventive, non–birth mothering. "There is a story that says that Anaisa was conceived in Africa, but born in Aiti/Quisqueya," Sancista Luis narrates. "Her mother Metresili and her father Ogun Balendjo tried to raise her, but they had their hands full as the suffering of their people in the New World had them very occupied."[51] Ezili Freda (Metresili) and Ogun placed their daughter in a convent, where her own GranGran Sili transformed into a Spanish nun to raise her granddaughter. "Gran Sili raised Anaisa until she was 13," Sance Luis concludes. "At this age Anaisa wanted her freedom and became the Loa she is today."[52] At birth, Anaisa's life seemed scripted to become a tragedy bound up in the suffering of enslaved black folk that preoccupied her parents. But Gran Sili's creative mothering instead prepared her, at the witchy age of thirteen, to step into freedom and divinity that remained—indeed, *still remain*—distant aspirations for black women in the Americas. Anaisa's divine freedom is made possible by mothering that not only becomes literally intergenerational, but mythically exemplifies what Alexis Pauline Gumbs calls *queer intergenerationality*. Intergenerational because it links the African past (Gran Sili) to the Caribbean future (Anaisa), Gran Sili's choice to parent Anaisa into lwa-hood is queer because it defies normative politico-economic structures that seek to reproduce only violent futures for black bodies. Such black mothering relationships, Gumbs writes beautifully, raise the "queer potential for an outlawed future": a future black women create by caring for themselves, other black women, and black girls not out of birth-motherly duty, but out of desire to create generations in which "Black women can actually 'generate' desire, speech, narrative, critique and social relationships, a production silenced by the reproduction of these desires as pathologies in the dominant narratives."[53] Generations of carefree black girls talking story and talking back, feeling flawless and "not afraid to let ya know ok."

Creative black mothering consists of more than thoughtful child-rearing, though. It also means black women and girls mothering their own creativity. Anaisa's sheltered, woman-centered childhood allowed her years to sit still in convent gardens, luxuriating in the scent of roses, lilies, marigolds, rosemary, and virgin's bower grown in honor of the Virgin Mary. From this she developed her power to create and heal with perfumes, which she works to bring love, luck, and healing. "Many a perfume have been created and administered under her point to resolve a problem," Houngan Hector writes of her perfumer's art. "There are several mixes that are aimed at specifically obtaining her help, and there are others that she will mix together for a person as needed on an individual case basis. Perfumes can be for money, love, luck—usually she mixes perfumes to attract these things to the person whom she is giving it to."[54] When Anaisa leaves the convent at thirteen, she emerges at the age of puberty ready to create perfume, not babies; she's matured composition skills rather than ovaries. More comfortable as a godmother than a full-time mother, the Rihanna who performed at the 2015 Grammys was in the throes of completing her eighth album *Anti*, and "treating delivery of the project like 'making a baby.'"[55] A music source explained that, relative to the speed with which she produced earlier albums, *Anti* has "taken so long because she's a complete perfectionist. She's treating this record like, 'I'm going to make a baby.'"[56] The album's cover art, by Roy Nachum, centers a photorealist image of Rihanna as a little girl in Barbados, red paint veiling her face and torso, a gold crown covering her eyes and a black balloon—"a metaphor of escaped reality," Nachum explains—clasped in her left hand. In her art, then, Rihanna is literally re-creating and remothering the little girl she was, recoloring her realities and possibilities.[57] The image is "tinted with naïvety—here is a picture of Rihanna when she was not yet Rihanna but Robyn Fenty of Barbados—yet, with the red and the crown, also with an innate, inevitable power."[58] Yes, the power of a carefree black girl who's mothered herself, brought beauty into the world and is ready to pass it on and on.

∞

Near the midpoint of her life, Arties became the owner of a small house in Collegeville, North Birmingham. How she got funds to purchase this house isn't clear: my grandfather told my mother that he bought it for her, while my cousin counters that she bought it herself with settlement money from the railroad after her son's death. Both stories could be true, of course, but what's certain is that buying this house marked a turning point in her life. The building is no longer standing—a tree-bordered lot of lush green grass now spills out into the street there—but I visited its former site in 2007 with my mother Helen, cousin John Robert, his wife Sue, and their daughter Savannah. Across the street two older gentlemen greeted us, enjoying an afternoon of shared whiskey on their front porch. When we told them we were Arties Phillips's grandchildren come to look for her old place, they obligingly remembered the house and its matriarch. Miss Arties! Yes, she had a white clapboard house three rooms deep with a front porch, all kinds of neighborhood children running in and out—if you lived on the block and needed someone to watch your kids for a day or a week, Miss Arties was the one.

Arties lived in that house with her oldest son until she died in 1975, and there they raised a handful of well-behaved black children. They raised Hattie Pearl's daughter and sons—including John Robert, who led us back to the block he grew up on that day—and Arties offered to take in my uncle John Talmadge when he was a boy (much to my grandmother's dismay). Other children stayed there from time to time too, children whose names and stories John and Arties's neighbors have forgotten but whose presence they knew as a neighborhood fixture. Blood kin and play family, overnight guests and forever family, high yellows and deep browns, tomboys and church girls: the children who passed through Arties's house were many and varied, filling the white shotgun house with even more ways to love than her lovers ever could.

From the Gulf Coast to Birmingham, Alabama boasts thousands of shot-gun houses like my great-grandmother's. The region's most enduring African American architectural form, shotgun houses were first built in New Orleans at the turn of the nineteenth century by Haitian migrants who replicated the houses they left behind in revolutionary Haiti "in every detail, from height and floor space, to door and window placement."[59] Shotgun houses are long and narrow, one room opening into another, so allowing breezes to move through easily and cool the space. The compactness of their design also allowed black folk to group their houses together the way their Congo and Yoruba ancestors had, opening into a common space—the lakou in Haiti, the block in Birming-ham. With housing difficult and municipal services as scarce as they were in North Birmingham, Arties always had enough space to raise her children and anyone else's because her family's living area was never limited to her three rooms. Her home was also that shared in-between space where folks crossed from one house to the next, called to each other from porches, sent children to ask neighbors for a favor, cursed each other out, collected for the church, shared gossip and whiskey, laughed and kissed goodbye. Now that the struc-ture of Arties's house is no more, our onetime family home has become the open space that her house always was figuratively, and now is literally. The "inexhaustible tangle" of the black extended family, as Edouard Glissant calls it, extended beyond bloodlines and heartlines into its own messy, overflowing work of art.[60]

Great-grandmother Arties, this book has been written in the black woman's space you created: a space of endless, unfinished loves; of everyday, imperfect, forward-dawning goddesses.

NOTES

Bridge: Read This Book Like a Song

1. Barbara Christian, "The Race for Theory," *Cultural Critique* 6 (spring 1987): 52.
2. Christian, "The Race for Theory," 52, 61.

Introduction: For the Love of Laveau

1. Several spelling variations of this spirit's name are common in English, including Erzulie, Erzuli, and Ezili. For consistency, I have opted to use "Ezili"— the most common spelling in Kreyòl—throughout.
2. Karen McCarthy Brown, *Mama Lola: A Vodou Priestess in Brooklyn* (Berkeley: University of California Press, 1991), 221.
3. Lisa Ze Winters citing Brent Hayes Edwards in "Specter, Spectacle and the Imaginative Space: Unfixing the Tragic Mulatta" (PhD diss., University of California, Berkeley, 2005), 23.
4. Barbara Christian, "The Race for Theory," in *Making Face, Making Soul: Haciendo Caras*, ed. Gloria Anzaldúa (San Francisco: Aunt Lute, 1990), 336.
5. Song for Ezili cited by Marie-Jose Alcide Saint-Lot, *Vodou: A Sacred Theatre—the African Heritage in Haiti* (Miami: Educa Vision, 2004), 154–155.
6. Marilyn Houlberg, "Sirens and Snakes: Water Spirits in the Arts of Haitian Vodou," *African Arts* (Spring 1996): 31, 32.
7. See, for example, Ursula Szeles, "Sea Secret Rising: The Lwa Lasirennn in Haitian Vodou," *Journal of Haitian Studies* 17, no. 1 (spring 2011): 193–210.
8. Luce Irigaray, *This Sex That Is Not One* (Ithaca, NY: Cornell University Press, 1985), 209.
9. For these statistics and others relating to Haiti's water supply, see Paul Farmer et al., "Meeting Cholera's Challenge to Haiti and the World: A Joint

Statement on Cholera Prevention and Care," PLoS *Neglected Tropical Diseases* 5, no. 5 (May 31, 2011).

10. Quoted in GreenCOM, "Haitian Urban Sanitation Project Formative Research," USAID, 1996, 6, http://pdf.usaid.gov/pdf_docs/pnacd457.pdf.

11. GreenCOM, "Haitian Urban Sanitation Project Formative Research," 19.

12. Romulo E. Colindres et al., "After the Flood: An Evaluation of In-Home Drinking Water Treatment Combined with Flocculent-Disinfectant Following Tropical Storm Jeanne—Gonaives, Haiti, 2004," *Journal of Water and Health* 5, no. 3 (March 2007): 368.

13. Michel Desse, "Les difficultés de gestion d'un littoral de survie à Haïti: L'exemple du golfe de la Gonave," *Cahiers de Geographie du Québec* 47, no. 130 (April 2003): 79, 72. Translation mine.

14. See Nice Rodriguez, "Throw It to the River," in *Throw It to the River* (Toronto: Women's Press, 1993), 93–101.

15. On this haunted history see "Top Ten Most Haunted New Orleans Locations," Haunted New Orleans Tours, accessed April 30, 2012, http://www.hauntedne worleanstours.com/toptenhaunted/toptenhauntedNewOrleanslocations.

16. Carolyn Morrow Long, *A New Orleans Voudou Priestess: The Legend and Reality of Marie Laveau* (Gainesville: University Press of Florida, 2006), xxxvii.

17. Sallie Ann Glassman, *Vodou Visions: An Encounter with Divine Mystery* (New York: Villard, 2000), 53. Martha Ward describes this vèvè in *Vodou Queen: The Spirited Lives of Marie Laveau* (Jackson: University Press of Mississippi, 2004), 188.

18. Glassman, *Vodou Visions*, 53.

19. Quoted in Claudine Michel, Patrick Bellegarde-Smith, and Marlene Racine-Toussaint, "From the Horses' Mouths: Women's Words/Women's Worlds," in *Haitian Vodou: Spirit, Myth, and Reality*, ed. Patrick Bellegarde-Smith and Claudine Michel (Bloomington: University of Indiana Press, 2006), 80.

20. Quoted in Randy P. Conner with David Hatfield Sparks, *Queering Creole Spiritual Traditions: Lesbian, Gay, Bisexual, and Transgender Participation in African-Inspired Traditions in the Americas* (Binghamton, NY: Harrington Park, 2004), 96.

21. Marilyn Houlberg, "Magique Marasa: The Ritual Cosmos of Twins and Other Sacred Children," in *The Sacred Arts of Haitian Vodou*, ed. Daniel J. Cosentino (Los Angeles: UCLA Fowler Museum of Cultural History, 1995), 425, n. 27.

22. Quoted in Conner and Sparks, *Queering Creole Spiritual Traditions*, 97.

23. Kate Ramsey, *The Spirits and the Law: Vodou and Power in Haiti* (Chicago: University of Chicago Press, 2011), 48–49.

24. Ramsey, *The Spirits and the Law*, 44–45.

25. Brown, *Mama Lola*, 220.

26. George René and Marilyn Houlberg, "My Double Mystic Marriages to Two Goddesses of Love," in *The Sacred Arts of Haitian Vodou*, ed. Daniel J. Cosentino (Los Angeles: UCLA Fowler Museum of Cultural History, 1995), 299.

27. Quoted in Conner and Sparks, *Queering Creole Spiritual Traditions*, 60.

28. Katherine McKittrick, *Demonic Grounds: Black Women and the Cartographies of Struggle* (Minneapolis: University of Minnesota Press, 2006), xxv.

29. Jani Scandura, *Down in the Dumps: Place, Modernity, American Depression* (Durham, NC: Duke University Press, 2008), 21.

30. Carolyn Morrow Long gives thorough consideration to which of Laveau's biological daughters might have taken her mother's place and concludes that most likely it was a spiritual, rather than biological daughter. Long, *A New Orleans Voudou Priestess*, 200–205.

31. On the history of Haitian migration to New Orleans, see Shirley Thompson, *Exiles at Home: The Struggle to Become American in Creole New Orleans* (Cambridge, MA: Harvard University Press, 2009), 73–74.

32. Ina Johanna Fandrich, "Defiant African Sisterhoods: The Voodoo Arrests of the 1850s and 1860s in New Orleans," in *Fragments of Bone: Neo-African Religions in a New World*, ed. Patrick Bellegarde-Smith (Urbana: University of Illinois Press, 2005), 187.

33. Cited by Fandrich, "Defiant African Sisterhoods," 192.

34. Cited by Ward, *Vodou Queen*, 135.

35. Cited by Fandrich, "Defiant African Sisterhoods," 197.

36. Cited by Fandrich, "Defiant African Sisterhoods," 194, 195.

37. Ward, *Vodou Queen*, makes the point about nakedness, 142.

38. The color differences between these paths of Ezili—two of her emanations being mulatta, while Ezili Danto is dark skinned—have important implications for how race, class, and gender intersect in Haiti and elsewhere in the Caribbean. Although these divisions of racialized gender are not my focus here (as they are the focus of the film), they would deserve an in-depth look in a wider study of representations of Ezili.

39. On Ezili as the most textualized of lwa, see Joan Dayan, "Erzulie: A Women's History of Haiti," *African Literatures* 25 (1994), 18. On the presence of the lwa in the works of Saint and Gerestant, see Jana Evans Braziel, *Artists, Performers, and Black Masculinity in the Haitian Diaspora* (Bloomington: Indiana University Press, 2008), 85–142; and on Ana-Maurine Lara's novel *Erzulie's Skirt*, see Omise'eke Natasha Tinsley, "Black Atlantic, Queer Atlantic: Queer Imaginings of the Middle Passage," *GLQ* 14, no. 2/3 (April 2008): 191–215.

40. Elizabeth McAlister, "Love, Sex, and Gender Embodied: The Spirits of Haitian Vodou," in *Love, Sex, and Gender in the World Religions*, ed. Joseph Runzo and Nancy Martin (Oxford: Oneworld, 2000), 132.

41. Dayan, "Erzulie," 5, 6.

42. Dayan, "Erzulie," 6.

43. Dayan, "Erzulie," 6.

44. Maya Deren, *Divine Horsemen: The Living Gods of Haiti* (1953; reprint, Kingston, NY: Documentext, 1983), 138.

45. Saidiya Hartman, "Venus in Two Acts," *Small Axe* 26 (June 2008): 12.

46. Grace Hong, "The Ghosts of Transnational American Studies," *American Quarterly* 59, no. 1 (March 2007): 38.

47. Wade Davis, *The Serpent and the Rainbow: A Harvard Scientist's Astonishing Journey into the Secret Societies of Haitian Voodoo, Zombis, and Magic* (New York: Simon & Schuster, 1985), 160.

48. Nick Caistor, "Voodoo's Spell over Haiti," BBC News, August 4, 2003, http://news.bbc.co.uk/2/hi/americas/3122303.stm.

49. Caistor, "Voodoo's Spell over Haiti."

50. Daniel Cosentino, "It's All for You, Sen Jak!," in *The Sacred Arts of Haitian Vodou*, ed. Daniel J. Cosentino (Los Angeles: UCLA Fowler Museum of Cultural History, 1995), 243.

51. Roberto Strongman, "Transcorporeality in Haitian Vodou," *Journal of Haitian Studies* 14, no. 2 (2008): 5.

52. This song is cited and translated by Ward, *Vodou Queen*, 140.

53. This description is taken from Ward, *Vodou Queen*, 14.

54. On Laveau's relationship with Native American women, see Ward, *Vodou Queen*, 76–77.

55. See Ward, *Vodou Queen*, 113–115.

56. Cited and translated by Ward, *Vodou Queen*, 142.

57. Cited by Long, *A New Orleans Voudou Priestess*, 53.

58. Anonymous interviewee in Frank Perez and Jeffrey Palmquist, *In Exile: The History and Lore Surrounding New Orleans Gay Culture and Its Oldest Gay Bar* (Hurlford, Scotland: LL Publications, 2012), 107.

59. Ward, *Vodou Queen*, 111.

60. Zora Neale Hurston, *Mules and Men* (New York: Harper Perennial, 1990), 193.

61. Cited by Ward, *Vodou Queen*, 143.

62. "Marie Lavaux: Death of the Queen of the Voudous," *New Orleans Democrat*, June 18, 1881, available at Wendy Mae Chambers, Voodoo on the Bayou, accessed May 1, 2012, http://www.voodooonthebayou.net/marie_laveau.html.

63. Cited by Ward, *Vodou Queen*, 150.

64. Cathy Cohen, "Bulldaggers, Punks, and Welfare Queens," GLQ 3 (1997): 453.

65. M. Jacqui Alexander, *Pedagogies of Crossing: Meditations on Feminism, Sexual Politics, Memory, and the Sacred* (Durham, NC: Duke University Press, 2005), 293.

66. I take my inspiration for this description from George René's altar to Danto, photographed in René and Houlberg, "My Double Mystic Marriages to Two Goddesses of Love," 293.

67. Daniel Cosentino, "Imagine Heaven," in *The Sacred Arts of Haitian Vodou*, ed. Daniel J. Cosentino (Los Angeles: UCLA Fowler Museum of Cultural History, 1995), 28–29.

68. Keith McNeal, "Pantheons as Mythistorical Archives: Pantheonization and Remodeled Iconographies in Two Southern Caribbean Possession Religions," in *Activating the Past: History and Memory in the Black Atlantic World*, ed. Andrew Apter and Lauren Derby (Newcastle upon Tyne: Cambridge Scholars, 2010), 226.

69. McNeal, "Pantheons as Mythistorical Archives," 188.

70. Matthew Richardson, personal communication, September 13, 2011.

71. Sallie Ann Glassman, personal communication, May 2, 2012.

72. Sallie Ann Glassman, personal communication, May 2, 2012.

73. Sallie Ann Glassman, personal communication, May 2, 2012.

74. Sallie Ann Glassman, personal communication, May 2, 2012; Audre Lorde, "The Uses of the Erotic: The Erotic as Power," in *Sister Outsider: Essays and Speeches by Audre Lorde* (New York: Crossing Press, 1984), 54–55.

Bridge: A Black Cisfemme Is a Beautiful Thing

1. See Caryn Ganz, "The Curious Case of Nicki Minaj," *Out*, September 12, 2010, http://www.out.com/entertainment/music/2010/09/12/curious-case-nicki-minaj.

2. See Oprah Winfrey's interview with Raven-Symoné on the broadcast "Where Are They Now?," YouTube video, October 5, 2014, https://www.youtube.com/watch?v=QXAho8vlmAI.

3. See Cardi B's interview on *The Breakfast Club*, Power 105.1, March 8, 2016. http://www.vh1.com/news/249697/cardi-b-admits-bisexual-dabbles-with-women/.

4. Kanye West, "I Don't Like," on *Cruel Summer* (New York: G.O.O.D. Music, 2012).

5. Cyree Jarelle Johnson, "Femme Privilege Does Not Exist," *Femme Dreamboat* (blog), January 5, 2013, http://femmedreamboat.tumblr.com/post/39734380982/femme-privilege-does-not-exist.

6. Julia Serano, *Excluded: Making Feminist and Queer Movements More Inclusive* (New York: Seal, 2013), 62.

Chapter 1: To Transcender Transgender

1. Adia Whitaker, "Ezili," YouTube video, May 2012, http://www.youtube.com/watch?v=JDwN2DNschc.

2. Maya Deren, *Divine Horsemen: The Living Gods of Haiti* (1953; reprint, Kingston, NY: Documentext, 1983): 139, 140.

3. Whitaker, "Ezili." Transcription by author. Ellipses in original.

4. Kara Keeling, *The Witch's Flight: The Cinematic, the Black Femme, and the Image of Common Sense* (Durham, NC: Duke University Press, 2007), 84.

5. Keeling, *The Witch's Flight*, 9.

6. Keeling, *The Witch's Flight*, 143–144.

7. Quoted in Dora Silva Santana, "Trans-Atlantic Re-turnings: A Trans/Black/Diasporic/Feminist Auto-account of a Black Trans Brazilian Woman's Transitioning" (master's thesis, University of Texas at Austin, 2015), 30.

8. See Santana, "Trans-Atlantic Re-turnings," 29–36.

9. Quoted in Ulrika Dahl, *Femmes of Power* (London: Serpent's Tail, 2009), 45.

10. This performance appears in Gabriel Baur's film *Venus Boyz* (Onix Films, 1998).

11. Dréd cited in Ifalade TaShia Asanti, ed., *Tapestries of Faith: Black SGLBT Stories of Faith, Love, & Family* (Long Beach, CA: Glover Lane, 2011), 34.

12. Sarah Chinn and Kris Franklin, "King of the Hill: Changing the Face of Drag—an interview with Dred," in *Butch/Femme: Inside Lesbian Gender*, ed. Sally R. Munt and Cherry Smyth (London: Continuum, 1998), 152.

13. Jana Evans Braziel, *Artists, Performers, and Black Masculinity in the Haitian Diaspora* (Bloomington: Indiana University Press, 2008), 122.

14. TJ Bryan, "You've Got to Have Ballz to Walk in These Shoes," in *Brazen Femme: Queering Femininity*, ed. Chloe Brushwood Rose (Vancouver: Arsenal Pulp, 2003), 147.

15. Bryan, "You've Got to Have Ballz," 147.

16. Matt Richardson, personal communication, September 2011.

17. Storme Webber in Baur, *Venus Boyz*. Transcription by author

18. Janet Collins's autobiography, in Yael Tamar Lewin, *Night's Dancer: The Life of Janet Collins* (Middletown, CT: Wesleyan University Press, 2011), 4–5.

19. Collins in Lewin, *Night's Dancer*, 5.

20. Collins, in Lewin, *Night's Dancer*.

21. Collins in Lewin, *Night's Dancer*, 18.

22. Collins in Lewin, *Night's Dancer*, 20–21.

23. Elizabeth McAlister, "Love, Sex, and Gender Embodied: The Spirits of Haitian Vodou," in *Love, Sex, and Gender in the World Religions*, vol. 2, ed. Joseph Runzo and Nancy M. Martin (Oxford: One World, 2000), 132.

24. See Homi Bhabha, "Of Mimicry and Man," in *The Location of Culture* (New York: Routledge, 2004), 128.

25. See Hërsza Barjon, *Ezili Freda*; Gerard Fortune, *Erzulie Maitresse*; and Frohawk Two Feathers, *He Dead. Amen! La Donna, Inventor of the Hot Comb and Widow of the Emperor Andre I of Hispaniola as Maitresse Mambo Erzulie Freda Dahomey*.

26. McAlister, "Love, Sex, and Gender Embodied," 132; Mambo Vye Zo Komande LaMenfo, *Serving the Spirits: The Religion of Haitian Vodou* (CreateSpace, 2012), 144.

27. Zora Neale Hurston, *Tell My Horse* (1938; reprint, New York: Harper Perennial Classics, 2008), 128.

28. Lisa Duggan and Kathleen McHugh, "Fem(me)inist Manifesto," in *Brazen Femme: Queering Femininity*, ed. Chloe Brushwood Rose (Vancouver: Arsenal Pulp, 2003), 165.

29. LaMenfo, *Serving the Spirits*, 150.

30. Dayan, "Erzulie: A Women's History of Haiti?," *African Literatures* 25 (1994): 22.

31. See "About: Our Mission, Our Dream," Makandal, accessed July 24, 2013, http://makandal.org/about/.

32. Kirsty MacDonald, "Assume Nothing: MilDred Gerestant," YouTube video, October 31, 2010, http://www.youtube.com/watch?v=pWAg3DsEnaA.

33. MacDonald, "Assume Nothing," transcription by author.

34. MacDonald, "Assume Nothing."

35. Rinaldo Walcott, "Reconstructing Manhood; or, The Drag of Black Masculinity," *Small Axe* 13, no. 1 (March 2009): 77.

36. MilDred Gerestant, Tantra-zawadi, and Sokhna Heathyre Mabin, "A Night of Three Goddesses: Powerful Women." New York Public Library, June 28, 2010. http://www.nypl.org/events/programs/2010/06/28/night-three-goddesses -powerful-women.

37. Lewin, *Night's Dancer*, 146.

38. Quoted in Lewin, *Night's Dancer*, 131.

39. Quoted in Lewin, *Night's Dancer*, 137.

40. Quoted in Lewin, *Night's Dancer*, 104.

41. Lewin, *Night's Dancer*, 143.

42. Lewin, *Night's Dancer*, 143–144.

43. Collins quoted in Lewin, *Night's Dancer,* 104.

44. This picture is reproduced in Lewin, *Night's Dancer*, 131.

45. Quoted in Lewin, *Night's Dancer*, 261.

46. Quoted in Lewin, *Night's Dancer*, 106.

47. McAlister, "Love, Sex, and Gender Embodied," 132.

48. Hurston, *Tell My Horse*, 128.

49. Duggan and McHugh, "Fem(me)inist Manifesto," 166.

50. Bryan, "You've Got to Have Ballz," 147.

51. See Marie Vieux Chauvet, *La Danse sur le Volcan* (1957; reprint, Paris: Maison-neuve & Larose et Emina Soleil, 2004), 1.

52. Quoted in Sheena Boa, "Young Ladies and Dissolute Women: Conflicting Views of Culture and Gender in Public Entertainment, Kingstown, St. Vincent, 1838–1888," in *Gender and Slave Emancipation in the Atlantic World*, ed. Pamela Scully and Diana Paton (Durham, NC: Duke University Press, 2005), 258.

53. Quoted in Boa, "Young Ladies and Dissolute Women," 257.

54. Quoted in Boa, "Young Ladies and Dissolute Women," 257.

55. See Brenda Dixon Gottschild, *The Black Dancing Body: A Geography from Coon to Cool* (New York: Palgrave Macmillan, 2003), 133–134.

56. Gerestant, Tantra-zawadi, and Mabin, "A Night of Three Goddesses."

57. Randy P. Conner with David Hatfield Sparks, *Queering Creole Spiritual Traditions: Lesbian, Gay, Bisexual, and Transgender Participation in African-Inspired Traditions in the Americas* (New York: Routledge, 2004), 57.

58. See Dréd's performance at POW WOW in Chicago: Chelcie Porter, "Mildred 'Dred' Gerestant at POW WOW," YouTube video, December 11, 2011, https://www.youtube.com/watch?v=qtpBGLZgLrg.

59. MilDred Gerestant and Victoria Gaither, "A Night of Three Goddesses," At Home with Victoria, Blog Talk Radio, March 7, 2010, http://www.blogtalkradio.com/victoria-gaither/2010/03/07/a-night-of-3-goddesses-featuring-actress -mildred-g.

60. On the cultural politics of the gwo neg, see Braziel, *Artists, Performers, and Black Masculinity*, 1–24.

61. McAlister, "Love, Sex, and Gender Embodied," 138.

62. McAlister, "Love, Sex, and Gender Embodied," 139.

63. Judith "Jack" Halberstam and Del LaGrace Volcano, "Class, Race, and Masculinity: The Superfly, the Macdaddy, and the Rapper," in *The Drag King Book* (London: Serpent's Tail, 1999), 142.

64. MilDred Gerestant, "Who Am I—D.R.E.D.—Daring Reality Every Day," Women Writers in Bloom Poetry Salon, 2011, http://womenwritersinbloom poetrysalon.blogspot.com/p/poetry-garden-archives.html.

65. Lewin, *Night's Dancer*, 177.

66. Lewin, *Night's Dancer*, 187.

67. Lewin, *Night's Dancer*, 187.

68. Lewin, *Night's Dancer*, 205.

69. Bryan, "You've Got to Have Ballz," 156.

70. Steeve Buckridge, *The Language of Dress: Resistance and Accommodation in Jamaica, 1760–1890* (Kingston: University of the West Indies Press, 2004), 92.

71. Buckridge, *The Language of Dress*, 89–91.

72. Gloria Wekker, "Mati-ism and Black Lesbianism: Two Idealtypical Expressions of Female Homosexuality in Black Communities of the Diaspora," in *Classics in Lesbian Studies*, ed. Esther D. Rothblum (Binghamton, NY: Haworth, 1996), 16.

73. Gloria Wekker, *The Politics of Passion: Women's Sexual Culture in the Afro Surinamese Diaspora* (New York: Columbia University Press, 2006), 219.

74. Dréd's performance at POW WOW in Chicago, Porter, "Mildred 'Dred' Gerestant at POW WOW."

75. Sallie Ann Glassman, *Vodou Visions: An Encounter with Divine Mystery* (New York: Villard, 2000), 25.

76. Quoted in Jacob Anderson-Minshall, "Is Femme a Gender Identity?," *San Francisco Bay Times*, July 20, 2006, http://www.sfbaytimes.com/?sec=article&article _id=5213.

77. Anderson-Minshall, "Is Femme a Gender Identity?"

78. Alfred Metraux, *Voodoo in Haiti* (New York: Pantheon, 1989), 113.

79. MilDred Gerestant, interview with Stylelikeu, March 21, 2011, http://stylelikeu. com/closets/mildred-gerestant/.

80. Cited in Ulrike Dahl, *Femmes of Power* (London: Serpent's Tail, 2009), 105.

81. Collins in Lewin, *Night's Dancer*.

82. Lewin, *Night's Dancer*, 259.

83. Quoted in Lewin, *Night's Dancer*, 240.

84. Alvin Ailey quoted in Marc Ramirez, "The Blazing Steps of Janet Collins," *Seattle Times*, January 23, 2000, http://community.seattletimes.nwsource.com /archive/?date=20000123&slug=4000846.

85. Geoffrey Holder quoted in Lewin, *Night's Dancer*, 242.

86. Ramirez, "The Blazing Steps of Janet Collins."

87. Ramirez, "The Blazing Steps of Janet Collins."

88. Collins quoted in Ramirez, "The Blazing Steps of Janet Collins."

89. See Beverly Greene, "African American Lesbian and Bisexual Women," *Journal of Social Issues* 56 (2000): 239–249.
90. LaMenfo, *Serving the Spirits*, 150.

Bridge: Sissy Werk

1. See Big Freedia with Nicole Balin, *Big Freedia: God Save the Queen Diva!* (New York: Gallery, 2015), 236–237.
2. Big Freedia in Beyonce, "Formation," on *Lemonade* (New York: Parkwood Entertainment, 2016).
3. Quoted by Chevel Johnson, "Big Freedia Twerking Her Way to Stardom," AP: The Big Story, April 30, 2016, http://bigstory.ap.org/article/976f28971c3943999 3e27db5518f288f/big-freedia-twerks-her-way-stardom.
4. Big Freedia with Balin, *Big Freedia*, 52.
5. Big Freedia with Balin, *Big Freedia*, 82.
6. See Carole Boyce Davies, "Women, Labor, and the Transnational: From Work to Work," in *Caribbean Spaces: Escapes from Twilight Zones* (Urbana: University of Illinois Press, 2013), 107–128.
7. Saidiya Hartman, "The Belly of the World: A Note on Black Women's Labors," *Souls* 18, no. 1 (January–March 2016): 166.

Chapter 2: Mache Ansanm

1. Carolle Charles, quoted in Bob Corbett, "Dwa Fanm Celebrates the Voices of Women," Haiti Mailing List (e-mail group), March 19, 2003, http://faculty .webster.edu/corbetre/haiti-archive-new/msg15132.html.
2. See the description on the website of its distributor: Anne Lescot and Laurence Magloire, dirs., *Of Men and Gods* (Documentary Educational Resouces, 2002), http://www.der.org/films/of-men-and-gods.html.
3. Robert Koehler, "Review: 'Of Men and Gods,'" *Variety*, August 5, 2003, http:// variety.com/2003/film/reviews/of-men-and-gods-1200540075/.
4. Yasmine Chouaki with Anne Lescot, "En Sol Majeur," RFI, March 11, 2000, http://www.rfi.fr/contenu/20100302-1-anne-lescot.
5. Roberto Strongman, "Transcorporeality in Haitian Vodou," *Journal of Haitian Studies* 14, no. 2 (2008): 25.
6. Roderick Ferguson, "Sissies at the Picnic: The Subjugated Knowledges of a Black Rural Queer," in *Feminist Waves, Feminist Generations: Life Stories from the Academy*, ed. Hokulani Aikau, Karla Erickson, and Jennifer Pierce (Minneapolis: University of Minnesota Press, 2007), 193.
7. Renée Bergan and Mark Schuller, "Directors' Statements," in *Poto Mitan: Haitian Women, Pillars of the Global Economy* (Santa Barbara: Tet Ansanm Productions, 2009), http://potomitan.net/downloads/Poto_Mitan_EPK_NOPIX.pdf.
8. Régine Jean-Charles, "Poto Mitan: Haitian Women, Pillars of the Global Economy," *Films for the Feminist Classroom* 2, no. 1 (spring 2010), http://ffc.twu .edu/issue_2-1/rev_rjc_film_2-1.html.

9. Schuller and Bergan, *Poto Mitan*. Unless otherwise noted, the translations cited here follow those contained in the film's subtitles. Where the subtitles lost some nuances that I felt were important, however, I have added my own translations and transcriptions of the original Kreyòl.

10. Schuller and Bergan, *Poto Mitan*, transcription mine.

11. Karen McCarthy Brown, *Mama Lola: A Vodou Priestess in Brooklyn* (Berkeley: University of California Press, 1991), 220.

12. Brown, *Mama Lola*, 229; Mambo Vye Zo Komande LaMenfo, *Serving the Spirits: The Religion of Haitian Vodou* (CreateSpace, 2012), 178. "Dantor" is an alternate spelling of "Danto," used especially in French.

13. LaMenfo, *Serving the Spirits*, 177.

14. LaMenfo, *Serving the Spirits*, 177.

15. Junior Vazquez, "Just Like a Queen" (New York: Minimal Records, 1990).

16. Jacob Bernstein, "Paris Is Still Burning," *New York Times*, July 25, 2012, http://www.nytimes.com/2012/07/26/fashion/a-lively-house-of-xtravaganza-ball-scene-city.html?_r=0XL.

17. Father Jose Xtravaganza, "Xtravaganza Ball 'Wrath of the Gods & Goddesses,'" Facebook, July 22, 2012, https://www.facebook.com/events/151075545016950/?active_tab=highlights.

18. Bernstein, "Paris Is Still Burning."

19. Jennie Livingston, dir., *Paris Is Burning* (Miramax, 1991; reissue, 2005), transcription mine.

20. Livingston, *Paris Is Burning*, transcription mine.

21. Barbara Browning, *Infectious Rhythm: Metaphors of Contagion and the Spread of African Culture* (New York: Routledge, 1998), 159.

22. Xtravaganza, "Xtravaganza Ball."

23. Lescot and Magloire, *Of Men and Gods*. Unless otherwise noted, the translations cited here follow those contained in the film's subtitles. Where the subtitles lost some nuances that I felt were important, however, I have added my own translations and transcriptions of the original Kreyòl.

24. Lescot and Magloire, *Of Men and Gods*, transcription mine.

25. Lescot and Magloire, *Of Men and Gods*, transcription mine.

26. Lescot and Magloire, *Of Men and Gods*, transcription mine.

27. Brown, *Mama Lola*, 157.

28. Lescot and Magloire, *Of Men and Gods*, transcription mine.

29. Lescot and Magloire, *Of Men and Gods*, translation and transcription mine.

30. Carolle Charles, "Reflections on Being *Machann ak Machandiz*," *Meridians* 11, no. 1 (2011): 122.

31. Charles, "Reflections on Being *Machann ak Machandiz*."

32. Dan Irving, 162.

33. Charles, "Reflections on Being *Machann ak Machandiz*," 118–119.

34. Lescot and Magloire, *Of Men and Gods*, transcription mine.

35. Willi Coleman, "Among the Things That Used to Be," in *Home Girls: A Black Feminist Anthology*, ed. Barbara Smith (New York: Kitchen Table, Women of Color Press, 1983), 221–222.

36. Lescot and Magloire, *Of Men and Gods*, transcription mine.

37. Ginetta Candelario, "Hair Race-ing: Dominican Beauty Culture and Identity Production," *Meridians* 1, no. 1 (2000): 134.

38. Candelario, "Hair Race-ing," 152.

39. Schuller and Bergan, *Poto Mitan*, translation and transcription mine.

40. Schuller and Bergan, *Poto Mitan*, transcription mine.

41. Brown, *Mama Lola*, 244.

42. Quoted in Alexandra Boutros, "Lwa Like Me: Gender, Sexuality, and Vodou Online," in *Media, Religion and Gender: Key Issues and New Challenges*, ed. Mia Lovheim (New York: Routledge, 2013), 107.

43. Schuller and Bergan, *Poto Mitan*, transcription mine.

44. Houngan Hector, "Interview with a Houngan," Tripod, accessed March 13, 2016, http://hounganhector.tripod.com/id3.html.

45. Junior Vasquez, "Work This Pussy" (New York: House of Ellis Music, 1989).

46. Michael Cunningham, "The Slap of Love," *Open City* 6 (1995), http://opencity.org/archive/issue-6/the-slap-of-love.

47. Cunningham, "The Slap of Love."

48. Will Kohler, "Forgotten New York City—the Cock Ring and the Hotel Christopher," Back2Stonewall, August 14, 2013, http://www.back2stonewall.com/2013/08/forgotten-gay-york-city-cock-ring-hotel-christopher.html.

49. Hector Xtravaganza, quoted in Cunningham, "The Slap of Love."

50. Marlon M. Bailey, "Engendering Space: Ballroom Culture and the Spatial Practice of Possibility in Detroit," *Gender, Space, and Culture: A Journal of Feminist Geography* 21, no. 4 (2014): 5.

51. Livingston, *Paris Is Burning*, transcription mine.

52. Livingston, *Paris Is Burning*, transcription mine.

53. Lescot and Magloire, *Of Men and Gods*, transcription mine.

54. Lescot and Magloire, *Of Men and Gods*, transcription mine.

55. Lescot and Magloire, *Of Men and Gods*, translation and transcription mine.

56. Lescot and Magloire, *Of Men and Gods*.

57. Judi Moore Latta, "When the Spirit Takes Hold, What the Work Becomes!," in *Sister Circle: Black Women and Work*, ed. Sharon Harley and the Black Women and Work Collective (Newark, NJ: Rutgers University Press, 2002), 255.

58. Lescot and Magloire, *Of Men and Gods*, translation and transcription mine.

59. Lescot and Magloire, *Of Men and Gods*, translation and transcription mine.

60. Lescot and Magloire, *Of Men and Gods*, translation and transcription mine.

61. Lescot and Magloire, *Of Men and Gods*, translation and transcription mine.

62. Lescot and Magloire, *Of Men and Gods*, translation and transcription mine.

63. Lescot and Magloire, *Of Men and Gods*, transcription mine.

64. Schuller and Bergan, *Poto Mitan*.

65. Schuller and Bergan, *Poto Mitan*.

66. Schuller and Bergan, *Poto Mitan*, transcription mine.

67. Schuller and Bergan, *Poto Mitan*, translation and transcription mine.

68. Houngan Hector, "Ezili Danto," Gade Nou Leve Society, accessed March 13, 2016, http://www.ezilikonnen.com/the-lwa/ezili-danto/, bold in original.

69. LaMenfo, *Serving the Spirits*, 176.

70. LaMenfo, *Serving the Spirits*, 183.

71. See Linda Alcoff, "The Problem of Speaking for Others," *Cultural Critique* 20 (Winter 1991–1992): 21.

72. Schuller and Bergan, *Poto Mitan*, transcription mine.

73. Junior Vasquez, "Dream Drums" (New York: Eightball Records, 1999).

74. Marlon Bailey, *Butch Queens Up in Pumps: Gender, Performance, and Ballroom Culture in Detroit* (Ann Arbor: University of Michigan Press, 2013), 145.

75. Cunningham, "The Slap of Love."

76. Livingston, *Paris Is Burning*.

77. Cunningham, "The Slap of Love."

78. Bailey, *Butch Queens Up in Pumps*, 144.

79. Bailey, *Butch Queens Up in Pumps*, 108.

80. "LET IT SNOW . . . Vintage 1988 'SNOW BALL' invitation," accessed August 3, 2017, http://www.imgrum.org/media/906750726763592987_634791166.

81. Brown, *Mama Lola*, 47.

82. Livingston, *Paris Is Burning*, transcription mine.

83. Lescot and Magloire, *Of Men and Gods*, translation and transcription mine.

84. Lescot and Magloire, *Of Men and Gods*, translation and transcription mine.

85. Lescot and Magloire, *Of Men and Gods*, translation and transcription mine.

86. Lescot and Magloire, *Of Men and Gods*, translation and transcription mine.

87. Lescot and Magloire, *Of Men and Gods*, translation and transcription mine.

88. Lescot and Magloire, *Of Men and Gods*, translation and transcription mine.

89. Jasbir Puar, *Terrorist Assemblages: Homonationalism in Queer Times* (Durham, NC: Duke University Press, 2007), 211–212.

90. Maya Deren, *Divine Horsemen* (Mystic Fire Video, 1985), transcription mine.

91. Schuller and Bergan, *Poto Mitan*, transcription mine.

92. Schuller and Bergan, *Poto Mitan*, transcription mine.

93. Schuller and Bergan, *Poto Mitan*, transcription mine.

94. Mambo Racine Sans Bout, quoted in Maggie, "Our Lady Erzulie Dantor— Thoughts and Links," Tribe, July 28, 2010, http://tribes.tribe.net/global_vodou _2010/thread/5ed0dcd9-3d8a-40d3-b90b-5e76271e0c0f.

95. Mambo Racine Sans Bout, quoted in Maggie, "Our Lady Erzulie Dantor."

96. Houngan Matt, quoted in Boutros, "Lwa Like Me," 104.

97. "Helene," Poto Mitan, accessed March 13, 2016, http://www.potomitan.net /helene.html.

98. "Helene," Poto Mitan, transcription mine.

99. Junior Vazquez, "X" (New York: Tribal America, 1994).

100. Bailey, *Butch Queens Up in Pumps*, 80.

101. Cunningham, "The Slap of Love."

102. Cunningham, "The Slap of Love."

103. Livingston, *Paris Is Burning*, transcription mine.

104. Livingston, *Paris Is Burning*, transcription mine.

105. Livingston, *Paris Is Burning*, transcription mine.

106. Arbert Evisu, quoted in Edgar Rivera Colon, "Getting Life in Two Worlds: Power and Prevention in the New York City House Ball Community," PhD diss., Rutgers University, 2009, 108.

107. Livingston, *Paris Is Burning*, transcription mine.

108. Livingston, *Paris Is Burning*, transcription mine. These outtakes are included on the 2005 reissue of the film cited above.

109. Livingston, *Paris Is Burning*, transcription mine.

110. Brooke Cerda, "#GirlsLikeUs Ms. Tiffany Mathieu WE NEED TO BE UNITED," YouTube video, September 17, 2014, https://www.youtube.com/watch?v=neIHdXb8g7A.

111. See "About Us," Translatina Network, accessed March 13, 2016, http://www.translatinanetwork.org/#!about-us/c1ppg.

112. This information about Mathieu is reported by Julie Compton, "Is Transmisogyny Killing Transgender Women?," NBC News, August 25, 2015, http://www.nbcnews.com/news/nbc-out/transmisogyny-killing-transgender-women-n415286.

113. Brooke Cerda with Tiffany Mathieu, "#GirlsLikeUs: Ms. Tiffany Mathieu INTERVIEW," YouTube video, September 17, 2014, https://www.youtube.com/watch?v=CoZsV7IobBg.

Bridge: My Femdom, My Love

1. Chloe Wayne, "GHE20G0TH1K: A Conversation with Venus X," Creative New York, June 24, 2016, https://nyc.moma.org/ghe20goth1k-a-conversation-with-venus-x-2c3511a62977#.8ee1rf92e.

2. Quoted in Bobby Viteri, "Venus X on GHE20G0TH1K, the Best Party in New York," Vice, September 28, 2013, http://www.vice.com/en_ca/read/ghe20goth1ks-venus-x-is-devoted-to-the-art-of-moving-butts.

3. Venus X, Twitter post, February 19, 2016, https://twitter.com/venusxgg/status/700748839683284992.

4. Saidiya Hartman, "Venus in Two Acts," *Small Axe* 26 (June 2008): 1.

5. Ariane Cruz, "Beyond Black and Blue: BDSM, Internet Pornography, and Black Female Sexuality," *Feminist Studies* 14, no. 2 (summer 2015): 410.

6. Event announcement for Everything @ Bedlam, Gay New York, August 11, 2011, http://newyork.gaycities.com/events/84189-everything-bedlam-with-venus-x-ghe20goth1k-clarissa-the-teenage-witch.

7. Cruz, "Beyond Black and Blue," 411.

Chapter 3: Riding the Red

1. http://www.dominaerzulie.com/en/rantings-thoughtsblog-2/. Accessed July 11, 2014.

2. Domina Erzulie, "WHO I AM," *Domina Erzulie* (blog), May 20, 2013, http://dominaerzulie.blogspot.com/2013/05/who-i-am.html.

3. Edwidge Danticat, *Breath, Eyes, Memory* (New York: Vintage, 1998), 227.

4. Joan Dayan, "Erzulie: A Women's History of Haiti," *Research in African Literature* 25, no. 2 (summer 1994): 6; "Erzulie," Voodoo Loa, accessed July 11, 2014, http://voodoo.forourpla.net/loa/erzulie/; "Erzulie Red-Eyes," Tribe of the Sun, accessed July 11, 2014, http://www.tribeofthesun.com/ezulieredeyes.htm; Saundra Elise Ziyatdinova, "Erzulie Red Eyes, the Separate Entity," *ErzulieRedEyesArtAndSpirit*, November 26, 2011, https://erzulieredeyes.wordpress.com/2011/11/26/erzulie-red-eyes-the-separate-entity/.

5. Saundra Elise Ziyatdinova, "Erzulie Red Eyes (Ge Rouge)," *ErzulieRedEyesArtAndSpirit*, December 16, 2010, https://erzulieredeyes.wordpress.com/2010/12/16/erzulieredeyes-ge-rouge-ii/.

6. Maya Deren, *Divine Horsemen: The Living Gods of Haiti* (1953; reprint, Kingston, NY: Documentext, 1983), 62.

7. Pat Califia, "The Dominant Woman as Priestess," in *Bitch Goddess: The Spiritual Path of the Dominant Woman*, ed. Pat Califia and Drew Campbell (San Francisco: Greenery, 1997), 73–74.

8. http://www.dominaerzulie.com/en/my-description/. Accessed July 11, 2014.

9. Domina Erzulie, "What I Like about Being Dominant," *Domina Erzulie* (blog), April 5, 2008, http://dominaerzulie.blogspot.com/2008/04/heres-peek-of-who-i-am-and-why-i-love.html.

10. Mireille Miller-Young, *A Taste for Brown Sugar: Black Women in Pornography* (Durham, NC: Duke University Press, 2014), 273–274.

11. Miller-Young, *A Taste for Brown Sugar*, 274.

12. *Publishers Weekly*, Review of *The Salt Roads*, by Nalo Hopkinson, November 12, 2003, http://www.publishersweekly.com/978-0-446-53302-7.

13. Nalo Hopkinson, *The Salt Roads* (New York: Grand Central, 2004), 305.

14. Charles Baudelaire, "Sed Non Satiata," trans. Jacques LeClerc, accessed May 24, 2016, http://www.poemsabout.com/poet/charles-baudelaire/page-37/.

15. Nancy Johnston, " 'Happy That It's Here': An Interview with Nalo Hopkinson," in *Queer Universes: Sexualities in Science Fiction*, ed. Wendy Gay Pearson, Veronica Hollinger, and Joan Gordon (Liverpool: Liverpool University Press, 2008), 211.

16. Johnston, " 'Happy That It's Here.' "

17. Johnston, " 'Happy That It's Here.' "

18. See Sylvie Bérard, "BDSMSF(QF): Sadomasochistic Readings of Québécois Women's Science Fiction," in *Queer Universes: Sexualities in Science Fiction*, ed. Wendy Gay Pearson, Veronica Hollinger, and Joan Gordon (Liverpool: Liverpool University Press, 2008), 180–198.

19. Quoted in Johnston, " 'Happy That It's Here,' " 203.

20. Johnston, " 'Happy That It's Here,' " 211.

21. Elizabeth Freeman, *Time Binds: Queer Temporalities, Queer Histories* (Durham, NC: Duke University Press, 2010), 141.

22. M. Jacqui Alexander, *Pedagogies of Crossing: Meditations on Feminism, Sexual Politics, Memory, and the Sacred* (Durham, NC: Duke University Press, 2005), 309.

23. See "Erin Currier," Artistaday, accessed May 24, 2016, http://artistaday.com/?p=11349.

24. Susheel Bibbs, "Pleasant's Story," Mary Ellen Pleasant, accessed May 24, 2016, http://www.mepleasant.com/story.html.

25. Susheel Bibbs, "Pleasant's Story: San Francisco," Mary Ellen Pleasant, accessed May 24, 2016, http://www.mepleasant.com/story3.html.

26. Helen Holdredge, *Mammy Pleasant* (New York: Putnam, 1953), 111.

27. Lynn Hudson, *The Making of "Mammy Pleasant": A Black Entrepreneur in Nineteenth-Century San Francisco* (Urbana-Champaign: University of Illinois Press, 2002), 33.

28. Mistress A., "Confessions of a Black Dominatrix," Afropunk, December 9, 2011, http://www.afropunk.com/profiles/blogs/confessions-of-a-black-dominatrix?xg_source=activity.

29. Mistress A., "Confessions of a Black Dominatrix."

30. Mistress A., "Confessions of a Black Dominatrix."

31. Domina Erzulie, "About," accessed May 24, 2016, https://plus.google.com/115083255973291951873/about.

32. Mollena Williams, *The Toybag Guide to Playing with Taboo* (Gardena, CA: Greenery), 2010.

33. Colin Dayan, *Haiti, History, and the Gods* (Berkeley: University of California Press, 1995), 106.

34. Hannah Woolley, *The Compleat Servant-Maid; or, The Young Maidens Tutor* (London: T. Hamnet, 1670), available at LUNA, Folger Library, accessed May 25, 2016, http://luna.folger.edu/luna/servlet/detail/FOLGERCM1~6~6~372986~131888:The-compleat-servant-maid—or,-The-.

35. John Armstrong, *The Water of Life: A Treatise on Urine Therapy* (London: True Health, 1957).

36. Domina Erzulie, "About," Google+, accessed May 24, 2016, https://plus.google.com/115083255973291951873/.

37. Hopkinson, *The Salt Roads*, 15.

38. Hopkinson, *The Salt Roads*.

39. Hopkinson, *The Salt Roads*, 17.

40. See Johnston, " 'Happy That It's Here,' " 210.

41. Ann McClintock, "Maid to Order: Commercial Fetishization and Gender Power," *Signs* 37 (winter 1993): 100.

42. Hopkinson, *The Salt Roads*, 22.

43. Hopkinson, *The Salt Roads*.

44. Lynda Hart, *Between the Body and the Flesh* (New York: Columbia University Press, 1998), 181.

45. Hart, *Between the Body and the Flesh*.

46. This much-quoted phrase about BDSM comes from Pat Califia's introduction to *Macho Sluts* (New York: Alyson, 1994), 15.

47. Miller-Young, *A Taste for Brown Sugar*, 274.

48. Hopkinson, *The Salt Roads*, 56.

49. Quoted in Hudson, *The Making of "Mammy Pleasant,"* 11.

50. Susheel Bibbs, "Pleasant's Story: The Early Years," Mary Ellen Pleasant, accessed May 25, 2016, http://www.mepleasant.com/story2.html.

51. See Robert Tallant, *Voodoo in New Orleans* (New York: Pelican Publishing, 2003), 9–13.

52. Holdredge, *Mammy Pleasant*, 73.

53. Holdredge, *Mammy Pleasant*.

54. Holdredge, *Mammy Pleasant*, 77.

55. See Karen McCarthy Brown, *Mama Lola: A Vodou Priestess in Brooklyn* (Berkeley: University of California Press, 1991), 36.

56. Holdredge, *Mammy Pleasant*, 74.

57. Domina Erzulie, "Answer to Kolan Blanc," *Domina Erzulie* (blog), February 25, 2009, http://dominaerzulie.blogspot.com/2009/02/answer-to-kolan-blanc.html.

58. Domina Erzulie, "Answer to Kolan Blanc."

59. Domina Erzulie, "About."

60. Deren, *Divine Horsemen*, 107.

61. Califia, "The Dominant Woman as Priestess," 73.

62. Williams, *The Toybag Guide to Playing with Taboo*.

63. Williams, *The Toybag Guide to Playing with Taboo*.

64. McClintock, "Maid to Order," 102.

65. Deren, *Divine Horsemen*, 144.

66. Deren, *Divine Horsemen*, 145.

67. Domina Erzulie, accessed August 17, 2014, www.dominaerzulie.com/en/rantings-thoughtsblog-2/.

68. Hopkinson, *The Salt Roads*, 148.

69. Johnston, " 'Happy That It's Here,' " 211.

70. Johnston, " 'Happy That It's Here,' " 213.

71. Hopkinson, *The Salt Roads*, 148.

72. Hopkinson, *The Salt Roads*, 149.

73. Hopkinson, *The Salt Roads*.

74. Margot Weiss, *Techniques of Pleasure: BDSM and the Circuits of Sexuality* (Durham, NC: Duke University Press, 2011), 22.

75. Weiss, *Techniques of Pleasure*, 158

76. Weiss, *Techniques of Pleasure*, 155–156.

77. Freeman, *Time Binds*, 155.

78. Hopkinson, *The Salt Roads*, 150.

79. Hopkinson, *The Salt Roads*, 154.
80. Weiss, *Techniques of Pleasure*, 188–189.
81. Hopkinson, *The Salt Roads*, 152.
82. Hopkinson, *The Salt Roads*, 156.
83. Holdredge, *Mammy Pleasant*, 111.
84. Hudson, *The Making of "Mammy Pleasant,"* 76.
85. Quoted in Hudson, *The Making of "Mammy Pleasant,"* 77.
86. Hudson, *The Making of "Mammy Pleasant,"* 76.
87. Mistress A., "Confessions of a Black Dominatrix."
88. Hudson, *The Making of "Mammy Pleasant,"* 78.
89. "Popping Golden Balloons in Public Park," Voodoo Fetish Videos, accessed May 25, 2016, http://voodoofetish.c4slive.com/video_gallery.php?startLimit =0&limitPerPage=20&orderby=newtoold&search=EBONY.
90. See "Balloon Fetish," *Strange Sex*, TLC, August 1, 2010, http://www.tlc.com/tv -shows/strange-sex/videos/sex-and-toys-videos/.
91. Susan Donaldson James, " 'Looners' Substitute Balloons for Love, Sex and Intimacy," ABC News, August 15, 2012, http://abcnews.go.com/Health/balloon -fetishists-objects-love-sex-intimacy/story?id=17010057.
92. Hart, *Between the Body and the Flesh*, 199.
93. Williams, *The Toybag Guide to Playing with Taboo*.
94. Deren, *Divine Horsemen*, 145.
95. "Erzulie Red-Eyes," Tribe of the Sun, accessed May 25, 2016, http:// tribeofthesun.com/deities/ezulie-red-eyes/.
96. Hopkinson, *The Salt Roads*, 354.
97. Hopkinson, *The Salt Roads*, 355.
98. Hopkinson, *The Salt Roads*, 356.
99. Hopkinson, *The Salt Roads*, 357, 356.
100. *Petticoat Discipline Quarterly*, accessed August 17, 2014, http://www.petticoated.com/.
101. *Petticoat Discipline Quarterly*.
102. Saidiya Hartman, "Venus in Two Acts," *Small Axe* 26 (June 2008): 11.
103. Hartman, "Venus in Two Acts," 13, 10.
104. Hopkinson, *The Salt Roads*, 355.
105. Hopkinson, *The Salt Roads*, 366.
106. Hopkinson, *The Salt Roads*.
107. Hudson, *The Making of "Mammy Pleasant,"* 60.
108. Quoted in Hudson, *The Making of "Mammy Pleasant,"* 61.
109. Hudson, *The Making of "Mammy Pleasant,"* 61.
110. Quoted in Hudson, *The Making of "Mammy Pleasant,"* 71.
111. Quoted in Hudson, *The Making of "Mammy Pleasant,"* 73.
112. Quoted in Hudson, *The Making of "Mammy Pleasant,"* 92.
113. Hudson, *The Making of "Mammy Pleasant."*
114. John Thompson, "Mary Ellen Pleasant," *Obsidian Portal*, http://shadows-of-the -city.obsidianportal.com/characters/mary-ellen-pleasant.

115. Thompson, "Mary Ellen Pleasant."

116. Thompson, "Mary Ellen Pleasant."

117. Prince, "Scarlet Pussy," *The Hits/The B-Sides* (Chanhassen, MN: Paisley Park Records, 1993).

118. Ekundayo Afolayan, "Whether Prince Knew It or Not, He Was a Disability Icon to Me," BGD, April 22, 2016, http://www.blackgirldangerous.org/2016/04 /whether-or-not-prince-knew-it/.

119. Prince, "Shockadelica," *The Hits/The B-Sides* (Chanhassen, MN: Paisley Park Records, 1993).

120. K. T. Billey, "Prince and the Queer Body: Our Dirty Patron Saint of Pop Gave Me Permission to Think outside the Gender Binary," *Salon*, April 22, 2016, http:// www.salon.com/2016/04/22/prince_and_the_queer_body_our_dirty_patron _saint_of_pop_gave_me_permission_to_think_outside_the_gender_binary/.

Chapter 4: It's a Party

1. See Clive Davis's speech at Mark Morris, "Whitney Houston: Clive Davis' Tribute at Pre-Grammy Party," YouTube video, February 2012, https://www .youtube.com/watch?v=alr8IpVzyVg.

2. Alicia Keys' beautiful tribute is archived at "Alicia Keys Tribute to Whitney Houston Clive Davis 2012 Pre Grammy Party," YouTube video, February 20, 2012, https://www.youtube.com/watch?v=fyHlfX1c6VI.

3. See Alan Duke, "Whitney Houston Drowned in a Foot of Hot Water, Autopsy Says," CNN, April 4, 2012, http://www.cnn.com/2012/04/04/showbiz/whitney -houston-toxicology/.

4. Quoted by Kevin Dolak and Eileen Murphy, "Whitney Houston Cause of Death: How Cocaine Contributes to Heart Disease," ABC News, March 23, 2012, http://abcnews.go.com/Health/whitney-houston-death-cocaine -contributed-heart-disease/story?id=15984196.

5. Rickey Minor, "The 2012 Oral History: Whitney Houston, 1963–2012," *Esquire*, November 20, 2012, http://www.esquire.com/entertainment/a16739/whitney -houston-death-1212/.

6. Houston's interlude in this interview can be viewed at "Whitney Houston Last Kiss Goodbye to Clive Davis, Monica and Brandy at Interview," YouTube video, February 12, 2012, https://www.youtube.com/watch?v =1kGZ5q8YYrE.

7. Whitney Houston's notorious interview with Diane Sawyer aired on ABC's *Primetime: Special Edition* on December 4, 2002. Quotes from the interview appear at "Whitney Houston Tells Diane Sawyer: 'Crack Is Whack,'" ABC News, http://abcnews.go.com/Entertainment/whitney-houston-tells-diane-sawyer -crack-whack/story?id=131898.

8. Richard Rohr, *Breathing under Water: Spirituality and the Twelve Steps* (Cincinnati: Franciscan Media, 2011), xv.

9. Rohr, *Breathing under Water*, 123.

10. Peter Tatchell, "Whitney's REAL Tragedy Was Giving Up Her Greatest Love of All—Her Female Partner Robyn Crawford," *Daily Mail*, February 20, 2012, http://www.dailymail.co.uk/tvshowbiz/article-2103164/Whitney-Houstons -REAL-tragedy-giving-female-partner-Robyn-Crawford.html.

11. Tatchell, "Whitney's REAL Tragedy."

12. Eleanor Nealy, "April 30," in *Amazon Spirit: Daily Meditations for Lesbians in Recovery* (New York: Perigee Trade, 1995).

13. Robyn Crawford, "Whitney Elizabeth Houston, 1963–2012," *Esquire*, February 12, 2012, http://www.esquire.com/entertainment/music/a12753/whitney -houston-6654718/.

14. Crawford, "Whitney Elizabeth Houston."

15. MC Jack Mizrahi at Azealia Banks's Mermaid Ball in New York, June 3, 2012. Quoted at https://www.yahoo.com/?err=404&err_url=https%3a%2f%2fwww .yahoo.com%2fmovies%2fazealia-banks-throws-mermaid-ball-york-185017839 .html. Accessed June 1, 2015.

16. Matthew Trammell, "Azealia Banks Throws a Mermaid Ball in New York," *Rolling Stone*, June 4, 2012, http://www.rollingstone.com/music/news/azealia -banks-throws-a-mermaid-ball-in-new-york-20120604.

17. Quoted in Trammell, "Azealia Banks Throws a Mermaid Ball."

18. See Rachel Syme, "Azealia Banks on Why No One Really Wants to See Her Naked, Her Impure Thoughts about Barak Obama, and Why She's 'Not Here to Be Your Idol.'" *Billboard*, April 3, 2015, http://www.billboard.com/articles /news/6523916/billboard-cover-azealia-banks-broke-with-expensive-taste -barack-obama-twitter-controversy-playboy.

19. Quoted in Gavin Haynes, "Azealia Banks Interview: 'I Was Never Going to End Up a Broke Bitch,'" NME, May 13, 2015, http://www.nme.com/features/azealia -banks-interview-i-was-never-going-to-end-up-a-broke-bitch.

20. Azealia Banks, "Aquababe," released as free digital download June 13, 2012.

21. Azealia Banks, quoted by Syme, "Azealia Banks on Why No One Really Wants to See Her Naked."

22. Mambo Vye Zo Komande LaMenfo, *Serving the Spirits: The Religion of Haitian Vodou* (CreateSpace, 2012), 146.

23. LaMenfo, *Serving the Spirits*.

24. Sharon Bridgforth, "Dat Black Mermaid Man Lady," unpublished manuscript, 2. My thanks to Sharon Bridgforth for sharing this manuscript with me and welcoming me to rehearsals of the New York premiere.

25. Bridgforth, "Dat Black Mermaid Man Lady."

26. Bridgforth, "Dat Black Mermaid Man Lady."

27. See Bridgforth's blog post "Mermaids in NYC," Sharon Bridgforth (blog), October 2, 2014, https://sharonbridgforthblog.wordpress.com/2014/10/02 /mermaids-in-nyc/.

28. See Sharon Bridgforth, "Bio," Sharon Bridgforth, accessed May 26, 2016, http://www.findingvoice.co/bio-sharon-2–1/.

29. Will Buckingham, "Ocean of Existence," ThinkBuddha.org, May 7, 2008, http://www.thinkbuddha.org/article/336/the-ocean-of-existence.

30. Omi Oshun Joni L. Jones, *Theatrical Jazz: Performance, Ase, and the Power of the Present Moment* (Cincinnati: Ohio University Press, 2015), 158.

31. See Matt Richardson, *The Queer Limit of Black Memory: Black Lesbian Literature and Irresolution* (Cincinnati: Ohio University Press, 2013), 89.

32. Allison Reed, "Traumatic Utopias: Holding Hope in Sharon Bridgforth's Love Conjure/Blues," *Text and Performance Quarterly* 35, no. 2–3 (June 2015): 120.

33. Reed, "Traumatic Utopias," 121.

34. Connie Matthews, Peggy Lorah, and Jaime Fenton, "Toward a Grounded Theory of Lesbians' Recovery from Addiction," in *Making Lesbians Visible in the Substance Use Field*, ed. Elizabeth Ettore (Binghamton, NY: Harrington Park, 2005), 61.

35. See Matthews, Lorah, and Fenton, "Toward a Grounded Theory of Lesbians' Recovery," 62–66.

36. Quoted in Susan Schindehette, "Rock Bottom," *People*, March 29, 2004, http://www.people.com/people/archive/rock-bottom-vol-61-no-12/.

37. Fields quoted in "Houston Celebrates at Age 40 (and a Day)," All Whitney Houston, accessed May 26, 2016, http://whfan.free.fr/news/030811.htm.

38. Stephen Silverman, "Whitney Houston Out of Rehab after Only 5 Days," *People*, March 24, 2004, http://www.people.com/celebrity/whitney-out-of-rehab-after-only-5-days/.

39. See the brochure "Crossroads Centre: Antigua," accessed May 26, 2015, http://crossroadsantigua.org/pdf/Crossroads_12pageBrochure.pdf.

40. Antigua and Barbuda Tourism Authority, "Whitney Houston's Special A&B Connection," Antigua Nice, February 24, 2012, http://www.antiguanice.com/v2/client.php?id=775&news=3674.

41. Antigua and Barbuda Tourism Authority, "Whitney Houston's Special A&B Connection."

42. Lynn Norment, "The Awards, the Gossip, the Glory: Whitney's Wild and Wonderful Year," *Ebony* 49, no. 8 (July 1994): 125.

43. This quote comes from a partial transcript of the interview published by CBS News, "Whitney to Oprah 2009: Trying to Hide the Pain," February 13, 2012, http://www.cbsnews.com/news/whitney-to-oprah-2009-trying-to-hide-the-pain/.

44. Luchina Fisher and Sheila Marikar, "Whitney Houston Returns to Rehab," ABC News, May 9, 2011, http://abcnews.go.com/Entertainment/whitney-houston-returns-rehab/story?id=13563047.

45. Charles Duhigg, "Why Did Whitney Fail Rehab? Too Much Talent," Charles Duhigg (blog), February 13, 2012, http://charlesduhigg.com/rehab-for-whitney/.

46. Quoted in David W. Freeman, "Whitney Houston Back in Rehab: Why Is Addiction So Hard to Beat?," CBS News, May 10, 2011, http://www.cbsnews.com/news/whitney-houston-back-in-rehab-why-is-addiction-so-hard-to-beat/.

47. See the Minnesota PRIDE Institute brochure, accessed May 26, 2016, http://pride-institute.com/wp-content/uploads/2015/ . . . /PRIDE-Book-PRINT

-COPYv22.pdf; see "LGBT and Gay-Friendly Alcohol and Drug Rehab," Recovery Connection, accessed May 26, 2016, https://www.recoveryconnection.com /substance-abuse/treatment-programs/specialty-treatment-addictions/lgbt -gay-friendly-alcohol-drug-rehab/.

48. Emma Knock, "Live Review: Azealia Banks London Mermaid Ball," MTV, October 16, 2012, http://www.mtv.co.uk/the-wrap-up/blog/live-review-azelia -banks-london-mermaid-ball.

49. This description comes in the "Teacher Zone" of the London Aquarium's website, accessed May 26, 2016, https://www2.visitsealife.com/london/discover /teacher-zone/.

50. Quoted in Rob Tannenbaum, "Azealia Banks: Wild and Uncensored for Playboy," *Playboy*, March 16, 2015, https://www.playboy.com/articles/azealia-banks -playboy-photos.

51. Quoted by Sady Doyle, "Season of the Witch: Why Young Women Are Flocking to the Ancient Craft," *Guardian*, February 24, 2015, http://www.theguardian .com/world/2015/feb/24/witch-symbol-feminist-power-azealia-banks.

52. Haynes, "Azealia Banks Interview."

53. Azealia Banks on Twitter, https://twitter.com/AZEALIABANKS/status /617849504I4287257.

54. Azealia Banks retweeted by Ashley Forbes, accessed May 26, 2016, https://twitter .com/ashleymarie_11/status/491590251010605057.

55. Skye Alexander, *Mermaids: The Myths, Legends, and Lore* (Avon, MA: Adams Media, 2012), 195.

56. Timothy Leary and Richard Alpert, *The Psychedelic Experience: A Manual Based on the Tibetan Book of the Dead* (New York: Citadel Underground, 2000), 11.

57. Leary and Alpert, *The Psychedelic Experience*, 13.

58. Leary and Alpert, *The Psychedelic Experience*.

59. Quoted in Haynes, "Azealia Banks Interview."

60. Bridgforth, "Dat Black Mermaid Man Lady," 10.

61. Bridgforth, "Dat Black Mermaid Man Lady," 6, 7.

62. Bridgforth, "Dat Black Mermaid Man Lady," 9.

63. Bridgforth, "Dat Black Mermaid Man Lady," 10.

64. Bridgforth, "Dat Black Mermaid Man Lady," 15.

65. Bridgforth, "Dat Black Mermaid Man Lady," 16.

66. Vincent Ravalec, Mallendi, and Agnès Paicheler, *Iboga: The Visionary Root of African Shamanism* (South Paris, ME: Park Street, 2007), 39.

67. Bridgforth, "Dat Black Mermaid Man Lady," 12.

68. Bridgforth, "Dat Black Mermaid Man Lady," 13.

69. Nealy, "February 22," in *Amazon Spirit*.

70. See Ravalec, Mallendi, and Paicheler, *Iboga*, 57–60.

71. Bridgforth, "Dat Black Mermaid Man Lady," 13.

72. Bridgforth, "Dat Black Mermaid Man Lady," 2.

73. Ravalec, Mallendi, and Paicheler, *Iboga*, 86.

74. Jones, *Theatrical Jazz*, 195.

75. Jones, *Theatrical Jazz*.

76. Bridgforth, "Dat Black Mermaid Man Lady," 15.

77. Bridgforth, "Dat Black Mermaid Man Lady."

78. Quoted in "Whitney Houston Holds a Lavish Birthday Gala," *Jet* 76, no. 23 (September 11, 1989): 60.

79. Roger Friedman, "Flashback: Young Whitney Reflects on Fame and Sexuality," Showbiz 411, February 18, 2012, http://www.showbiz411.com/2012/02/18 /flashback-young-whitney-reflects-on-fame-and-sexuality.

80. Friedman, "Flashback."

81. Whitney's birthday interview with *The Insider* is available at https://www .youtube.com/watch?v=3b8uI8HPn30. Accessed May 26, 2016.

82. Whitney's birthday interview, *The Insider*.

83. Cissy Houston, *Remembering Whitney: My Story of Love, Loss, and the Night the Music Stopped* (New York: Harper, 2013), 145.

84. Hilton Als, "The Widow," accessed May 26, 2016, http://www.hiltonals.com /2012/02/the-widow/.

85. Quoted in James Robert Parish, *Whitney Houston 1963–2012: We Will Always Love You* (New York: John Blake, 2012), 68.

86. Quoted in Mark Seal, "The Devils in the Diva," *Vanity Fair*, June 2012, http:// www.vanityfair.com/hollywood/2012/06/whitney-houston-death-bathtub -drugs-rehab.

87. Narada Michael Walden and Richard Buskin, *Whitney Houston: The Voice, the Music, the Inspiration* (San Rafael, CA: Insight Editions, 2012), 96.

88. Walden and Buskin, *Whitney Houston*, 45.

89. Quoted in Friedman, "Flashback."

90. Houston, *Remembering Whitney*, 145.

91. Houston, *Remembering Whitney*, 121.

92. Houston, *Remembering Whitney*.

93. Quoted in Cavan Sieczkowski, "Cissy Houston on Whitney Houston Gay Relationship: I Would Have 'Absolutely' Disapproved," *Huffington Post*, January 29, 2013, http://www.huffingtonpost.com/2013/01/29/cissy-houston-whitney -houston-gay-rumors_n_2573718.html.

94. See Kevin Ammons, *Good Girl, Bad Girl: An Insider's Biography of Whitney Houston* (New York: Citadel, 1998), 62.

95. Als, "The Widow."

96. Houston, *Remembering Whitney*, 151.

97. Houston, *Remembering Whitney*.

98. Houston, *Remembering Whitney*, 152.

99. Azealia Banks quoted by Kat Bee, "Azealia Banks; Mermaid Ball Splashes Down with Charli xcx, Robyn & Rye Rye in Los Angeles," Idolator, July 16, 2012, http://www.idolator.com/6726311/azealia-banks-mermaid-ball-charli-xcx -robyn-rye-rye-in-los-angeles.

100. Brittany Graham, "Azealia Banks Channels Gay 'Ball Culture' at the Mermaid Ball in L.A.," Vibe, July 17, 2012, http://www.vibe.com/2012/07/azealia-banks -channels-gay-ball-culture-mermaid-ball-la/.

101. Bee, "Azealia Banks."

102. John Ortved, "Azealia Banks, Taking Her Cues and Lyrics from the Street," New York Times, February 2, 2012, http://www.nytimes.com/2012/02/02/fashion /azealia-banks-a-young-rapper-taking-cues-from-the-street.html?_r=0.

103. Syme, "Azealia Banks on Why No One Really Wants to See Her Naked."

104. Syme, "Azealia Banks on Why No One Really Wants to See Her Naked."

105. Tannenbaum, "Azealia Banks."

106. Azealia Banks, "Idle Delilah," Broke with Expensive Taste (New York: Prospect Park, 2014).

107. Banks, "212," Broke with Expensive Taste.

108. LaMenfo, Serving the Spirits, 146.

109. Ursula Szeles, "Sea Secret Rising: The Lwa Lasirenn in Haitian Vodou," Journal of Haitian Studies 17, no. 1 (spring 2011): 195.

110. Quoted in Alex Ostroff, "On Azealia Banks, Angel Haze, Sexuality, Biphobia, and Appropriation," Purplechrain, December 24, 2012, http://purplechrain .tumblr.com/post/38693856075/on-azealia-banks-angel-haze-sexuality-biphobia.

111. Quoted in Arye Dworken, "Interview: Azealia Banks Discusses the Self-Made World That Saved Her," Self-Titled, November 13, 2014, http://www.self -titledmag.com/2014/11/13/the-self-titled-interview-azealia-banks/.

112. Dworken, "Interview."

113. Bridgforth, "Dat Black Mermaid Man Lady," 20.

114. Bridgforth, "Dat Black Mermaid Man Lady," 22.

115. Bridgforth, "Dat Black Mermaid Man Lady," 23.

116. Bridgforth, "Dat Black Mermaid Man Lady."

117. Bridgforth, "Dat Black Mermaid Man Lady," 24.

118. Bridgforth, "Dat Black Mermaid Man Lady."

119. Bridgforth, "Dat Black Mermaid Man Lady," 25.

120. Leo Bersani, "Is the Rectum a Grave?," in Is the Rectum a Grave? And Other Essays (Chicago: University of Chicago Press, 2009), 25.

121. Bersani, "Is the Rectum a Grave?," 29.

122. Bridgforth, "Dat Black Mermaid Man Lady," 24.

123. Sharon Bridgforth, love conjure/blues (Washington, DC: Redbone, 2004).

124. Tiq Milan in "Love Is Revolutionary When You're Black and Transgender," NBC News, June 15, 2016, http://www.nbcnews.com/video/living-color-love-is -revolutionary-when-youre-black-and-transgender-464842307606, transcription mine.

125. Bridgforth, "Dat Black Mermaid Man Lady," 25.

126. E. Patrick Johnson, " 'Quare' Studies, or (Almost) Everything I Know about Queer Studies I Learned from My Grandmother," Text and Performance Quarterly 21, no. 1 (January 2001): 19.

127. Houston, *Remembering Whitney*, 74.

128. See Steve Strunsky, "Whitney Houston's Childhood Friends in N.J. Knew She Was Destined for Success," NJ.com, February 13, 2012, http://www.nj.com /news/index.ssf/2012/02/whitney_houstons_childhood_fri.html.

129. Houston, *Remembering Whitney*, 75.

130. John Leland, "In East Orange, Recalling Whitney Houston before She Was a Star," *New York Times*, February 17, 2012, http://www.nytimes.com/2012/02/17 /nyregion/in-east-orange-before-whitney-houston-was-a-star.html.

131. Houston, *Remembering Whitney*, 91.

132. Quoted in Leland, "In East Orange, Recalling Whitney Houston."

133. TMZ reported that Houston was reading these verses the morning of her death. "Whitney Houston Had Premonition about Death," TMZ, February 15, 2012, http:// www.tmz.com/2012/02/15/whitney-houston-premonition-death-jesus-bible/.

134. Linda Ocasio, "N.J.'s Black Churches Open Doors to Gay Congregants, but Not Right to Marry," NJ.com, December 11, 2011, http://www.nj.com/njvoices /index.ssf/2011/12/njs_black_churches_open_doors.html.

135. Quoted in Ocasio, "N.J.'s Black Churches Open Doors."

136. Quoted in Gayle R. Baldwin, "Whose Black Church? Voices of Oppression and Resistance in Response to the Murder of a 'Gay' Black Teenager," in *Churches, Blackness, and Contested Multiculturalism: Europe, Africa, and North America*, ed. R. Drew Smith, William Ackha, and Anthony Reddie (New York: Palgrave Macmillan, 2014), 242.

137. Ruth 1:16–17.

138. Crawford, "Whitney Elizabeth Houston."

139. Azealia Banks, Twitter, accessed May 26, 2016, https://twitter.com/hashtag /FantaseaMixTape?src=hash.

140. "Last Splash: Azealia Banks Explains Whole Mermaid Deal," SPIN, July 12, 2012, http://www.spin.com/2012/07/last-splash-azealia-banks-explains-whole -mermaid-deal/.

141. Banks quoted in Tannenbaum, "Azealia Banks."

142. Szeles, "Sea Secret Rising."

143. Quoted in Camilla Long, "Shooting from the Mouth," *Sunday Times*, October 6, 2013, http://www.thesundaytimes.co.uk/sto/style/fashion/People /article1321310.ece.

144. Quoted in Marlow Stern, "Azealia Banks Opens Up about Her Journey from Stripping to Rap Stardom," *Daily Beast*, November 17, 2014, http://www .thedailybeast.com/articles/2014/11/17/azealia-banks-opens-up-about-her -journey-from-stripping-to-rap-stardom.html.

145. Tannenbaum, "Azealia Banks."

146. Karen McCarthy Brown, *Mama Lola: A Vodou Priestess in Brooklyn* (Berkeley: University of California Press, 1991), 224.

147. Azealia Banks, Instagram, https://www.instagram.com/azealiabanks/.

148. Szeles, "Sea Secret Rising."

149. "Last Splash."
150. Quoted in Georgina Littlejohn, " 'The Token Sand N***a from 1D': Azealia Banks Launches Homophobic and Racist Attack on Zayn Malik," Sun, May 11, 2016. https://www.thesun.co.uk/archives/news/1170608/the-token -sand-n-from-1d-azealia-banks-launches-homophobic-and-racist-attack -on-zayn-malik/; quoted in Richard Godwin, "Azealia Banks: 'I've Realised You're Not Keeping It Real by Being the Crazy Girl," Evening Standard, October 17, 2016, http://www.standard.co.uk/showbiz/celebrity-news/azealia -banks-i-ve-realised-you-re-not-keeping-it-real-by-being-the-crazy-girl -a3371046.html.
151. Godwin, "Azealia Banks."
152. Bridgforth, "Dat Black Mermaid Man Lady," 26.
153. Bridgforth, "Dat Black Mermaid Man Lady," 27.
154. Bridgforth, "Dat Black Mermaid Man Lady," 28.
155. Bridgforth, "Dat Black Mermaid Man Lady," 28–29.
156. Bridgforth, "Dat Black Mermaid Man Lady," 30.
157. Bridgforth, "Dat Black Mermaid Man Lady."
158. Quoted in Richard Follett, The Sugar Masters: Planters and Slaves in Louisiana's Cane World, 1800–1860 (Baton Rouge: Louisiana State University Press, 2007), 46.
159. Quoted in Follett, The Sugar Masters, 130–131.
160. Quoted in Follett, The Sugar Masters, 131.
161. Bridgforth, "Dat Black Mermaid Man Lady," 30.
162. Follett, The Sugar Masters, 227; Elizabeth Ross Hite quoted in Follett, The Sugar Masters, 226.
163. Bridgforth, "Dat Black Mermaid Man Lady," 36.
164. Bridgforth, "Dat Black Mermaid Man Lady."
165. Bridgforth, "Dat Black Mermaid Man Lady," 41.
166. Bridgforth, "Dat Black Mermaid Man Lady."
167. Bridgforth, "Dat Black Mermaid Man Lady," 42.

Bridge: Baía and Marigo

1. Omise'eke Tinsley, "Black Atlantic, Queer Atlantic: Queer Imaginings of the Middle Passage," GLQ 14, no. 2–3 (2008): 199.
2. Omise'eke Tinsley, "The Myths Surrounding Black Women and Miscarriage," Ebony, October 22, 2015, http://www.ebony.com/life/the-myths-surrounding -black-women-and-miscarriage#axzz4LZu2WglH.

Conclusion: Arties's Song

1. Ana-Maurine Lara, Erzulie's Skirt (Washington, DC: Redbone, 2006), xiv.
2. Lara, Erzulie's Skirt, xvi.
3. Polyamory Society, "Introduction to Polyamory," accessed May 27, 2016, http:// www.polyamorysociety.org/page6.html.

4. Hector Salva, "Introduction to Las 21 Divisiones," Las 21 Divisiones, accessed May 27, 2016, http://las21divisiones.com/.

5. Lara, *Erzulie's Skirt*, xvi.

6. Quoted in Cheryl Wischhover, "Chinese Couturier Guo Pei Reveals How Rihanna Ended Up Wearing Her Gown to the Met Gala," Fashionista, May 5, 2015, http://fashionista.com/2015/05/guo-pei-rihanna-met-ball-dress -interview.

7. Hannah Giorgis, "Rihanna and the Radical Power of 'Carefree Black Girl' Celebrity," Pinoria, April 8, 2015, https://pinoria.wordpress.com/2015/04/08 /rihanna-and-the-radical-power-of-carefree-black-girl-celebrity-2/. Rihanna is a complicated media figure, whose image is haunted by images of her as a survivor of intimate partner violence. While I gesture toward some of these complexities, I've chosen to focus on her carefree black girl persona partly to speak back to images of her as always already damaged by violence. And partly just because I love her sexy, BBHM version of carefree black girl.

8. Jamala Johns, "Who Exactly Is 'the Carefree Black Girl'?," Refinery 29, January 30, 2014, http://www.refinery29.com/2014/01/61614/carefree-black-girls.

9. Giorgis, "Rihanna and the Radical Power."

10. Giorgis, "Rihanna and the Radical Power."

11. For this and more on Anaisa Pye see Sancista Luis, "The Mistress Anaisa Pye," Sociedad de Sance Rio Tempestuoso, March 25, 2013, http://sansespiritismo. blogspot.com/2013/03/the-mistress-anaisa-pye.html.

12. Ashleigh Shackelford, "Trap Queens and Freak Hoes: On Exclusivity in the Carefree Black Girl Movement," For Harriet, September 2015, http://www.forharriet.com/2015/09/trap-queens-and-freak-hoes-on .html#axzz49tadmR8v.

13. Lara, *Erzulie's Skirt*, 135–136.

14. Omise'eke Natasha Tinsley, *Thiefing Sugar: Eroticism between Women in Caribbean Literature* (Durham, NC: Duke University Press, 2010), 37–38.

15. This Twitter exchange was reproduced at Atl Night Spots, May 19, 2012, http:// www.atlnightspots.com/forum/showthread.php?5184-Rihanna-Responds-to -Celebuzz-For-Criticizing-Her-Recent-Outfit-on-Twitter-Today.

16. Quoted by Katt D., "Rihanna Jokes She's Dating Girls Now & Wishes It Was Nicki Minaj," Magic 107.5, 2011, http://majicatl.hellobeautiful.com/873521 /rihanna-jokes-shes-dating-girls-now-wishes-it-was-nicki-minaj-video/.

17. Rihanna, Twitter post, April 20, 2012, https://twitter.com/rihanna/status /193203884762738688.

18. Sugarscape, "Rihanna and Katy Perry's Big Lesbian Love Story Continues . . . ," accessed May 28, 2016, http://www.sugarscape.com/celebs/news/a730198 /rihanna-and-katy-perrys-big-lesbian-love-story-continues/.

19. Deja Jones, "The Struggle to Find Your Identity as a Carefree Black Girl," Madamenoire, April 2, 2015, http://madamenoire.com/522771/struggle-finding -identity-carefree-black-girl/.

20. Quoted in Sowmya Krishnamurthy, "The 11 Most Eye-Opening Quotes from Rihanna's Interview with Oprah," Vibe, August 20, 2012, http://www.vibe.com /2012/08/11-most-eye-opening-quotes-rihannas-interview-oprah/.
21. Lizzy Goodman, "The Big Reveal," Elle 352 (December 2014): 312.
22. Goodman, "The Big Reveal."
23. Houngan Hector, "Anaisa Pye," Gade Nou Leve Society, accessed May 28, 2016, http://www.ezilikonnen.com/dominican/anaisa-pye/.
24. Sancista Luis, "The Mistress Anaisa Pye."
25. Sancista Luis, "The Mistress Anaisa Pye."
26. See Rebecca Ann Shrugg, "How Does She Look?," in Femme: Feminists, Lesbians, and Bad Girls, ed. Laura Harris and Elizabeth Crocker (London: Routledge, 1997), 181–183.
27. Josune Urbistondo, "Bodies Scared Sacred at the Crossroads: Vodou Loa Erzulie in Mayra Montero's The Red of His Shadow and Ana-Maurine Lara's Erzulie's Skirt," Hispanet Journal 6 (March 2013): 17; Yingjin Zhang, Cinema, Space, and Polylocality in a Globalizing China (Honolulu: University of Hawai'i Press, 2009), 9.
28. Ana-Maurine Lara, "Vudú in the Dominican Republic: Resistance and Healing," Phoebe 17, no. 1 (spring 2005): 17.
29. Patricia Hill Collins, Black Feminist Thought: Knowledge, Consciousness, and the Politics of Empowerment (New York: Routledge: 2008), 32.
30. Quoted in Ayana Malaika Crichlow, "Rihanna Queen of Crop Over," Huffington Post, August 7, 2015, http://www.huffingtonpost.com/ayana-malaika-crichlow /rihanna-queen-of-crop-ove_b_7952880.html.
31. Crichlow, "Rihanna Queen of Crop Over."
32. National Cultural Foundation of Barbados, "The Story behind the Crop Over Festival," accessed May 28, 2016, http://www.ncf.bb/crop-over/.
33. Crichlow, "Rihanna Queen of Crop Over."
34. Quoted by Sancista Luis, "The Mistress Anaisa Pye."
35. Sancista Luis, "The Mistress Anaisa Pye."
36. Wilson Fallin Jr., The African American Church in Birmingham, Alabama, 1815–1963: A Shelter in the Storm (New York: Garland, 1997), 154.
37. Beyoncé, "Upgrade U," on B'Day (New York: Sony Legacy, 2006).
38. Quoted in Herbert C. Covey, African American Slave Medicine: Herbal and Non-herbal Treatments (Lanham, MD: Lexington, 2007), 76.
39. Lara, Erzulie's Skirt, 242.
40. Gloria Wekker, The Politics of Passion: Women's Sexual Culture in the Afro-Surinamese Diaspora (New York: Columbia University Press, 2006), 23.
41. José Muñoz, Cruising Utopia: The Then and There of Queer Futurity (New York: New York University Press, 2009), 1.
42. Muñoz, Cruising Utopia.
43. Maya Deren, Divine Horsemen: The Living Gods of Haiti (1953; reprint, Kingston, NY: Documentext, 1983), 138.

44. Sally Holmes, "Rihanna and Blue Ivy Had a Princess Moment at the Grammys," Elle, February 8, 2015, http://www.elle.com/culture/celebrities/news /a26644/rihanna-blue-ivy-grammys/.

45. Quoted in Holmes, "Rihanna and Blue Ivy."

46. Rihanna on Twitter, August 20, 2014, https://twitter.com/adoringrihanna /status/502225919084593154.

47. Shyam Dodge, "Aunty OhNaNa! Rihanna Bonds with Baby Cousin Majesty as She Carries the Tot to Her Christening in Barbados," Daily Mail, September 15, 2014, http://www.dailymail.co.uk/tvshowbiz/article-2756749/Rihanna-bonds -baby-cousin-Majesty-carries-tot-Christening-Barbados.html.

48. Quoted by Dodge, "Aunty OhNaNa!"

49. Simone Jones, "When You're a Carefree Black Girl Disguised as a Mama," The Shy Peacock (blog), August 12, 2015, https://theshypeacock.com/2015/08/12 /when-youre-a-carefree-black-girl-disguised-as-a-mama/.

50. Jones, "When You're a Carefree Black Girl."

51. Sancista Luis, "The Mistress Anaisa Pye."

52. Sancista Luis, "The Mistress Anaisa Pye."

53. Alexis Pauline Gumbs, "We Can Learn to Mother Ourselves: The Queer Survival of Black Feminism," PhD diss., Duke University, 2010, 62, 75.

54. Houngan Hector, "Anaisa Pye."

55. Carlos Greer, "Rihanna Treats Her New Album Like She's 'Going Make a Baby,'" Page Six, October 24, 2015, http://pagesix.com/2015/10/24/rihanna -treats-her-new-album-like-shes-going-make-a-baby/.

56. Greer, "Rihanna Treats Her New Album."

57. Quoted by Zara Golden, "Artist Roy Nachum Reveals the Meaning behind Rihanna's ANTi Cover," Fader, October 9, 2015, http://www.thefader.com/2015 /10/09/rihanna-anti-artist-roy-nachum.

58. Golden, "Artist Roy Nachum Reveals."

59. John Michael Vlach, The Afro-American Tradition in Decorative Arts (Athens: University of Georgia Press, 1990), 129.

60. Edouard Glissant, The Poetics of Relation, trans. Betsy Wing (Ann Arbor: University of Michigan Press, 1997), 58.

GLOSSARY

bull dyke: African American English; masculine-of-center lesbian

dyaspora: Kreyòl, diaspora

houngan: Kreyòl, male priest in Vodou

Ifa: Yoruba, Yoruba system of divination and, by extension, religion

istwa: Kreyòl, story or history

Iyawo: Yoruba, literally new bride, figuratively new initiate

mambo: Kreyòl, female priest in Vodou

Metres: Kreyòl, mistress

prodomme: American English, professional dominatrix

Regla de Ocha: Spanish, Yoruba-based religion in western Cuba

sevite: Kreyòl, literally servitor, participant in Vodou religion

Udana: Pali, Buddhist scripture

Vèvè: a religious symbol used to evoke a specific lwa in Vodou, often drawn on the ground during ceremonies

Yemoja: Yoruba, spirit of salt water, maternity, creativity

BIBLIOGRAPHY

"About: Our Mission, Our Dream." Makandal. Accessed July 24, 2013. http://makandal.org/about/.

"About Us." Translatina Network. Accessed March 13, 2016. http://www.translatinanetwork.org/#!about-us/c1ppg.

Afolayan, Ekundayo. "Whether Prince Knew It or Not, He Was a Disability Icon to Me." BGD, April 22, 2016. http://www.blackgirldangerous.org/2016/04/whether-or-not-prince-knew-it/.

Alcoff, Linda. "The Problem of Speaking for Others." *Cultural Critique* 20 (Winter 1991–1992): 5–32.

Alexander, M. Jacqui. *Pedagogies of Crossing: Meditations on Feminism, Sexual Politics, Memory, and the Sacred.* Durham, NC: Duke University Press, 2005.

Alexander, Skye. *Mermaids: The Myths, Legends, and Lore.* Avon, MA: Adams Media, 2012.

"Alicia Keys Tribute to Whitney Houston Clive Davis 2012 Pre Grammy Party." YouTube video, February 20, 2012. https://www.youtube.com/watch?v=fyHlfX1c6VI.

Als, Hilton. "The Widow." Accessed May 26, 2016. http://www.hiltonals.com/2012/02/the-widow/.

Ammons, Kevin. *Good Girl, Bad Girl: An Insider's Biography of Whitney Houston.* New York: Citadel, 1998.

Anderson-Minshall, Jacob. "Is Femme a Gender Identity?" *San Francisco Bay Times,* July 20, 2006. Accessed July 24, 2013. http://www.sfbaytimes.com/?sec=article&article_id=5213.

Antigua and Barbuda Tourism Authority. "Whitney Houston's Special A&B Connection." Antigua Nice, February 24, 2012. http://www.antiguanice.com/v2/client.php?id=775&news=3674.

Armstrong, John. *The Water of Life: A Treatise on Urine Therapy*. London: True Health, 1957.

Asanti, Ifalade TaShia, ed. *Tapestries of Faith: Black SGLBT Stories of Faith, Love, & Family*. Long Beach, CA: Glover Lane, 2011.

Bailey, Marlon. *Butch Queens Up in Pumps: Gender, Performance, and Ballroom Culture in Detroit*. Ann Arbor: University of Michigan Press, 2013.

Bailey, Marlon M. "Engendering Space: Ballroom Culture and the Spatial Practice of Possibility in Detroit." *Gender, Space, and Culture: A Journal of Feminist Geography* 21 (2014): 489–507.

Baldwin, Gayle R. "Whose Black Church? Voices of Oppression and Resistance in Response to the Murder of a 'Gay' Black Teenager." In *Churches, Blackness, and Contested Multiculturalism: Europe, Africa, and North America*, edited by R. Drew Smith, William Ackha, and Anthony Reddie. New York: Palgrave Macmillan, 2014.

"Balloon Fetish." *Strange Sex*. TLC, August 1, 2010. http://www.tlc.com/tv-shows /strange-sex/.

Banks, Azealia. *Broke with Expensive Taste*. New York: Prospect Park, 2014.

Baudelaire, Charles. "Sed Non Satiata." Translated by Jacques LeClerc. Accessed May 24, 2016. http://www.poemsabout.com/poet/charles-baudelaire/page-37/.

Baur, Gabriel, dir. *Venus Boyz*. Onix Films, 1998.

Bee, Kat. "Azealia Banks; Mermaid Ball Splashes Down with Charli XCX, Robyn & Rye Rye in Los Angeles." Idolator, July 16, 2012. http://www.idolator.com/6726311 /azealia-banks-mermaid-ball-charli-xcx-robyn-rye-rye-in-los-angeles.

Bérard, Sylvie. "BDSMSF(QF): Sadomasochistic Readings of Québécois Women's Science Fiction." In *Queer Universes: Sexualities in Science Fiction*, edited by Wendy Gay Pearson, Veronica Hollinger, and Joan Gordon, 180–199. Liverpool: Liverpool University Press, 2008.

Bergan, Renée, and Mark Schuller, dirs. *Poto Mitan: Haitian Women, Pillars of the Global Economy*. Santa Barbara: Tet Ansanm Productions, 2009.

Bernstein, Jacob. "Paris Is Still Burning." *New York Times*, July 25, 2012. http://www .nytimes.com/2012/07/26/fashion/a-lively-house-of-xtravaganza-ball-scene-city .html?_r=0XL.

Bersani, Leo. "Is the Rectum a Grave?" In *Is the Rectum a Grave? And Other Essays*, 3–30. Chicago: University of Chicago Press, 2009.

Beyoncé. "Upgrade U." *B'Day*. New York: Sony Legacy, 2006.

Bhabha, Homi. "Of Mimicry and Man." In *The Location of Culture*, 121–131. New York: Routledge, 2004.

Bibbs, Susheel. "Pleasant's Story." Mary Ellen Pleasant. Accessed May 24, 2016. http://www.mepleasant.com/story.html.

Big Freedia, with Nicole Balin. *Big Freedia: God Save the Queen Diva!* New York: Gallery, 2015.

Billey, K. T. "Prince and the Queer Body: Our Dirty Patron Saint of Pop Gave Me Permission to Think outside the Gender Binary." *Salon*, April 22, 2016. http://www.salon.com/2016/04/22/prince_and_the_queer_body_our_dirty

_patron_saint_of_pop_gave_me_permission_to_think_outside_the_gender
_binary/.

Boa, Sheena. "Young Ladies and Dissolute Women: Conflicting Views of Culture and Gender in Public Entertainment, Kingstown, St. Vincent, 1838–1888." In *Gender and Slave Emancipation in the Atlantic World*, edited by Pamela Scully and Diana Paton. Durham, NC: Duke University Press, 2005.

Boutros, Alexandra. "Lwa Like Me: Gender, Sexuality, and Vodou Online." In *Media, Religion and Gender: Key Issues and New Challenges*, edited by Mia Lovheim. New York: Routledge, 2013.

Braziel, Jana Evans. *Artists, Performers, and Black Masculinity in the Haitian Diaspora.* Bloomington: Indiana University Press, 2008.

Bridgforth, Sharon. "Bio." Sharon Bridgforth. Accessed May 26, 2016. http://www .findingvoice.co/bio-sharon-2-1/.

Bridgforth, Sharon. "Dat Black Mermaid Man Lady." Unpublished manuscript.

Bridgforth, Sharon. *love conjure/blues*. Washington, DC: Redbone, 2004.

Bridgforth, Sharon. "Mermaids in NYC." Sharon Bridgforth (blog), October 2, 2014. https://sharonbridgforthblog.wordpress.com/2014/10/02/mermaids-in-nyc/.

Brown, Karen McCarthy. *Mama Lola: A Vodou Priestess in Brooklyn.* Berkeley: University of California Press, 1991.

Browning, Barbara. *Infectious Rhythm: Metaphors of Contagion and the Spread of African Culture.* New York: Routledge, 1998.

Bryan, TJ. "You've Got to Have Ballz to Walk in These Shoes." In *Brazen Femme: Queering Femininity*, edited by Chloe Brushwood Rose. Vancouver: Arsenal Pulp, 2003.

Buckingham, Will. "Ocean of Existence." ThinkBuddha.org, May 7, 2008. http:// www.thinkbuddha.org/article/336/the-ocean-of-existence.

Buckridge, Steeve. *The Language of Dress: Resistance and Accommodation in Jamaica, 1760–1890.* Kingston: University of the West Indies Press, 2004.

Caistor, Nick. "Voodoo's Spell over Haiti." BBC News, August 4, 2003. http://news .bbc.co.uk/2/hi/americas/3122303.stm.

Califia, Pat. "The Dominant Woman as Priestess." In *Bitch Goddess: The Spiritual Path of the Dominant Woman*, edited by Pat Califia and Drew Campbell. San Francisco: Greenery, 1997.

Califia, Pat. *Macho Sluts.* New York: Alyson, 1994.

Candelario, Ginetta. "Hair Race-ing: Dominican Beauty Culture and Identity Production." *Meridians* 1 (2000): 128–156.

Cardi B. Interview. *The Breakfast Club.* Power 105.1, March 8, 2016. https://www .youtube.com/watch?v=dSkTtwYAFI8.

Cerda, Brooke. "#GirlsLikeUs Ms. Tiffany Mathieu: WE NEED TO BE UNITED." YouTube video, September 17, 2014. https://www.youtube.com/watch?v =neIHdXb8g7A.

Cerda, Brooke, and Tiffany Mathieu. "#GirlsLikeUs Ms. Tiffany Mathieu INTERVIEW." YouTube video, September 17, 2014. https://www.youtube.com /watch?v=CoZsV7IobBg.

Charles, Carolle. "Reflections on Being *Machann ak Machandiz*." *Meridians* 11 (2011): 118–123.

Chauvet, Marie Vieux. *La Danse sur le Volcan*. 1957. Reprint, Paris: Maisonneuve & Larose et Emina Soleil, 2004.

Chinn, Sarah, and Kris Franklin. "King of the Hill: Changing the Face of Drag—An Interview with Dred." In *Butch/Femme: Inside Lesbian Gender*, edited by Sally R. Munt and Cherry Smyth. London: Continuum, 1998.

Chouaki, Yasmine, and Anne Lescot. "En Sol Majeur." RFI, March 11, 2000. http://www.rfi.fr/contenu/20100302-1-anne-lescot.

Christian, Barbara. "The Race for Theory." *Cultural Critique* 6 (Spring 1987): 51–63.

Christian, Barbara. "The Race for Theory." In *Making Face, Making Soul: Haciendo Caras*, edited by Gloria Anzaldúa. San Francisco: Aunt Lute, 1990.

Cohen, Cathy. "Bulldaggers, Punks, and Welfare Queens." GLQ 3 (1997): 437–465.

Coleman, Willi. "Among the Things That Used to Be." In *Home Girls: A Black Feminist Anthology*, edited by Barbara Smith. New York: Kitchen Table, Women of Color Press, 1983.

Colindres, Romulo E., Seema Jain, Anna Bowen, Eric Mintz, and Polyana Domond. "After the Flood: An Evaluation of In-Home Drinking Water Treatment Combined with Flocculent-Disinfectant Following Tropical Storm Jeanne—Gonaives, Haiti, 2004." *Journal of Water and Health* 5 (March 2007): 367.

Collins, Patricia Hill. *Black Feminist Thought: Knowledge, Consciousness, and the Politics of Empowerment*. New York: Routledge, 2008.

Colon, Edgar Rivera. "Getting Life in Two Worlds: Power and Prevention in the New York City House Ball Community." PhD diss., Rutgers University, 2009.

Compton, Julie. "Is Transmisogyny Killing Transgender Women?" NBC News, August 25, 2015. http://www.nbcnews.com/news/nbc-out/transmisogyny-killing -transgender-women-n415286.

Conner, Randy P., with David Hatfield Sparks. *Queering Creole Spiritual Traditions: Lesbian, Gay, Bisexual, and Transgender Participation in African-Inspired Traditions in the Americas*. Binghamton, NY: Harrington Park, 2004.

Corbett, Bob. "Dwa Fanm Celebrates the Voices of Women." Haiti Mailing List (e-mail group), March 19, 2003. http://faculty.webster.edu/corbetre/haiti-archive -new/msg15132.html.

Cosentino, Daniel. "Imagine Heaven." In *The Sacred Arts of Haitian Vodou*, edited by Daniel J. Cosentino. Los Angeles: UCLA Fowler Museum of Cultural History, 1995.

Cosentino, Daniel. "It's All for You, Sen Jak!" In *The Sacred Arts of Haitian Vodou*, edited by Daniel J. Cosentino. Los Angeles: UCLA Fowler Museum of Cultural History, 1995.

Covey, Herbert C. *African American Slave Medicine: Herbal and Non-herbal Treatments*. Lanham, MD: Lexington, 2007.

Crawford, Robyn. "Whitney Elizabeth Houston, 1963–2012." *Esquire*, February 12, 2012. http://www.esquire.com/entertainment/music/a12753/whitney-houston -6654718/.

Crichlow, Ayana Malaika. "Rihanna Queen of Crop Over." *Huffington Post*, August 7, 2015. http://www.huffingtonpost.com/ayana-malaika-crichlow/rihanna-queen -of-crop-ove_b_7952880.html.

Cruz, Ariane. "Beyond Black and Blue: BDSM, Internet Pornography, and Black Female Sexuality." *Feminist Studies* 14 (summer 2015): 409–436.

Cunningham, Michael. "The Slap of Love." *Open City* 6 (1995). http://opencity.org /archive/issue-6/the-slap-of-love.

D., Katt. "Rihanna Jokes She's Dating Girls Now & Wishes It Was Nicki Minaj." *Magic* 107.5, 2011. http://majicatl.hellobeautiful.com/873521/rihanna-jokes-shes -dating-girls-now-wishes-it-was-nicki-minaj-video/.

Dahl, Ulrika. *Femmes of Power*. London: Serpent's Tail, 2009.

Danticat, Edwidge. *Breath, Eyes, Memory*. New York: Vintage, 1998.

Davies, Carole Boyce. "Women, Labor, and the Transnational: From Work to Work." In *Caribbean Spaces: Escapes from Twilight Zones*, 107–128. Urbana: University of Illinois Press, 2013.

Davis, Wade. *The Serpent and the Rainbow: A Harvard Scientist's Astonishing Journey into the Secret Societies of Haitian Voodoo, Zombis, and Magic*. New York: Simon & Schuster, 1985.

Dayan, Colin. *Haiti, History, and the Gods*. Berkeley: University of California Press, 1995.

Dayan, Joan. "Erzulie: A Women's History of Haiti." *African Literatures* 25 (1994): 5–32.

Deren, Maya. *Divine Horsemen: The Living Gods of Haiti*. 1953. Reprint, Kingston, NY: Documentext, 1983.

Desse, Michel. "Les difficultés de gestion d'un littoral de survie à Haïti: L'exemple du golfe de la Gonave." *Cahiers de Geographie du Québec* 47 (2003): 63–83.

Dodge, Shyam. "Aunty OhNaNa! Rihanna Bonds with Baby Cousin Majesty as She Carries the Tot to Her Christening in Barbados." *Daily Mail*, September 15, 2014. http://www.dailymail.co.uk/tvshowbiz/article-2756749/Rihanna-bonds-baby -cousin-Majesty-carries-tot-Christening-Barbados.html.

Dolak, Kevin, and Eileen Murphy. "Whitney Houston Cause of Death: How Cocaine Contributes to Heart Disease." ABC News, March 23, 2012. http:// abcnews.go.com/Health/whitney-houston-death-cocaine-contributed-heart -disease/story?id=15984196.

Doyle, Sady. "Season of the Witch: Why Young Women Are Flocking to the Ancient Craft." *Guardian*, February 24, 2015. http://www.theguardian.com/world/2015/feb /24/witch-symbol-feminist-power-azealia-banks.

Duggan, Lisa, and Kathleen McHugh. "Fem(me)inist Manifesto." In *Brazen Femme: Queering Femininity*, edited by Chloe Brushwood Rose. Vancouver: Arsenal Pulp, 2003.

Duhigg, Charles. "Why Did Whitney Fail Rehab? Too Much Talent." Charles Duhigg (blog), February 13, 2012. http://charlesduhigg.com/rehab-for-whitney/.

Duke, Alan. "Whitney Houston Drowned in a Foot of Hot Water, Autopsy Says." CNN, April 4, 2012. http://www.cnn.com/2012/04/04/showbiz/whitney-houston -toxicology/.

Dworken, Arye. "Interview: Azealia Banks Discusses the Self-Made World That Saved Her." *Self-Titled*, November 13, 2014. http://www.self-titledmag.com/2014/11/13/the-self-titled-interview-azealia-banks/.

"Erin Currier." Artistaday. Accessed May 24, 2016. http://artistaday.com/?p=11349.

Erzulie, Domina. "About." Google+. Accessed May 24, 2016. https://plus.google.com/115083255973291951873/.

Erzulie, Domina. "I'm Back!!" Domina Erzulie (blog), April 13, 2008. http://dominaerzulie.blogspot.com/2008/04/im-back.html.

Erzulie, Domina. Blog post. Accessed July 11, 2014. http://www.dominaerzulie.com/en/my-description/.

Erzulie, Domina. Blog post. Accessed July 11, 2014. http://www.dominaerzulie.com/en/rantings-thoughtsblog-2/.

Erzulie, Domina. "Answer to Kolan Blanc." Domina Erzulie (blog), February 25, 2009. http://dominaerzulie.blogspot.com/2009/02/answer-to-kolan-blanc.html.

"Erzulie Red-Eyes." Tribe of the Sun. Accessed May 25, 2016. http://tribeofthesun.com/deities/ezulie-red-eyes/.

Everything @ Bedlam. Event announcement, Gay New York, August 11, 2011. http://newyork.gaycities.com/events/84189-everything-bedlam-with-venus-x-ghe20goth1k-clarissa-the-teenage-witch.

Fallin, Wilson, Jr. *The African American Church in Birmingham, Alabama, 1815–1963: A Shelter in the Storm*. New York: Garland, 1997.

Fandrich, Ina Johanna. "Defiant African Sisterhoods: The Voodoo Arrests of the 1850s and 1860s in New Orleans." In *Fragments of Bone: Neo-African Religions in a New World*, edited by Patrick Bellegarde-Smith. Urbana: University of Illinois Press, 2005.

Farmer, Paul, Charles Patrick Almazor, Emily T. Bahnsen, Donna Barry, Junior Bazile, Barry R. Bloom, and Niranjan Bose. "Meeting Cholera's Challenge to Haiti and the World: A Joint Statement on Cholera Prevention and Care." *PLoS Neglected Tropical Diseases* 5 (2011): e1145.

Ferguson, Roderick. "Sissies at the Picnic: The Subjugated Knowledges of a Black Rural Queer." In *Feminist Waves, Feminist Generations: Life Stories from the Academy*, edited by Hokulani Aikau, Karla Erickson, and Jennifer Pierce, 188–196. Minneapolis: University of Minnesota Press, 2007.

Fisher, Luchina, and Sheila Marikar. "Whitney Houston Returns to Rehab." ABC News, May 9, 2011. http://abcnews.go.com/Entertainment/whitney-houston-returns-rehab/story?id=13563047.

Follett, Richard. *The Sugar Masters: Planters and Slaves in Louisiana's Cane World, 1800–1860*. Baton Rouge: Louisiana State University Press, 2007.

Freeman, David W. "Whitney Houston Back in Rehab: Why Is Addiction So Hard to Beat?" CBS News, May 10, 2011. http://www.cbsnews.com/news/whitney-houston-back-in-rehab-why-is-addiction-so-hard-to-beat/.

Freeman, Elizabeth. *Time Binds: Queer Temporalities, Queer Histories*. Durham, NC: Duke University Press, 2010.

Friedman, Roger. "Flashback: Young Whitney Reflects on Fame and Sexuality." *Showbiz 411*, February 18, 2012. http://www.showbiz411.com/2012/02/18/flashback-young-whitney-reflects-on-fame-and-sexuality.

Ganz, Caryn. "The Curious Case of Nicki Minaj." *Out*, September 12, 2010. http://www.out.com/entertainment/music/2010/09/12/curious-case-nicki-minaj.

Gerestant, MilDred. Interview. Stylelikeu. March 21, 2011. http://stylelikeu.com/closets/mildred-gerestant/.

Gerestant, MilDred. "Who Am I—D.R.E.D.—Daring Reality Every Day." Women Writers in Bloom Poetry Salon, 2011. http://womenwritersinbloompoetrysalon.blogspot.com/p/poetry-garden-archives.html.

Gerestant, MilDred, and Victoria Gaither. "A Night of Three Goddesses." *At Home with Victoria*. Blog Talk Radio, March 7, 2010. http://www.blogtalkradio.com/victoria-gaither/2010/03/07/a-night-of-3-goddesses-featuring-actress-mildred-g.

Gerestant, MilDred, Tantra-zawadi, and Sokhna Heathyre Mabin. "A Night of Three Goddesses: Powerful Women." New York Public Library, June 28, 2010. http://www.nypl.org/events/programs/2010/06/28/night-three-goddesses-powerful-women.

Giorgis, Hannah. "Rihanna and the Radical Power of 'Carefree Black Girl' Celebrity." *Pinoria*, April 8, 2015. https://pinoria.wordpress.com/2015/04/08/rihanna-and-the-radical-power-of-carefree-black-girl-celebrity-2/.

Glassman, Sallie Ann. *Vodou Visions: An Encounter with Divine Mystery*. New York: Villard, 2000.

Glissant, Edouard. *The Poetics of Relation*. Translated by Betsy Wing. Ann Arbor: University of Michigan Press, 1997.

Godwin, Richard. "Azealia Banks: 'I've Realised You're Not Keeping It Real by Being a Crazy Girl.'" *Evening Standard*, October 17, 2016. http://www.standard.co.uk/showbiz/celebrity-news/azealia-banks-i-ve-realised-you-re-not-keeping-it-real-by-being-the-crazy-girl-a3371046.html.

Golden, Zara. "Artist Roy Nachum Reveals the Meaning behind Rihanna's ANTi Cover." *Fader*, October 9, 2015. http://www.thefader.com/2015/10/09/rihanna-anti-artist-roy-nachum.

Goodman, Lizzy. "The Big Reveal." *Elle* 352 (December 2014).

Gottschild, Brenda Dixon. *The Black Dancing Body: A Geography from Coon to Cool*. New York: Palgrave Macmillan, 2003.

Graham, Brittany. "Azealia Banks Channels Gay 'Ball Culture' at the Mermaid Ball in L.A." Vibe, July 17, 2012. http://www.vibe.com/2012/07/azealia-banks-channels-gay-ball-culture-mermaid-ball-la/.

GreenCOM. "Haitian Urban Sanitation Project Formative Research." USAID, 1996. http://pdf.usaid.gov/pdf_docs/pnacd457.pdf.

Greene, Beverly. "African American Lesbian and Bisexual Women." *Journal of Social Issues* 56 (2000): 239–249.

Greer, Carlos. "Rihanna Treats Her New Album Like She's 'Going Make a Baby.'" Page Six, October 24, 2015. http://pagesix.com/2015/10/24/rihanna-treats-her -new-album-like-shes-going-make-a-baby/.

Gumbs, Alexis Pauline. "We Can Learn to Mother Ourselves: The Queer Survival of Black Feminism." PhD diss., Duke University, 2010.

Halberstam, Judith "Jack," and Del LaGrace Volcano. "Class, Race, and Masculinity: The Superfly, the Macdaddy, and the Rapper." In The Drag King Book. London: Serpent's Tail, 1999.

Hart, Lynda. Between the Body and the Flesh. New York: Columbia University Press, 1998.

Hartman, Saidiya. "The Belly of the World: A Note on Black Women's Labors." Souls 18 (2016).

Hartman, Saidiya. "Venus in Two Acts." Small Axe 26 (June 2008): 1–14.

Haynes, Gavin. "Azealia Banks Interview: 'I Was Never Going to End Up a Broke Bitch.'" NME, May 13, 2015. http://www.nme.com/features/azealia-banks -interview-i-was-never-going-to-end-up-a-broke-bitch.

"Helene." Poto Mitan. Accessed March 13, 2016. http://www.potomitan.net/helene .html.

Holdredge, Helen. Mammy Pleasant. New York: Putnam, 1953.

Holmes, Sally. "Rihanna and Blue Ivy Had a Princess Moment at the Grammys." Elle, February 8, 2015. http://www.elle.com/culture/celebrities/news/a26644 /rihanna-blue-ivy-grammys/.

Hong, Grace. "The Ghosts of Transnational American Studies: A Response to the Presidential Address." American Quarterly 59 (March 2007): 33–39.

Hopkinson, Nalo. The Salt Roads. New York: Grand Central, 2004.

Houlberg, Marilyn. "Magique Marasa: The Ritual Cosmos of Twins and Other Sacred Children." In The Sacred Arts of Haitian Vodou, edited by Daniel J. Cosentino. Los Angeles: UCLA Fowler Museum of Cultural History, 1995.

Houlberg, Marilyn. "Sirens and Snakes: Water Spirits in the Arts of Haitian Vodou." African Arts 29 (spring 1996): 30–101.

Houngan Hector. "Anaisa Pye." Gade Nou Leve Society. Accessed May 28, 2016. http://www.ezilikonnen.com/dominican/anaisa-pye/.

Houngan Hector. "Ezili Danto." Gade Nou Leve Society. Accessed March 13, 2016. http://www.ezilikonnen.com/the-lwa/ezili-danto/.

Houngan Hector. "Interview with a Houngan." Haitian Vodou—Lwa Ginen. Accessed March 13, 2016. http://hounganhector.tripod.com/id2.html.

"Houston Celebrates at Age 40 (and a Day)." All Whitney Houston. Accessed May 26, 2016. http://whfan.free.fr/newsfile.htm.

Houston, Cissy. Remembering Whitney: My Story of Love, Loss, and the Night the Music Stopped. New York: Harper, 2013.

Houston, Whitney. Primetime: Special Edition. Interview by Diane Sawyer. December 4, 2002.

Hudson, Lynn. *The Making of "Mammy Pleasant": A Black Entrepreneur in Nineteenth-Century San Francisco.* Urbana-Champaign: University of Illinois Press, 2002.

Hurston, Zora Neale. *Mules and Men.* 1935. Reprint, New York: Harper Perennial, 1990.

Hurston, Zora Neale. *Tell My Horse.* 1938. Reprint, New York: Harper Perennial Classics, 2008.

"The Insider: Rewind Whitney Houston's 26th Birthday Party, 1989." August 2012. YouTube https://www.youtube.com/watch?v=3b8uI8HPn30.

Irigaray, Luce. *This Sex That Is Not One.* Ithaca, NY: Cornell University Press, 1985.

James, Susan Donaldson. " 'Looners' Substitute Balloons for Love, Sex and Intimacy." ABC News, August 15, 2012. http://abcnews.go.com/Health/balloon-fetishists-objects-love-sex-intimacy/story?id=17010057.

Jean-Charles, Régine. "Poto Mitan: Haitian Women, Pillars of the Global Economy." *Films for the Feminist Classroom* 2 (Spring 2010). http://ffc.twu.edu/issue_2-1/rev_rjc_film_2-1.html.

Johns, Jamala. "Who Exactly Is 'the Carefree Black Girl'?" Refinery 29, January 30, 2014. http://www.refinery29.com/2014/01/61614/carefree-black-girls.

Johnson, Chevel. "Big Freedia Twerking Her Way to Stardom." AP: The Big Story, April 30, 2016. http://bigstory.ap.org/article/976f28971c39439993e27db5518f288f/big-freedia-twerks-her-way-stardom.

Johnson, Cyree Jarelle. "Femme Privilege Does Not Exist." Femme Dreamboat (blog), January 5, 2013. http://femmedreamboat.tumblr.com/post/39734380982/femme-privilege-does-not-exist.

Johnson, E. Patrick. " 'Quare' Studies, or (Almost) Everything I Know About Queer Studies I Learned from My Grandmother." *Text and Performance Quarterly* 21 (January 2001): 1–25.

Johnston, Nancy. " 'Happy That It's Here': An Interview with Nalo Hopkinson." In *Queer Universes: Sexualities in Science Fiction*, edited by Wendy Gay Pearson, Veronica Hollinger, and Joan Gordon, 200–215. Liverpool: Liverpool University Press, 2008.

Jones, Deja. "The Struggle to Find Your Identity as a Carefree Black Girl." Madamenoire, April 2, 2015. http://madamenoire.com/522771/struggle-finding-identity-carefree-black-girl/.

Jones, Omi Oshun Joni L. *Theatrical Jazz: Performance, Ase, and the Power of the Present Moment.* Cincinnati: Ohio University Press, 2015.

Jones, Simone. "When You're a Carefree Black Girl Disguised as a Mama." The Shy Peacock (blog), August 12, 2015. https://theshypeacock.com/2015/08/12/when-youre-a-carefree-black-girl-disguised-as-a-mama/.

Keeling, Kara. *The Witch's Flight: The Cinematic, the Black Femme, and the Image of Common Sense.* Durham, NC: Duke University Press, 2007.

Knock, Emma. "Live Review: Azealia Banks London Mermaid Ball." MTV, October 16, 2012. http://www.mtv.co.uk/the-wrap-up/blog/live-review-azealia-banks-london-mermaid-ball.

Knowles, Beyoncé, and Kahlil Joseph, dirs. *Lemonade*. New York: Parkwood Entertainment, 2016.

Koehler, Robert. "Review: 'Of Men and Gods.'" *Variety*, August 5, 2003. http://variety.com/2003/film/reviews/of-men-and-gods-1200540075/.

Kohler, Will. "Forgotten New York City—the Cock Ring and the Hotel Christopher." Back2Stonewall, August 14, 2013. http://www.back2stonewall.com/2013/08/forgotten-gay-york-city-cock-ring-hotel-christopher.html.

Krishnamurthy, Sowmya. "The 11 Most Eye-Opening Quotes from Rihanna's Interview with Oprah." Vibe, August 20, 2012. http://www.vibe.com/2012/08/11-most-eye-opening-quotes-rihannas-interview-oprah/.

LaMenfo, Mambo Vye Zo Komande. *Serving the Spirits: The Religion of Haitian Vodou*. CreateSpace, 2012.

Lara, Ana-Maurine. *Erzulie's Skirt*. Washington, DC: Redbone, 2006.

Lara, Ana-Maurine. "Vudú in the Dominican Republic: Resistance and Healing." *Phoebe* 17 (spring 2005).

"Last Splash: Azealia Banks Explains Whole Mermaid Deal." *Spin*, July 12, 2012. http://www.spin.com/2012/07/last-splash-azealia-banks-explains-whole-mermaid-deal/.

Latta, Judi Moore. "When the Spirit Takes Hold, What the Work Becomes!" In *Sister Circle: Black Women and Work*, edited by Sharon Harley and the Black Women and Work Collective. Newark, NJ: Rutgers University Press, 2002.

Leary, Timothy, and Richard Alpert. *The Psychedelic Experience: A Manual Based on the Tibetan Book of the Dead*. New York: Citadel Underground, 2000.

Leland, John. "In East Orange, Recalling Whitney Houston before She Was a Star." *New York Times*, February 17, 2012. http://www.nytimes.com/2012/02/17/nyregion/in-east-orange-before-whitney-houston-was-a-star.html.

Lescot, Anne, and Laurence Magloire, dirs. *Of Men and Gods*. Documentary Educational Resources, 2002. http://www.der.org/films/of-men-and-gods.html.

"LET IT SNOW . . . Vintage 1988 'SNOW BALL' Invitation." Accessed August 3, 2017. http://www.imgrum.org/media/906750726763592987_634791166.

Lewin, Yael Tamar. *Night's Dancer: The Life of Janet Collins*. Middletown, CT: Wesleyan University Press, 2011.

"LGBT and Gay-Friendly Alcohol and Drug Rehab." Recovery Connection. Accessed May 26, 2016. https://www.recoveryconnection.com/substance-abuse/treatment-programs/specialty-treatment-addictions/lgbt-gay-friendly-alcohol-drug-rehab/.

Littlejohn, Georgina. "'The Token Sand N***a from ID': Azealia Banks Launches Homophobic and Racist Attack on Zayn Malik." Sun, May 11, 2016. https://www.thesun.co.uk/archives/news/1170608/the-token-sand-n-from-id-azealia-banks-launches-homophobic-and-racist-attack-on-zayn-malik/.

Livingston, Jennie, dir. *Paris Is Burning*. Miramax, 1991; reissue, 2005.

Long, Camilla. "Shooting from the Mouth." *Sunday Times*, October 6, 2013. http://www.thesundaytimes.co.uk/sto/style/fashion/People/article1321310.ece.

Long, Carolyn Morrow. *A New Orleans Voudou Priestess: The Legend and Reality of Marie Laveau*. Gainesville: University Press of Florida, 2006.

Lorde, Audre. "The Uses of the Erotic: The Erotic as Power." In *Sister Outsider: Essays and Speeches by Audre Lorde*, 53–59. New York: Crossing Press, 1984.

"Love Is Revolutionary When You're Black and Transgender." NBC News, June 15, 2016. http://www.nbcnews.com/video/living-color-love-is-revolutionary-when-youre-black-and-transgender-464842307606.

Luis, Sancista. "The Mistress Anaisa Pye." Sociedad de Sance Rio Tempestuoso, March 25, 2013. http://sansespiritismo.blogspot.com/2013/03/the-mistress-anaisa-pye.html.

MacDonald, Kirsty. "Assume Nothing: MilDred Gerestant." YouTube video, October 31, 2010. http://www.youtube.com/watch?v=pWAg3DsEnaA.

Maggie. "Our Lady Erzulie Dantor—Thoughts and Links." Tribe, July 28, 2010. http://tribes.tribe.net/global_vodou_2010/thread/5edodcd9-3d8a-40d3-b90b-5e76271eocof.

"Marie Lavaux: Death of the Queen of the Voudous." *New Orleans Democrat*, June 18, 1881. Available at Wendy Mae Chambers, Voodoo on the Bayou. Accessed May 1, 2012. http://www.voodooonthebayou.net/marie_laveau.html.

Matthews, Connie, Peggy Lorah, and Jaime Fenton. "Toward a Grounded Theory of Lesbians' Recovery from Addiction." In *Making Lesbians Visible in the Substance Use Field*, edited by Elizabeth Ettore. Binghamton, NY: Harrington Park, 2005.

McAlister, Elizabeth. "Love, Sex, and Gender Embodied: The Spirits of Haitian Vodou." In *Love, Sex, and Gender in the World Religions*, edited by Joseph Runzo and Nancy Martin. Oxford: Oneworld, 2000.

McClintock, Ann. "Maid to Order: Commercial Fetishization and Gender Power." *Signs* 37 (Winter 1993).

McKittrick, Katherine. *Demonic Grounds: Black Women and the Cartographies of Struggle*. Minneapolis: University of Minnesota Press, 2006.

McNeal, Keith. "Pantheons as Mythistorical Archives: Pantheonization and Remodeled Iconographies in Two Southern Caribbean Possession Religions." In *Activating the Past: History and Memory in the Black Atlantic World*. Newcastle upon Tyne: Cambridge Scholars, 2010.

Metraux, Alfred. *Voodoo in Haiti*. New York: Pantheon, 1989.

Michel, Claudine, Patrick Bellegarde-Smith, and Marlene Racine-Toussaint. "From the Horses' Mouths: Women's Words/Women's Worlds." In *Haitian Vodou: Spirit, Myth, and Reality*, edited by Patrick Bellegarde-Smith and Claudine Michel. Bloomington: University of Indiana Press, 2006.

Miller-Young, Mireille. *A Taste for Brown Sugar: Black Women in Pornography*. Durham, NC: Duke University Press, 2014.

Minor, Rickey. "The 2012 Oral History: Whitney Houston, 1963–2012." *Esquire*, November 20, 2012. http://www.esquire.com/entertainment/a16739/whitney-houston-death-1212/.

Mistress A. "Confessions of a Black Dominatrix." Afropunk, December 9, 2011. http://www.afropunk.com/profiles/blogs/confessions-of-a-black-dominatrix?xg _source=activity.

Morris, Mark. "Whitney Houston: Clive Davis' Tribute at Pre-Grammy Party." YouTube video, February 2012. https://www.youtube.com/watch?v=alr8IpVzyVg.

Muñoz, José. *Cruising Utopia: The Then and There of Queer Futurity*. New York: New York University Press, 2009.

National Cultural Foundation of Barbados. "The Story Behind the Crop Over Festival." Accessed May 28, 2016. http://www.ncf.bb/crop-over/.

Nealy, Eleanor. "April 30." In *Amazon Spirit: Daily Meditations for Lesbians in Recovery*. New York: Perigee Trade, 1995.

Norment, Lynn. "The Awards, the Gossip, the Glory: Whitney's Wild and Wonderful Year." *Ebony* 49 (July 1994).

Ocasio, Linda. "N.J.'s Black Churches Open Doors to Gay Congregants, but Not Right to Marry." NJ.com, December 11, 2011. http://www.nj.com/njvoices/index .ssf/2011/12/njs_black_churches_open_doors.html.

Ortved, John. "Azealia Banks, Taking Her Cues and Lyrics from the Street." *New York Times*, February 2, 2012. http://www.nytimes.com/2012/02/02/fashion/azealia -banks-a-young-rapper-taking-cues-from-the- street.html.

Ostroff, Alex. "On Azealia Banks, Angel Haze, Sexuality, Biphobia, and Appropriation." Purplechrain, December 24, 2012. http://purplechrain.tumblr .com/post/38693856075/on-azealia-banks-angel-haze-sexuality-biphobia.

Parish, James Robert. *Whitney Houston 1963–2012: We Will Always Love You*. New York: John Blake, 2012.

Perez, Frank, and Jeffrey Palmquist. *In Exile: The History and Lore Surrounding New Orleans Gay Culture and Its Oldest Gay Bar*. Hurlford, Scotland: LL Publications, 2012.

Polyamory Society. "Introduction to Polyamory." Accessed May 27, 2016. http:// www.polyamorysociety.org/page6.html.

Porter, Chelcie. "Mildred 'Dred' Gerestant at POW WOW." YouTube video, December 11, 2011. https://www.youtube.com/watch?v=qtpBGLZgLrg.

Prince. "Scarlet Pussy." On *The Hits/The B-Sides*. Chanhassen, MN: Paisley Park Records, 1993.

Prince. "Shockadelica." On *The Hits/The B-Sides*. Chanhassen, MN: Paisley Park Records, 1993.

Puar, Jasbir. *Terrorist Assemblages: Homonationalism in Queer Times*. Durham, NC: Duke University Press, 2007.

Publishers Weekly. Review of *The Salt Roads*, by Nalo Hopkinson. November 12, 2003. http://www.publishersweekly.com/978-0-446-53302-7.

Ramirez, Marc. "The Blazing Steps of Janet Collins." *Seattle Times*, January 23, 2000. http://community.seattletimes.nwsource.com/archive/?date=20000123&slug =4000846.

Ramsey, Kate. *The Spirits and the Law: Vodou and Power in Haiti*. Chicago: University of Chicago Press, 2011.

Ravalec, Vincent, Mallendi, and Agnès Paicheler. *Iboga: The Visionary Root of African Shamanism*. South Paris, ME: Park Street, 2007.

Reed, Allison. "Traumatic Utopias: Holding Hope in Sharon Bridgforth's Love Conjure/Blues." *Text and Performance Quarterly* 35 (June 2015): 119.

René, George, and Marilyn Houlberg. "My Double Mystic Marriages to Two Goddesses of Love." In *The Sacred Arts of Haitian Vodou*, edited by Daniel J. Cosentino. Los Angeles: UCLA Fowler Museum of Cultural History, 1995.

Richardson, Matt. *The Queer Limit of Black Memory: Black Lesbian Literature and Irresolution*. Cincinnati: Ohio University Press, 2013.

Rodriguez, Nice. "Throw It to the River." In *Throw It to the River*. Toronto: Women's Press, 1993.

Rohr, Richard. *Breathing under Water: Spirituality and the Twelve Steps*. Cincinnati: Franciscan Media, 2011.

Saint-Lot, Marie-Jose Alcide. *Vodou: A Sacred Theatre—the African Heritage in Haiti*. Miami: Educa Vision, 2004.

Salva, Hector. "Introduction to Las 21 Divisiones." Las 21 Divisiones. Accessed May 27, 2016. http://las21divisiones.com/.

Santana, Dora Silva. "Trans-Atlantic Re-turnings: A Trans/Black/Diasporic/ Feminist Auto-Account of a Black Trans Brazilian Woman's Transitioning." Master's thesis, University of Texas at Austin, 2015.

Scandura, Jani. *Down in the Dumps: Place, Modernity, American Depression*. Durham, NC: Duke University Press, 2008.

Schindehette, Susan. "Rock Bottom." *People*, March 29, 2004. http://www.people .com/people/archive/rock-bottom-vol-61-no-12/.

Seal, Mark. "The Devils in the Diva." *Vanity Fair*, June 2012. http://www.vanityfair .com/hollywood/2012/06/whitney-houston-death-bathtub-drugs-rehab.

Serano, Julia. *Excluded: Making Feminist and Queer Movements More Inclusive*. New York: Seal, 2013.

Shackelford, Ashleigh. "Trap Queens and Freak Hoes: On Exclusivity in the Carefree Black Girl Movement." For Harriet, September 2015. http://www .forharriet.com/2015/09/trap-queens-and-freak-hoes-on.html#axzz49tadmR8v.

Shrugg, Rebecca Ann. "How Does She Look?" In *Femme: Feminists, Lesbians, and Bad Girls*, edited by Laura Harris and Elizabeth Crocker. London: Routledge, 1997.

Sieczkowski, Cavan. "Cissy Houston on Whitney Houston Gay Relationship: I Would Have 'Absolutely' Disapproved." *Huffington Post*, January 29, 2013. http://www.huffingtonpost.com/2013/01/29/cissy-houston-whitney-houston-gay -rumors_n_2573718.html.

Silverman, Stephen. "Whitney Houston out of Rehab after Only 5 Days." *People*, March 24, 2004. http://www.people.com/celebrity/whitney-out-of-rehab-after -only-5-days/.

Stern, Marlow. "Azealia Banks Opens Up about Her Journey from Stripping to Rap Stardom." *Daily Beast*, November 17, 2014. http://www.thedailybeast.com/articles

/2014/11/17/azealia-banks-opens-up-about-her-journey-from-stripping-to-rap
-stardom.html.

Strongman, Roberto. "Transcorporeality in Haitian Vodou." *Journal of Haitian Studies*
14 (2008): 4–29.

Strunsky, Steve. "Whitney Houston's Childhood Friends in N.J. Knew She Was
Destined for Success." NJ.com, February 13, 2012. http://www.nj.com/news
/index.ssf/2012/02/whitney_houstons_childhood_fri.html.

Sugarscape. "Rihanna and Katy Perry's Big Lesbian Love Story Continues . . ."
Accessed May 28, 2016. http://www.sugarscape.com/celebs/news/a730198
/rihanna-and-katy-perrys-big-lesbian-love-story-continues/.

Syme, Rachel. "Azealia Banks on Why No One Really Wants to See Her Naked, Her
Impure Thoughts about Barack Obama, and Why She's 'Not Here to Be Your
Idol.' " *Billboard*, April 3, 2015. http://www.billboard.com/articles/news/6523916
/billboard-cover-azealia-banks-broke-with-expensive-taste-barack-obama
-twitter-controversy-playboy.

Szeles, Ursula. "Sea Secret Rising: The Lwa Lasirenn in Haitian Vodou." *Journal of
Haitian Studies* 17 (Spring 2011): 193–210.

Tatchell, Peter. "Whitney's REAL Tragedy Was Giving Up Her Greatest Love of
All—Her Female Partner Robyn Crawford." *Daily Mail*, February 20, 2012.
http://www.dailymail.co.uk/tvshowbiz/article-2103164/Whitney-Houstons-REAL
-tragedy-giving-female-partner-Robyn-Crawford.html.

Tannenbaum, Rob. "Azealia Banks: Wild and Uncensored for Playboy." *Playboy*,
March 16, 2015. https://www.playboy.com/articles/azealia-banks-playboy-photos.

"Teacher Zone." London Aquarium. Accessed May 26, 2016. https://www2
.visitsealife.com/london/discover/teacher-zone/.

Thompson, Shirley. *Exiles at Home: The Struggle to Become American in Creole New
Orleans.* Cambridge, MA: Harvard University Press, 2009.

Tinsley, Omise'eke Natasha. "Black Atlantic, Queer Atlantic: Queer Imaginings of
the Middle Passage." *GLQ* 14 (April 2008): 191–215.

Tinsley, Omise'eke Natasha. "The Myths Surrounding Black Women and
Miscarriage." *Ebony*, October 22, 2015. http://www.ebony.com/life/the-myths
-surrounding-black-women-and-miscarriage#axzz4LZu2WglH.

Tinsley, Omise'eke Natasha. *Thiefing Sugar: Eroticism between Women in Caribbean Literature.* Durham, NC: Duke University Press, 2010.

"Top Ten Most Haunted New Orleans Locations." Haunted New Orleans
Tours. Accessed April 30, 2012. http://www.hauntednewworleanstours.com
/toptenhaunted/toptenhauntedNewOrleanslocations.

Trammell, Matthew. "Azealia Banks Throws a Mermaid Ball in New York." *Rolling
Stone*, June 4, 2012. http://www.rollingstone.com/music/news/azealia-banks
-throws-a-mermaid-ball-in-new-york-20120604.

Urbistondo, Josune. "Bodies Scared Sacred at the Crossroads: Vodou Loa Erzulie
in Mayra Montero's *The Red of His Shadow* and Ana-Maurine Lara's *Erzulie's Skirt*."
Hispanet Journal 6 (March 2013).

Vasquez, Junior. "Dream Drums." New York: Eightball Records, 1999.

Vazquez, Junior. "Just Like a Queen." New York: Minimal Records, 1990.

Vasquez, Junior. "Work This Pussy." New York: House of Ellis Music, 1989.

Vazquez, Junior. "X." New York: Tribal America, 1994.

Viteri, Bobby. "Venus X on GHE20G0TH1K, the Best Party in New York." Vice, September 28, 2013. http://www.vice.com/en_ca/read/ghe20goth1ks-venus-x-is -devoted-to-the-art-of-moving-butts.

Vlach, John Michael. The Afro-American Tradition in Decorative Arts. Athens: University of Georgia Press, 1990.

Walcott, Rinaldo. "Reconstructing Manhood; or, The Drag of Black Masculinity." Small Axe 13 (March 2009): 75–89.

Walden, Narada Michael, and Richard Buskin. Whitney Houston: The Voice, the Music, the Inspiration. San Rafael, CA: Insight Editions, 2012.

Ward, Martha. Vodou Queen: The Spirited Lives of Marie Laveau. Jackson: University Press of Mississippi, 2004.

Wayne, Chloe. "GHE20G0TH1K: A Conversation with Venus X." Creative New York, June 24, 2016. https://nyc.moma.org/ghe20goth1k-a-conversation-with-venus-x -2c3511a62977#.8ee1rf92e.

Weiss, Margot. Techniques of Pleasure: BDSM and the Circuits of Sexuality. Durham, NC: Duke University Press, 2011.

Wekker, Gloria. "Mati-ism and Black Lesbianism: Two Idealtypical Expressions of Female Homosexuality in Black Communities of the Diaspora." In Classics in Lesbian Studies, edited by Esther D. Rothblum. Binghamton, NY: Haworth, 1996.

Wekker, Gloria. The Politics of Passion: Women's Sexual Culture in the Afro Surinamese Diaspora. New York: Columbia University Press, 2006.

West, Kanye. "I Don't Like." On Cruel Summer. New York: G.O.O.D. Music, 2012.

Whitaker, Adia. "Ezili." YouTube video, May 2012. http://www.youtube.com/watch ?v=JDwN2DNschc.

"Whitney Houston Had Premonition about Death." TMZ, February 15, 2012. http://www.tmz.com/2012/02/15/whitney-houston-premonition-death-jesus -bible/.

"Whitney Houston Holds a Lavish Birthday Gala." Jet 76 (September 11, 1989).

"Whitney Houston Last Kiss Goodbye to Clive Davis, Monica and Brandy at Interview." YouTube video, February 12, 2012. https://www.youtube.com/watch?v =1kGZ5q8YYrE.

"Whitney to Oprah 2009: Trying to Hide the Pain." CBS News, February 13, 2012. http://www.cbsnews.com/news/whitney-to-oprah-2009-trying-to-hide-the-pain/.

Williams, Mollena. The Toybag Guide to Playing with Taboo. Gardena, CA: Greenery, 2010.

Winfrey, Oprah, and Raven-Symoné. "Where Are They Now?" YouTube video, October 2014. https://www.youtube.com/watch?v=QXAho8vlmAI.

Winters, Lisa Ze. "Specter, Spectacle and the Imaginative Space: Unfixing the Tragic Mulatta." PhD diss., University of California, Berkeley, 2005.

Wischhover, Cheryl. "Chinese Couturier Guo Pei Reveals How Rihanna Ended Up Wearing Her Gown to the Met Gala." Fashionista, May 5, 2015. http://fashionista .com/2015/05/guo-pei-rihanna-met-ball-dress-interview.

Woolley, Hannah. *The Compleat Servant-Maid; or, The Young Maidens Tutor.* London: T. Hamnet, 1670. Available at LUNA, Folger Library. Accessed May 25, 2016. http://luna.folger.edu/luna/servlet/detail/FOLGERCM1~6~6~372986~131888 :The-compleat-servant-maid—or,-The-.

Zhang, Yingjin. *Cinema, Space, and Polylocality in a Globalizing China.* Honolulu: University of Hawai'i Press, 2009.

INDEX